Benefits *and* Compensation Glossary

Eleventh Edition

Benefits *and* Compensation Glossary

Eleventh Edition

Edited by Judith A. Sankey, CEBS

International Foundation

EDUCATION – BENEFITS • COMPENSATION

International Foundation of Employee Benefit Plans
18700 W. Bluemound Road
Post Office Box 69
Brookfield, WI 53008-0069
www.ifebp.org

Copies of this book may be obtained from:

Publications Department
International Foundation of Employee Benefit Plans
18700 West Bluemound Road
P.O. Box 69
Brookfield, Wisconsin 53008-0069
(262) 786-6710, option 4

Payment must accompany order.

Call (888) 334-3327, option 4, for price information;
or see www.ifebp.org/bookstore

Published in 2005 by the International Foundation of Employee Benefit Plans, Inc.
©2005 International Foundation of Employee Benefit Plans, Inc.
All rights reserved.
Library of Congress Control Number: 2004117620
ISBN 0-89154-597-2
Printed in the United States of America

4M-105

Contents

Foreword

The first edition of *Employee Benefit Plans: A Glossary of Terms* was compiled in 1975 to bring together, in one volume, terms applicable to the employee benefits field. This eleventh edition, newly christened *Employee Benefits and Compensation Glossary*, contains over 300 new definitions of terms from the benefits and compensation areas. Definitions are derived from current Canadian and U.S. sources covering the following:

Compensation
Employee benefits design and administration
Financial planning
Government regulations and legislation
Health care and health care cost-containment strategies
HIPAA privacy legislation
Human resources
Insurance
Investments
Labor law
Labor relations.

A special feature of the 11th edition is an updated list of almost 600 acronyms and abbreviations, covering a wide range of benefits-related topics.

This glossary is designed to provide a practical, easy-to-use guide to terminology used in the context of employee benefits and compensation. It is intended to provide assistance and should not be viewed as a definitive source. We have made every effort to present accurate and up-to-date information. The employee benefits and compensation area is complex and rapidly changing, and it would be impossible to include every applicable term and acronym. Use the glossary as a resource, not as an authority. Users should refer to standard texts and reference works for more detailed analyses of the definitions presented. Seek professional assistance in making decisions involving benefit and compensation planning and administration.

The International Foundation of Employee Benefit Plans welcomes feedback for future updates of this glossary. Please contact the Publications Department directly with any suggestions.

Acknowledgments

The International Foundation extends its sincere appreciation to all the dedicated individuals who contributed to the numerous source materials used to compile this glossary.

A

Ability to Pay—The ability of a firm to pay a given level of wages or benefit cost increase while remaining profitable. Dependent upon a firm's ability to be competitive in its market, it is a frequent issue in contract negotiating.

Absence Management—Various efforts by employers to manage planned and unplanned time off such as paid-time-off programs, focused attendance management, integrated disability management, family medical leave, work/life and wellness programs to reduce or deter lost productivity and employee absence.

Access—
—The ability to obtain health care. Elements of access include affordability; approachability, such as clinic location; and availability of health services.
—The ability or the means necessary to read, write, modify or communicate data/information or otherwise use any system resource.

Access Discrimination—Denial of certain jobs, promotions or training opportunities to qualified minorities. Illegal under Title VII of the Civil Rights Act.

Accident Insurance—A form of health insurance against loss by accidental bodily injury.

Accidental Death and Dismemberment (AD&D)—AD&D provides coverage for death or dismemberment resulting directly from accidental causes. Provides benefits in the event of loss of life, limbs or eyesight as the result of an accident.

Accidental Death Benefit (ADB)—A provision added to an insurance policy for payment of an additional benefit in case of death by accidental means. It is often referred to as *double indemnity*.

Accommodation—Modifications or changes made by an employer to assist an individual with a disability in the performance of a job.

Account Limit—The maximum addition to a qualified asset account of a welfare benefit fund that an employer is permitted to deduct. It equals the amount reasonably and actuarially necessary to fund benefit claims incurred but unpaid as of the end of the taxable year, plus administrative costs and certain contributions to an additional reserve for post-retirement medical or life insurance benefits.

Accounting Principles Board (APB)—Predecessor group to FASB. Opinions published as APB releases are applicable today unless superseded or revoked by FASB opinions.

Accreditation—Formal recognition by an agency or organization that evaluates and recognizes a program of study or an institution as meeting certain predetermined or industry-specific standards; may be either permanent or for a specified period of time. See also Certification; Licensure.

Accrual of Benefits—In the case of a defined benefit pension plan, the process of accumulating pension credits for years of credited service, expressed in the form of an annual benefit to begin payment at normal retirement age. In the case of a defined contribution plan, the process of accumulating funds in the individual employee's pension account.

Accrue—When actuaries say that pension benefits, actuarial costs and actuarial liabilities have accrued, they ordinarily mean that the amounts are associated, either specifically or by a process of allocation, with years of employee service before the date of a particular valuation of a pension plan.

Accrued Benefit—For any retirement plan that is not a defined benefit pension plan, a participant's accrued benefit is the balance in his or her plan account, whether vested or not. In the case of a defined benefit pension plan, a participant's accrued benefit is his or her benefit as determined under the terms of the plan expressed in the form of an annual benefit commencing at normal retirement age. Under ERISA, three alternative methods of benefit accrual are allowed. See also Backloading; Fractional Rule; 3% Rule.

Accrued Future Service Benefit—That portion of a participant's retirement benefit that relates to his or her period of credited service after the effective date of the plan and before a specified current date.

Accrued Interest—
—Interest earned on a bond since the last interest payment was made. The buyer of the bond pays the market price plus accrued interest.
—Interest that has already been earned; accumulated interest that is due and payable.

Accrued Liability—See Actuarial Accrued Liability.

Accumulated Benefit Obligation (ABO)—The actuarial present value of benefits (whether vested or nonvested) attributed by the pension benefit formula to employee service rendered before a specified date and based on employee service and compensation (if applicable) prior to that date. The accumulated benefit obligation differs from the projected benefit obligation in that it includes no assumption about future compensation levels. For plans with flat benefit or non-pay-related pension benefit formulas, the accumulated benefit obligation and the projected benefit obligation are the same. See also Projected Benefit Obligation (PBO).

Accumulated Funding Deficiency—
—In connection with ERISA's minimum funding standards, the excess of the total charges to the funding standard account for all plan years (beginning with the first plan year to which the funding provisions apply) over the total credits to such account for such years or, if less, the excess of the total charges to the alternative minimum funding standard account for such plan years over the total credits to such account for such years.
—If the minimum contributions have not been made to a covered plan, the funding standard account will show a deficiency, called the *accumulated funding deficiency*. A plan will meet the minimum funding standard for a plan year if, at the end of that year, it does not have an accumulated funding deficiency.

Accumulation Period—
—The period during which funds accumulate for later payment on a deferred annuity.
—The period during which the insured person must incur eligible medical expenses at least equal to the deductible to establish a benefit period under a major medical expense or comprehensive medical expense policy.

Acid Test Ratio—A measure of financial liquidity (also known as the *quick assets ratio*): quick assets (current assets less inventories) divided by current liabilities.

Active Account—A brokerage account with securities that are bought and sold frequently.

Active Management—A style of investment management that seeks to attain above-average risk-adjusted performance. Active managers buy and sell frequently.

Active Market—A market where securities are heavily traded and the volume of sales is above normal.

Active Participant—An individual who is a participant in an employer-sponsored plan and for whom at any time during the taxable year benefits are accrued under the plan on his or her behalf, or for whom the employer is obligated to contribute to or under the plan on his or her behalf, or for whom the employer would have been obligated to contribute to or under the plan on his or her behalf if any contributions were made to or under the plan. See also Plan Participant.

Activities of Daily Living (ADL)—Activities, such as bathing, dressing and toileting, that are needed for self-care. ADLs are measured to evaluate the continued feasibility of self-care.

Actual Contribution Percentage (ACP)—In a qualified retirement plan, the average of the ratios of aggregate contributions (matching contributions and after-tax employee contributions) to compensation. It is figured for two groups: highly compensated employees and nonhighly compensated employees. The ratio for each employee is calculated, and then it is averaged for the group. See also Alternative Limitation.

Actual Deferral Percentage (ADP)—In a qualified retirement plan such as a 401(k) plan, the average of the ratios of elective contributions to compensation is figured for two groups: highly compensated employees and nonhighly compensated employees. The ratio first is figured for each employee, and then averaged for each group. See also Alternative Limitation.

Actuarial Accrued Liability—
—The actuarial accrued liability of a pension plan at any time is the excess of the present value, as of the date of valuation, of total prospective benefits of the plan (plus administrative expenses if included in the normal cost) over the present value of future normal cost accruals, determined by the actuarial cost method in use.
—That portion, as determined by a particular actuarial cost method, of the actuarial present value of pension plan benefits and expenses that is not provided for by future normal costs. The presentation of an actuarial accrued liability

should be accompanied by reference to the actuarial cost method used.

Actuarial Adjustment—The result of offsetting the actuarial gains and losses in an annual actuarial valuation.

Actuarial Asset Value—See Actuarial Value of Assets.

Actuarial Assumptions—Factors used by the actuary in forecasting uncertain future events affecting pension cost. They involve such things as interest and investment earnings, inflation, unemployment, mortality rates and retirement patterns.

Actuarial Cost—A cost is characterized as actuarial if it is derived through the use of present values. An actuarial cost is often used to associate the costs of benefits under a retirement system with the approximate time the benefits are earned.

Actuarial Cost Method—
—A system for determining either the contributions to be made under a retirement plan or the level of benefits when the contributions are fixed. In addition to forecasts of mortality, interest and expenses, some of the methods involve estimates as to future labor turnover, salary scales and retirement rates. The methods of prime importance are those such as the entry age method, attained age method and unit credit method, which have been recognized by the Internal Revenue Service.
—A recognized technique for establishing the amount and incidence of the actuarial cost of pension plan benefits, or benefits and expenses, and the related actuarial liabilities.

Actuarial Equivalent—
—If the present value of two series of payments is equal, taking into account a given interest rate and mortality according to a given table, the two series are said to be actuarially equivalent. For example, under a given set of actuarial assumptions, a lifetime monthly benefit of $67.60 beginning at the age of 60 can be said to be the actuarial equivalent of $100 a month beginning at the age of 65. The actual benefit amounts are different but the present value of the two benefits, considering mortality and interest, is the same.
—A benefit having the same present value as the benefit it replaces.
—Of equal actuarial present value.

Actuarial Funding Method—Any of several techniques that actuaries use in determining the amounts and incidence of employer contributions to provide for pension benefits.

Actuarial Gain or Loss—The effects on actuarial costs of deviations or differences between the past events predicted by actuarial assumptions, and the events that actually occurred. An *actuarial gain* results where the actual experience under the plan is more favorable than the actuary's estimate, while an *actuarial loss* reflects an unexpectedly adverse deviation.

Actuarial Present Value (APV)—The value of an amount or series of amounts payable or receivable at various times, determined as of a given date by the application of a particular set of actuarial assumptions.

Actuarial Reduction—The reduction in the normal retirement benefit that offsets a cost increase to the plan when a participant retires ahead of schedule.

Actuarial Report—
—An actuary's report to the company recommending how much to contribute yearly to the pension fund to fund promised benefits.
—A report filed with the IRS by the administrator of a defined benefit pension plan that is subject to the minimum funding standards of ERISA.

Actuarial Valuation—
—An examination of a pension plan to determine whether contributions are being accumulated at a rate sufficient to provide the funds out of which the promised pensions can be paid when due. The valuation shows the actuarial liabilities of the plan and the applicable assets.
—The determination, as of a valuation date, of the normal cost, actuarial accrued liability, actuarial value of assets and related actuarial present values for a pension plan.

Actuarial Value of Assets—The value of cash, investments and other property belonging to a pension plan, as used by the actuary for the purpose of an actuarial valuation. The statement of actuarial assumptions should set forth the particular procedures used in determining this value.

Actuary—
—(Pension) A person professionally trained in the technical and mathematical aspects of insurance, pensions and related fields. The actuary esti-

mates how much money must be contributed to a pension fund each year in order to support the benefits that will become payable in the future.
—(Insurance) A person trained in the insurance field who determines policy rates, reserves and dividends, as well as conducts various other statistical studies.

Adequate Consideration—In the case of a security for which there is a generally recognized market value, *adequate consideration* means either (1) the price of the security prevailing on a national securities exchange or (2) if the security is not traded on a national securities exchange, a price not less favorable to the plan than the offering price for the security as established by current bid and asked prices quoted by persons independent of the issuer and of any party in interest; in the case of an asset other than a security for which there is a generally recognized market, *adequate consideration* means the fair market value of the asset as determined in good faith by the trustee or named fiduciary.

Adjudication—The exercise of judicial power by hearing, trying and determining the claims of litigants before the court.

Adjustable Rate Mortgage (ARM)—See Variable Rate Mortgage.

Adjusted Gross Income—The total of annual income such as wages, interest and dividends minus certain deductions such as contributions to a 401(k) account. This figure determines taxable income.

Administrative Agent—See Third-Party Administrator.

Administrative Manager (Employee Benefit Plans)—Firm or individual providing professional administrative services to an employee benefit plan. May be compensated under either a salaried or contract arrangement.

Administrative Policy Regarding Self-Correction (APRSC)—Part of the IRS policy that allows plan sponsors to correct insignificant operational failures at any time and to correct significant operational failures within a two-year period, without penalty of disqualification. No fees or filings with the IRS are required. See also Employee Plans Compliance Resolution System (EPCRS).

Administrative Safeguards—In HIPAA privacy legislation, administrative actions, and policies and procedures to manage the selection, development, implementation and maintenance of security measures to protect electronic protected health information, and to manage the conduct of the covered entity's workforce in relation to the protection of that information.

Administrative Services Only (ASO)—An arrangement in which a plan hires a third party to deliver administrative services to the plan such as claims processing and billing; the plan bears the risk for claims. Common in self-funded health care plans.

Administrator (Employee Benefit Plans)—Under ERISA, the person designated as such by the instrument under which the plan is operated. If the administrator is not so designated, *administrator* means the plan sponsor. If the administrator is not designated and the plan sponsor cannot be identified, the administrator may be such person as is prescribed by regulation of the secretary of labor. The administrator's responsibilities are as follows:
1. Act solely in the interest of plan participants and beneficiaries, and for the exclusive purpose of providing benefits and defraying reasonable administrative expenses.
2. Manage the plan's assets to minimize the risk of large losses.
3. Act in accordance with the documents governing the plan.
(Canada) The individual or company responsible for administering a group insurance contract including such services as accounting, issuance of certificates and settlement of claims.

Admission Certification—A form of utilization review in which assessment is made of the necessity—based on health status and treatment needs—of a patient's admission to a hospital or other inpatient institution; health status considerations include both physical and psychological conditions.

Admitted Carriers—Insurance companies licensed to conduct specific types of business in a given country.

Adoption Assistance Program—Benefit programs created to reimburse employees who legally adopt a child, including such costs as adoption agency fees, legal fees, pregnancy and hospital expenses of the natural mother, and immigration and naturalization expenses.

Adult Day Care—Provision during the day, on a regular basis, of a range of services that may include health, medical, psychological, social, nutritional and educational services that allow a disabled or elderly person to function in the home or at a center.

Advance Directives—See Durable Power of Attorney.

Advance Funding—
—An approach to funding retirement or other benefits whereby the employer sets aside monies for each employee or for the group of active employees as a whole on some systematic basis during their working years.
—An employer sets aside funds on a systematic basis to provide pension benefits; involves periodic contributions on behalf of the active employee group.

Adverse Impact—A negative discriminatory effect of an employment action, such as hiring or promotion of employees at a rate of less than 80% of the best achieving group.

Adverse Selection—The tendency of an individual to recognize his or her health status in selecting the option under a retirement system or insurance plan that tends to be most favorable to him or her (and more costly to the plan). In insurance usage, a person with an impaired health status or with expected medical care needs applies for insurance coverage financially favorable to himself or herself and detrimental to the insurance company. Also known as *antiselection.*

Advisory Opinion—A short written opinion by the Department of Labor regarding the legality of a given situation under ERISA.

Affidavit—A sworn statement in writing, made before an authorized official, generally a notary.

Affiliated Health Care Provider—A provider such as a hospital, clinic, outpatient services facility, individual physician or surgeon, or group of physicians or surgeons that by contract provides professional health care services to patients and others according to stated initiatives of the named insurer.

Affiliated Service Group—Two or more service or management organizations operating in separate units but providing common services to outsiders or for each other. Interlocking ownership is more concentrated than in a controlled group. Treated as a single employer for purposes of plan qualification.

Affirmative Action—A positive program developed in response to civil rights laws and executive orders. Its purpose is to eliminate all forms of discrimination, both overt and subtle, within the employment processes and to provide minorities, women and members of other protected classes with the opportunity to compete for jobs on an equal basis. It is concerned with equality of results, not just equality of opportunity.

Affirmative Action Program (AAP)—A written, results-oriented program in which an employer or contractor details the steps it will take to ensure equal employment opportunity including, where appropriate, remedying discrimination against an affected class and so forth. Sometimes required by law or court order.

Aftercare—Continued contact that will support and increase the gains made to date in a health treatment process and prevent relapse.

After-Tax Contribution—A portion of a person's income that has already been taxed by the IRS that is contributed to a qualified plan. After-tax contributions are not as tax efficient as contributions with before-tax income.

Age Discrimination—To discharge, refuse to hire or to otherwise discriminate against any individual with respect to the individual's compensation benefits, terms, conditions or privileges of employment because the individual is aged 40 or over.

Age Discrimination in Employment Act (ADEA)—Protects workers over 40 from compulsory retirement at any age as long as they are capable of performing their jobs adequately. It also protects them from adverse job actions based on age (e.g., refusal to hire; discriminatory layoff) and against benefits discrimination. Employers are subject to ADEA if they engage in an industry affecting interstate commerce and had 20 or more employees in each working day of 20 or more weeks in the current or preceding calendar year.

Age 50 Catch-Up Contributions—See Catch-Up Contributions.

Age-Weighted Profit-Sharing Plan—Combines the flexibility of a profit-sharing plan with the ability of a pension plan to skew benefits in favor of older employees. This type of plan applies an age factor to the allocation formula of the profit-sharing plan.

Each participant receives a contribution based on age as well as compensation.

Agency/Agent—A relationship in which one person acts for or represents another by the latter's authority.

Agency Bonds (Agencies)—The full faith and credit of the U.S. government is normally not pledged to payment of principal and interest on the majority of government agencies issuing these bonds, with maturities of up to ten years, so they are one step below Treasury issues on the marketing scale. Their yields, therefore, are normally higher and their marketability is good, thereby qualifying them as a low-risk/high-liquidity type of investment. They are eligible as security for advances to the member banks by the Federal Reserve, which attests to their standing.

Agent—See Agency/Agent.

Aggregate Funding Method—A method of accumulating money for future payment of pensions whereby the actuary determines the present value of all future benefit payments, deducts from this value whatever funds may be on hand with the trustee or the insurance company, and distributes the cost of the balance over the future on a reasonable basis. No distinction is made between present and past service liability.

Aggregation—Considering separate plans or companies as one plan or company to determine whether they satisfy certain requirements under ERISA or the Internal Revenue Code.

Aggressive Growth Fund—A mutual fund that aims to provide maximum long-term capital growth primarily from stocks of smaller companies or narrow market segments.

Aggressive Portfolio—A securities portfolio containing issues held primarily on the assumption that they will appreciate in value, as opposed to securities that provide greater yield or have good defensive qualities. Compare with Defensive Portfolio.

Alienation of Benefits—ERISA provides that plan benefits cannot be assigned to an individual other than the participant or alienated under a tax-qualified plan. Plan benefits cannot be paid to the employer or to a third party (except under a QDRO) when they would otherwise be paid to the participant. See also Assignment of Benefits.

All Payers System—This subjects all third-party payers that are reimbursing hospitals for services, including both public and private payers, to the same rules. Especially used in reference to hospital rate-setting programs.

All Salaried Workforce—A pay policy that makes exempt/nonexempt status invisible to workers. All employees are paid on a salaried basis and all pay is defined in the same terms, such as a monthly or annual salary. Fair Labor Standards Act requirements for overtime and minimum wage must still be met, but exempt status is not made a basis for status differentials in the organization.

Allied Health Professional—A specially trained non-physician health care provider, including paramedics, physician's assistants (PAs), certified nurse midwives (CNMs), phlebotomists, social workers, nurse practitioners (NPs) and other caregivers who perform tasks that supplement physician services.

Allocated Contract—A contract with an insurance company under which payments to the insurance company are currently used to purchase immediate or deferred annuities for individual participants. See also Annuity Contract.

Allocated Funding Instrument—A pension funding instrument by which contributions are assigned to provide benefits for specific employees. Examples are individual insurance and annuity contracts, group permanent contracts and group deferred annuity contracts.

Allocation—The distribution of the employer's contribution to the account of each participant. In a profit-sharing plan, it also refers to the distribution of earnings and forfeitures for the various accounts.

Allowed Charges—Charges for services rendered or supplies furnished by a health provider that would qualify as covered expenses and for which the program will pay in whole or in part, subject to any deductible, coinsurance or table of allowance included in the program.

Alpha—The premium a fund would be expected to earn if the market rate of return were equal to the Treasury bill rate—that is, a premium of zero for the market rate of return. A positive alpha indicates that a fund has earned on the average a premium above that expected for the level of market variability. A negative alpha would indicate that a fund received on the average a premium lower than that expected for the level of market variability. Sometimes alpha is used as a performance indicator or as a surrogate for selectivity.

Alternate Payee—See Qualified Domestic Relations Order.

Alternate Ranking Method—A variation of the straight ranking method of performance appraisal in which the appraiser alternates the ranking by starting with the best employee and the worst employee.

Alternative Delivery System (ADS)—An organized, nontraditional system of financing and delivering health care services from participating providers on a prepaid basis to a voluntarily enrolled population. Examples include HMOs and PPOs.

Alternative Dispute Resolution (ADR) Procedure—A procedure designed to settle disputes and avoid costly litigation. It involves a written complaint, an automatic appeal to arbitration in termination cases, and a final and binding decision in all cases.

Alternative Limitation—An alternate nondiscrimination test. The ACP and ADP percentage of highly compensated employees cannot be more than double the ACP and ADP of nonhighly compensated employees. In addition, the difference cannot exceed two percentage points.

Alternative Medicine—See Complementary and Alternative Medicine.

Alternative Minimum Tax—
—During the year certain incentive stock options are exercised, the paper gains must be included in a separate alternative minimum calculation. Either the regular or alternative minimum tax, whichever is higher, must be paid by the person exercising the option.
—(Canada) A supplemental tax payable in addition to regular income tax or the minimum tax payable on adjusted income greater than a certain dollar amount.

Amalgamation (Canada)—Merger; combining of two or more companies or corporations.

Ambulatory Care Benefits—Benefits for health care services received as an outpatient.

Ambulatory Care Facility—A freestanding or hospital-based facility providing preventive or diagnostic services, emergency or therapeutic services, surgery or other treatment not requiring overnight confinement.

Ambulatory Surgery Center (ASC)—An establishment that performs surgery of an uncomplicated nature that has traditionally been done in the more expensive inpatient setting but can be done with equal efficiency without hospital admission; centers may be hospital-based, sponsored, or independently owned; also called *same-day surgery center*. See also Freestanding Ambulatory Facility.

Amendment—
—(General) An addition, deletion or change in a legal document.
—(Employee Benefit Plans) A change in the terms of an existing plan or the initiation of a new plan. A plan amendment may increase benefits, including those attributed to years of service already rendered. See also Retroactive Benefits.
—(Insurance) A formal document changing the provisions of an insurance policy signed jointly by the insurance company officer and the policyholder or his or her authorized representative.

American Depository Receipts (ADRs)—American certificates of deposit are dollar-denominated certificates that represent equity ownership in non-U.S. companies. They are issued by an approved New York bank or trust company against the deposit of the original (foreign) shares with a European branch of the New York institution. These receipts facilitate the financing of foreign companies in this country. As foreign shares are deposited abroad, the equivalent ADRs are issued to buyers in New York. When transactions are made, the ADRs change hands, not the certificates. This eliminates the actual shipment of stock certificates between the United States and foreign countries and expedites transactions in securities traded on foreign exchanges.

American Federation of Labor (AFL)—Formed in 1881 as a national federation of local unions organized originally on trade or craft lines, today it also grants charters to industrial unions. Each local retains the right to govern its own affairs. In 1955, the AFL and the CIO merged to form the AFL-CIO, with which most, although not all, major U.S. unions are affiliated. See also Congress of Industrial Organizations.

American Stock Exchange (AMEX)—The second largest U.S. stock exchange, after the New York Stock Exchange. Since listing requirements are seen as less stringent than those for NYSE, small-to-medium-sized stocks are traded on this exchange. Foreign securities are also traded on this exchange.

American Stock Exchange (AMEX) Market Value Index—A capitalization-weighted index measuring the change in the aggregate market value of common shares, American depository receipts and warrants.

Americans with Disabilities Act (ADA)—A law enacted in 1990 that prohibits discrimination against persons with disabilities in areas such as terms and conditions of employment. Requires employers to make reasonable accommodations to enable employees with disabilities to perform the essential parts of a job.

Amortization—Paying off an interest-bearing liability by gradual reduction through a series of installments as opposed to paying it off by one lump-sum payment. A technique for gradually extinguishing a liability, deferred charge or capital expenditure over a period of time. Includes such practices as depreciation, depletion, write-off of intangibles, prepaid expenses and deferred charges (e.g., mortgages are amortized by periodically retiring part of the face amount). The liquidation of a debt on an installment basis.

Amortized Value—The amount at a given point in time to which the purchase price of a bond purchased at a discount or premium has been increased or decreased.

Ancillary Benefits—See Supplemental Benefits; Voluntary Benefits.

Ancillary Benefits (Canada)—Benefits in addition to regular pension and survivor benefits, such as bridging and enriched early retirement benefits.

Ancillary Services—Supplemental services and procedures, diagnostic or therapeutic, offered in hospital or outpatient settings. Some examples are radiography, laboratory tests and physical therapy.

Annual Addition—Under a profit-sharing plan, and other plans that use individual account balances, it is the contributions made to a participant's account. An annual addition includes employer and employee (participant) contributions, and forfeitures under a formula provided by federal law.

Annual Audit—The federally required independent audit of ERISA plans with more than 100 participants. Also refers to a DOL or IRS examination of a plan.

Annual Benefits Statement—A report containing specific information about the status of a participant's projected pension income or account balance. Can include a description of the value and cost of health and welfare benefits, and is often distributed to employees to promote awareness and appreciation of benefits.

Annual Bonus—See Annual Incentive.

Annual Incentive—Additional pay in cash or stock beyond an employee's normal pay for a fiscal or calendar year, based on individual, business unit and/or company performance. It is usually a lump-sum payment; also known as an *annual bonus*.

Annual Information Return (Canada)—Pension plans must file financial and other information each year with the appropriate provincial or federal government.

Annual Report—
—(Corporate) A formal financial statement issued annually by a corporation that depicts assets, liabilities, earnings—how the company stood at the close of the business year, how it fared profitwise during the year and other information of interest to shareholders.
—(Employee Benefit Plans) The employer or plan administrator is required to file an annual information return with the IRS regarding the qualification, financial condition and operations of any funded deferred compensation plan, health and welfare plan or qualified pension plan. This comprehensive information report is required for HR 10 plans and individual retirement accounts and annuities as well as for regular corporate plans. Uses Form 5500 series.

Annual Supplemental Cost—See Amortization.

Annual Yield—The money income or percentage of

8

return in dividends or interest received annually from an investment.

Annualize—To express a rate of return for a period greater than one year or less than one year in terms of 12 months.

Annualized Linked-Median Return—Rates of return calculated by compounding the annual median returns and annualizing the result.

Annuitant—A person entitled to receive payments under an annuity; a person receiving such payments.

Annuity—
—A contract that provides an income for a specified period of time such as a number of years or for life.
—The periodic payments provided under an annuity contract.
—The specified monthly or annual payment to a pensioner. Often used synonymously with *pension*.

Annuity, Cash Refund—See Refund Annuity.

Annuity Certain—A contract that provides an income for a specified number of years, regardless of life or death. If an annuitant dies, his or her beneficiary will receive payments for the remaining number of specified years. Also referred to as *period certain, term certain* or *dollar temporary annuity*.

Annuity Consideration—The payment, or one of the regular periodic payments, an annuitant makes for an annuity.

Annuity, Contingent—See Contingent Annuity Option.

Annuity Contract—A contract in which an insurance company unconditionally undertakes a legal obligation to provide specified pension benefits to specific individuals in return for a fixed consideration or premium. An annuity contract is irrevocable and involves the transfer of significant risk from the employer to the insurance company. Annuity contracts are also called *allocated contracts*. See also Allocated Contract.

Annuity, Deferred—See Deferred Annuity.

Annuity, Fixed—See Fixed Annuity.

Annuity, Joint and Survivor—See Joint and Survivor (J&S) Annuity.

Annuity Purchase Fund—The fund established to hold annuity purchase payments transferred from the unallocated active life fund under a deposit administration contract. Also known as the *retired life fund*.

Annuity Rate (Canada)—The price charged by an issuer of annuities to provide a dollar of annuity (usually per month) under specified conditions to an individual based on the person's age, interest rates, etc.

Annuity, Refund—See Refund Annuity.

Annuity Starting Date—The first day of the first period for which an amount is received as an annuity.

Annuity, Tax-Deferred—See Tax-Deferred Annuity.

Annuity, Variable—See Variable Annuity.

Antialienation/Antiassignment Rule—This rule requires that a qualified retirement plan must provide that participants' benefits may not be assigned to someone other than the employee or otherwise pledged (e.g., to a creditor), either voluntarily or involuntarily, while they are held by the plan's trust. An exception to the general antialienation rule of ERISA exists for payments made under a qualified domestic relations order (QDRO). See also Assignment of Benefits.

Anticutback Rule—A provision in the Internal Revenue Code that prohibits an employer from reducing accrued benefits under a qualified retirement plan by a plan amendment, other than an amendment that has been approved by the secretary of labor freezing benefit accruals only for the most recent plan year. Applies to benefits already accrued under the terms of the plan, early retirement benefits, early retirement-type subsidies and optional forms of benefits.

Antidiscrimination Rules—See Nondiscrimination Rules.

Any Willing Provider—Legislation requiring insurers to accept any provider (such as a pharmacy or physician) that agrees to abide by the same contractual terms and payment levels as other providers. The intent of the law is to preserve the patient's freedom of choice. However, this regulation directly affects managed care organizations, which attempt to control health care costs and quality by selecting the most efficient providers. See also Open Panel.

Appreciation—Increase in asset value. Synonymous with *price improvement,* one of the fundamental investment objectives. A stock advancing from 70 to 80 is said to have appreciated ten points.

Apprenticeship Plan—An employee welfare benefit plan consisting of a training plan connected to a union as established under a trust format.

Arbitrage—A technique employed to take advantage of price differences in separate markets. This is accomplished by purchasing in one market for immediate sale in another at a better price. Such transactions may be executed in the same type or similar types of securities.

Arbitrary and Capricious Standard—The standard employed by courts under which a plan trustee's decision to deny benefits must be upheld unless it is found to be arbitrary and capricious.

Arbitration/Arbitrator—The submitting of a matter in dispute to the judgment of a specified number of disinterested persons called *arbitrators,* whose decision, called an *award,* is binding upon the parties. See also Fact Finding.

Archer Medical Savings Account (MSA)—An account that can be used by employees to pay medical expenses not covered by insurance. Contributions to the account are tax-deductible for the employee. Self-employed individuals may contribute to and accumulate funds in the accounts from year to year. Employers with small group MSAs may contribute to the accounts, or employees may make the entire contribution.

Asked (Asking) or Offering Price—
—The lowest quoted round lot price that any potential seller will accept for a security at any given time.
—The price of a mutual fund, usually including current net asset value plus sales charge.

Assessed Valuation—Assessment of real estate by a unit of government for taxation purposes.

Asset Allocation—A process that determines the optimal distribution of funds among various types of as-

sets that offer the highest probability of consistently achieving investment objectives within the confines of a predetermined level of risk. The process often includes the use of a computer model program to assist in the processing of a myriad of data. See also Asset Classes.

Asset Allocation Models—The modern portfolio theory application area that addresses the problem of the amount of assets to be allocated among various investment alternatives.

Asset Classes—Broad groups of securities including stocks and bonds that share common financial traits and respond similarly to economic factors. They are key factors in investment decisions. See also Asset Allocation.

Asset/Liability Modeling—A tool that can be used by pension plan sponsors to explore a pension's risks and possible futures. By considering a possible range of outcomes, plan sponsors can make better decisions in the present. Asset liability modeling provides projections of plan funding on various assumptions about future experiences, such as demographic trends, the effects of inflation and the performance of capital markets. These financial studies are financial planning and risk management tools that are especially useful when plan changes, such as mergers, are contemplated.

Asset Reversion—Following the termination of a pension plan, the recovery—by the sponsoring employer—of any pension fund assets in excess of those required to pay accrued benefits. The recovered assets are subject to regular corporate income tax as well as an excise tax of either 20% or 50%, depending on subsequent retirement arrangements made for employees.

Assets—The valuable resources, property rights and properties owned by a company, such as cash, investments, money due it, materials and inventories, which are called *current assets;* buildings and machinery, which are known as *fixed assets;* and patents and good will, called *intangible assets.*

Assigned Payment—In the Medicare program, the right to receive reimbursement for medical expenses may be *assigned* to the physician by the beneficiary. If the physician accepts assignment, he or she agrees to accept the amount allowed by Medicare for a given service as payment in full for that service, and agrees not to charge the beneficiary for any difference between what Medicare approves and what he or she charged.

Assignment of Benefits—
  —(Health Care) The signed transfer of certain benefits by the insured person to a third party, e.g., to a health care provider such as a physician or a hospital.
  —(Pension) Includes any arrangement that pays plan benefits to the employer when they would otherwise be paid to the participant. This is generally *prohibited* by ERISA so as to assure that the accrued benefits will be available to the employee when he or she retires. An exception permits assignments, not in excess of 10% of any benefit payment, which are voluntary and revocable. This provision is not intended to interfere with the practice of using vested benefits as collateral for reasonable loans from a plan. Under the Retirement Equity Act of 1984, the creation, assignment or recognition of a right to any benefit payable with respect to a participant pursuant to a qualified domestic relations order is not treated as an assignment or alienation prohibited by ERISA. See also Qualified Domestic Relations Order.
  —(Canada) Assignment of group life insurance normally is not allowed under most plan provisions. Hospital and dental benefits, however, may be assigned to most providers.

Assisted Living Facilities—Shared and supervised housing for those who cannot function independently. Various types of homes serve those who need minimal support to those more severely impaired. Offer less skilled service than a nursing home.

Associate of the Society of Actuaries (ASA)—Holders of this designation must pass five examinations covering such topics as general mathematics, probability and statistics, and numerical analysis.

Association Group—A group formed from members of a trade or a professional association for group insurance under one master health insurance contract.

Assumptions, Actuarial—See Actuarial Assumptions.

Assurance (International Benefits)—Commonly used in Canada and Great Britain, it is synonymous with *insurance.*

At the Market—An order that the broker will execute at the best price obtainable after he or she receives it on the trading floor. Synonymous with *market order.*

At the Money—An option in which the underlying stock is trading precisely at the exercise price of that option.

Attained Age—An individual's age at his or her last birthday.

Attitude Survey—A device such as a questionnaire designed to elicit information about employee ideas, feelings, concerns, expectations and preferences on a broad range of managerial issues. The survey can uncover the causes of problems, probe feelings about situations or conditions, and draw out ideas for prevention.

Attribution—The process of assigning pension benefits or cost to periods of employee service.

Audit—Any systematic investigation of procedures or operations for the purpose of determining conformity with prescribed criteria. The purpose of an audit by a CPA is to lend credibility to a company's financial statements.

Audit Finding—A weakness in internal controls or noncompliance with applicable laws presented in the audit report. Findings are ordinarily presented together with a response from management which states management's concurrence or disagreement with the finding and any plan for corrective action.

Audit of Provider Treatment or Charges—The qualitative or quantitative review of services rendered or proposed by a health provider, which may take the form of a comparison of patient records and claim form information, a patient questionnaire, a review of hospital and practitioner records, an examination of pre- or postoperative radiographs or a pre- or posttreatment clinical examination of a patient. Also may involve fee verification.

Audit Trail—The availability of a manual or machine readable means for tracing the status and contents of an individual transaction record backward or forward and between output, processing and source.

Authentication—The corroboration that a person is the one claimed.

Automatic Enrollment—Employers can enroll all eligible employees in a plan and begin participant deferrals without requiring the employees to submit a salary deferral request. Plan design specifies the percentage of earnings to be contributed and how these deferrals will be invested; participants can generally change the percentage and allocations if they stay in the plan. Employees who do not wish to participate in the plan must actively file a request to be excluded from the plan. Also known as *negative enrollment*.

Automatic Retirement—See Compulsory Retirement.

Automatic Survivor Coverage—Under the Retirement Equity Act of 1984, a defined benefit plan or a money purchase plan is required to provide automatic survivor benefits to the surviving spouse of a participant (1) in the case of a vested participant who retires under the plan, in the form of a qualified joint and survivor annuity and (2) in the case of a vested participant who dies before retirement, in the form of a qualified preretirement survivor annuity. The automatic survivor coverage rule also applies to a profit-sharing or stock bonus plan unless (1) the plan provides that the participant's full vested account balance will be paid to his or her surviving spouse (or to another beneficiary if the spouse consents or if there is no surviving spouse), (2) the participant does not elect payment of benefits in the form of a life annuity and (3) with respect to the participant, the plan is not a transferee of a plan required to provide automatic survivor benefits (for example, a defined benefit plan). A participant may, with his or her spouse's consent, elect out of joint and survivor annuity or preretirement survivor annuity coverage. See also Contingent Annuity Option; Joint and Survivor Annuity.

Auxiliary Fund—See Conversion Fund.

Availability—Availability of data or accessibility and usability of information on demand by an authorized person.

Average Age at Entry—The average age of members under a retirement plan at the time of entry. Frequently used for estimating cost.

Average Annual Compensation—An employee's average annual compensation is his or her annual compensation averaged over at least three consecutive years, under a uniform rule used for all employees.

For this purpose, it is acceptable to use for each employee the period of consecutive years which will produce his or her highest average. See also Final Average Salary.

Average Daily Census—The average number of hospital or health institution inpatients (other than newborns) each day throughout a given period. The census is calculated by dividing the number of patient days during a period by the number of calendar days in the period.

Average Indexed Monthly Earnings (AIME)—A computation for determining a worker's Social Security benefits. Benefits are indexed ("updated") to reflect their relative values in comparison to earnings levels that prevail just prior to attaining age 62, disability or death. Indexed earnings are determined by multiplying the worker's actual earnings for that year by the ratio of average total wages of all workers in the indexing year to average total wages in the given year. The AIME is average monthly earnings adjusted for wage inflation over the employee's working career.

Average Length of Stay (ALOS)—The average number of patient days of service rendered to each inpatient (excluding newborns) during a given period. Varies for patients by diagnosis, age, hospital efficiency, etc. One measure of use of health facilities.

Average Life—Used in connection with the sale of mortgages or mortgage-backed securities. The prepayment expectations of a loan or a group of mortgages. An artificial number used primarily to allow comparison of one loan or pool of mortgages as opposed to another bearing a similar interest rate.

Average Price—The mean, or average, price obtained in the purchase, or sale, of a security by the process of averaging.

Average Wholesale Price (AWP)—The published suggested wholesale price of a drug. It is often used by pharmacies as a cost basis for pricing prescriptions. While a reliable pricing reference for brand-name drugs, it can be misleading in the case of generic drugs since each manufacturer establishes its own AWP for the generic drug. This can result in a broad range of prices for the identical product.

Averages—Various ways of measuring the trend of securities prices, one of the most popular of which is the Dow Jones Average of 30 industrial stocks listed on the New York Stock Exchange. Formulas—some very elaborate—have been devised to compensate for stock splits and stock dividends and thus give continuity to the average. In the case of the Dow Jones Industrial Average, the prices of the 30 stocks are totaled and then divided by a divisor that is intended to compensate for past stock splits and stock dividends and that is changed from time to time. As a result, point changes in the average have only the vaguest relationship to dollar price changes in stocks included in the average.

Averaging Up or Down—The practice of purchasing the same security at various price levels, thereby arriving at a higher or lower average cost.

B

Baby Bonuses (International Benefits)—Payments made under social systems for support of one or more children in a family. Frequently funded by the social security system of the country.

Baby Boomers—Individuals born between 1946 and 1964.

Back Bond—Debt issued with a debt warrant.

Back End Load—A sales charge due upon the sale, transfer or disposition of securities, partnership interests, annuities, life insurances or mutual funds. Also called *exit* or *redemption fee*.

Backloading—The practice of providing a faster rate of benefit accrual after an employee has attained a specified age or has completed a specified number of years of service. For example, backloading occurs in a plan that provides a benefit of 1.5% of compensation for each year of service before age 50 and 2% per year thereafter. The practice is limited under ERISA. See also Accrued Benefit.

Balance Billing—The practice of charging full fees in excess of covered amounts and then billing the patient for that portion of the bill that the payer does not cover.

Balance Sheet—A condensed financial statement showing the nature and amount of a company's assets, liabilities and capital on a given date. In one column all the company's assets are listed with their values, and in the other all its liabilities and the equity of the stockholders.

Balance Sheet Approach—As used for setting expatriate compensation, an accounting term meaning that debits and credits must agree. Purchasing power in the home country should be matched to that abroad.

Balanced Budget Act of 1997—Includes provisions for Medicare, Medicaid and children's health; amendments to existing legislation that allow for establishment of the Medicare+Choice plan; special rules for Medical Savings Accounts; the addition of high-deductible Medigap policies; and broad health prevention measures. See also Medicare Advantage.

Balanced Funds—Investment companies that diversify their portfolio holdings over a wide list of common stocks, bonds and/or preferred issues to provide current income and long-term growth.

Balloon Maturity—A type of maturity schedule for an issue of bonds that shows a relatively small number of bonds among the earlier maturities and a large number near the final maturity date. This kind of maturity schedule is sometimes called a *serial maturity*.

Balloon Mortgage—Though it starts off like a conventional mortgage, this mortgage requires the borrower to pay the balance or arrange new financing after a fixed period, usually three to five years. This allows borrowers to take advantage of lower rates, should they occur. If financing is difficult to get when the mortgage expires, however, the borrower may be forced to sell the house.

Bank Draft—A bank check drawn on its own funds in another bank; however, it is not necessary for the drawer to cover the amount until the draft reaches the bank and the bank requests payment.

Bank Investment Contract (BIC)—A contract similar to a guaranteed investment contract (GIC), but issued by a bank. See also Guaranteed Investment Contract (GIC).

Bank of Canada—The central bank of Canada, similar to the Federal Reserve System in the United States. It is responsible for managing the nation's banking system, including issuing currency and administering monetary policy.

Bank of Hours—See Hour Bank.

Bankers Acceptance (BA)—An irrevocable obligation of an issuing bank and the borrower whereby both are liable for payment. Used in domestic and/or international trade or commerce to finance the shipment and storage of goods or to facilitate dollar exchange transactions with foreign banks. A stronger instrument than a bank CD; there is no record of an investor sustaining a principal loss on an acceptance of a U.S. bank. Because of the varying dollar amounts involved in international and domestic trade transactions, acceptances are available in a wide variety of principal amounts. Maturities can range from any number of days (usually 30-60-90) up to a legal maximum of 180. Rates are posted and changed infrequently.

Bankruptcy—The inability to repay debts in full because liabilities exceed assets. The Bankruptcy Act provides procedures for various situations of bankruptcy: Chapter 7 refers to a business entity that must be liquidated due to insolvency; Chapter 11 applies to a business that is reorganizing; Chapter 12 refers to family farms; and Chapter 13 allows for consumer debt adjustments.

Bargaining Contract—A contract under which both (or all) parties, as equals, set the terms and conditions of the contract.

Barrister (International Benefits)—A law provider who has the right to plead at the bar in courts of law.

Base Benefit Percentage—The percentage of compensation at which employer-derived benefits are accrued with respect to compensation of participants at or below the integration level.

Base Contribution Percentage—The percentage of compensation contributed by an employer with respect to compensation of participants at or below the integration level.

Base Country (International Compensation)—The country on which an expatriate's compensation is based. It is usually the expatriate's home country but may be the country of original employment.

Base Rate; Base Wage Rate—The hourly money rate for a job performed at standard pace. Does not include bonuses or incentive premiums, shift differentials or overtime.

Basic Financial Statements—The financial statements necessary for a fair presentation of the entity's financial position and results of operations. Generally accepted accounting principles require the statement of financial position, operating statement, a budget comparison statement (if applicable) and the notes to the financial statement.

Basic Medical Benefits—Generally represent benefits for hospital, surgical, medical and other miscellaneous employee benefits, excluding major medical insurance.

Basic Value—The rate of interest on a bond or obligation that serves as the basis on which bond values are compared. Bonds are generally bought according to basis, as a "5% basis," or "to yield x%."

Basis—The yield to maturity at a given price when related to bonds as shown in bond tables.

Basis Points (bps)—100 bps equal 1%. The term is most often associated with fees or investment performance and is mathematically defined as $\frac{1}{100}$ of 1%.

Basket of Securities—A group of securities that have aggregate characteristics which cause the group to replicate the performance of a referenced index. Used in program trading strategies.

Bay Street (Canada)—A street in Toronto housing the headquarters of many financial institutions; similar to Wall Street in the United States.

Bear—Someone who believes the stock market will decline.

Bear Market—A market where prices decline sharply against a background of widespread pessimism, growing unemployment and business recession. The opposite of bull market.

Bearer Bond—A bond made payable to its holder. The opposite of registered bond.

Bearer Form—A note or bond payable to the bearer of the instrument. Coupon bonds fall into this classification.

Behavior-Based Appraisal—Any performance evaluation system that considers the behaviors of those being rated (such as behavioral expectation scales, behaviorally anchored rating scales or behavioral observation scales), as compared to systems concentrating on results, such as management by objectives (MBO).

Benchmarking—The process of comparing a standard unit or index with similar classifications. For example, an organization can be compared with best practices and industry standards to establish measurable goals for improvement of products and services. Investors can compare the performance of their investments with major market indices like the S&P 500 and quantify how far they are from their investment goals.

Benchmark Job—A job used as a reference point for comparing compensation within and outside the company. Published surveys provide pay data for benchmark jobs.

Beneficiary—
—A person named by the participant in an insurance policy or pension plan to receive any benefits provided by the plan if the participant dies.
—A person designated by a participant, or by the terms of an employee benefit plan, who is or may become entitled to a benefit thereunder.

Beneficiary, Absolute or Irrevocable—An unalterable beneficiary. The owner relinquishes the right to change the beneficiary designation when such a beneficiary is named.

Beneficiary, Contingent—An alternate beneficiary. One whose rights under a contract are dependent upon the death of the original beneficiary or some other contingency.

Benefit—The rights of the participant or beneficiary to either cash or services after meeting the eligibility requirements of the pension or other benefit plans. Pension benefits usually refer to monthly payments payable on retirement or disability.

Benefit Accrual—See Accrued Benefit.

Benefit Formula—See Pension Benefit Formula.

Benefit Fund—The monies set aside by the plan sponsor with a trustee or insurance company for the payment of benefits.

Benefit Multiplier—A percentage that is multiplied by a participant's salary/pay (definitions of salary/pay vary from plan to plan) to determine a monthly benefit.

Benefit Package—A listing of specific benefits provided by an employee benefit plan. The total value of noncash compensation.

Benefit Period—The period for application of deductibles, after which time deductibles must again be satisfied.

Benefit Plan Summary—See Summary Plan Description (SPD).

Benefits Specialist—An individual in an organization, typically in the human resource management function, whose responsibility it is to administer the employee benefits program.

Best Practices—Superior performance by an organization in both management and operational processes. See also Benchmarking.

Beta—A risk statistic that measures how an investment's price moves in relation to the market, usually the Standard & Poor's 500 index. Beta is a statistical estimate of the average change in the fund's rate of return corresponding to a 1% change in the market. See also Systematic Risk.

Bid and Asked—Often referred to as a *quotation* or *quote*. The bid is the highest price anyone has indicated that he or she will pay for a security at a given time, and the asked is the lowest price anyone will accept at the same time.

Bid Price—The highest quoted price that any prospective buyer will pay for a security at a specific moment of time. The *bid price* is the real established market for a stock, regardless of the price of the last sale.

Big Board—A general name for the New York Stock Exchange.

Birthday Rule—Coordination-of-benefits rule whereby, if both spouses are working and carry dependent coverage, the responsibility for primary coverage falls to the parent having the earlier birthday in the calendar year, regardless of which parent is older. In the event that the birthdays occur on the same day, the employer-provided health insurance plan that has covered a parent the longest pays first. (May not apply to self-funded programs.)

Birth Rate—Generally, the number of live births per 1,000 population, calculated by dividing the total population into the number of live births and multiplying by 1,000.

Biweekly Pay Systems—A pay system whereby employees receive their pay every two weeks. Under this system, there are normally 26 pay periods in a year.

Black Box—A projected working model of a wholly electronic stock exchange that some predict will eventually replace the traditional stock exchanges.

Black Monday—October 19, 1987; the day that the Dow Jones Industrial Average plummeted a record-shattering 508 points.

Blackout Period—Any time period of three consecutive days' duration or more during which plan participants or corporation insiders, such as executives or directors, cannot access their accounts because of insufficient information. Blackout periods can be caused by changes in plan recordkeepers, trustees, vendors and valuation systems or company mergers or acquisitions. Also known as a *lockdown*. See also Sarbanes-Oxley Act of 2002.

Block—A large holding or transaction of stock—often 1,000 shares or more—held or traded as a single unit.

Blue Chip—The stock of a leading company that is known for excellent management and a conservative financial structure.

Blue Cross Association (BCA)—The national nonprofit organization to which Blue Cross plans in the United States voluntarily belong. BCA administers programs of licensure and approval for Blue Cross; provides national services to local Blue Cross and Blue Shield plans; and contracts with the federal government as an administrative agency for federal health programs.

Blue Cross/Blue Shield Plans—Independent, usually nonprofit, voluntary membership organizations formed for the purpose of insuring medical and hospital expenses for their subscribers in a limited geographical area. Blue Shield covers mainly physician services, while Blue Cross covers hospital services.

Blue Sky Laws—State statutes that attempt to ensure that the terms of securities offerings are fair, just and equitable and meet minimum standards of investment quality. Blue sky laws impose requirements that are unique to securities offerings in a particular state and require registration with the appropriate public agency.

Board Certified—A physician or other health professional who has passed an examination given by a medical specialty board and has been certified by that board as a specialist in the subject in question.

Board Eligible—A physician who is eligible to take a specialty board examination as a result of completion of medical school and a relevant residency. Some HMOs and other health facilities accept board-eligible physicians.

Bona Fide Occupational Qualification (BFOQ)—A legal term referring to permissible discriminatory job requirements as exceptions to Title VII of the Civil Rights Act of 1964. A BFOQ is a legitimate reason why an employer can exclude persons on otherwise illegal bases of consideration.

Bona Fide Purchaser—A person who buys real property, in good faith, for a fair value and without notice of any adverse claims or rights of third parties.

Bond—A type of debt instrument similar to an IOU issued by a company, municipality or government agency. A bond investor lends money to the issuer and in exchange the issuer promises to repay the loan amount on a specified date of maturity, while paying the bondholder a specific amount of fixed interest at specified times. A bond is typically a promise to repay the principal loan along with interest on a certain date.

Bond Discount—The discount is the amount by which the face value of a bond exceeds the issue price. A discount occurs when the coupon rate on the bonds is less than the market interest rate at the time the bonds are issued.

Bond Fund—An investment company that holds corporate, municipal or U.S. Treasury bonds. Such companies concentrate variously on high-grade bonds, medium grade bonds, convertible bonds, or a combination of bonds and preferred stocks. Their main objective is securing the principal with as much income as possible.

Bond Immunization—See Immunization (Bonds).

Bond Premium—The premium is the amount by which the issue price of a bond exceeds the face value. A premium occurs when the coupon rate of interest on a bond is higher than the market interest rate at the time the bonds are issued.

Bond Quality Ratings—A grading system for measuring the relative investment qualities of bonds by the use of rating symbols, which range from the highest investment quality (at least investment risk) to the lowest investment quality (greatest investment risk). These ratings according to Standard & Poor's are A1+, highest grade; A1, high grade; A, upper medium grade; B1+, medium grade; B1, lower medium grade; B, speculative; C1+ and C1, outright speculations; C, income bonds paying no interest and the best defaulted bonds; and D1 and D, in default, with the D symbol assigned to issues that appear to have little recoverable value.

Bond Swap—A technique used by investors in bonds that involves the sale of a bond or bonds and the simultaneous purchase of entirely different bonds in a like amount with comparable coupons and maturities.

Bond Tables—Mathematical tables that facilitate the conversion of bond yields into dollar values. They are employed for the pricing of municipal bonds, which frequently are quoted on a "yield basis"; for example, they are sold at a certain price which, taking into consideration both interest rate and maturity, will result in definite return on the amount paid.

Bond Yield—The rate of return on bonds.

Bonding—ERISA-required protection for fiduciaries and any plan officials handling plan assets to safeguard the plan against loss through acts of fraud or dishonesty, directly or indirectly.

Book Reserve (International Benefits)—A system of recognizing pension liabilities through the creation of a reserve on the employer's balance sheet. The corresponding reserves may or may not be segregated from the assets of the employer. In some countries, it is possible for the employer to take a deduction for income or other taxes, even when assets are not segregated.

Book Value—An accounting term determined by adding all of the company's assets, then deducting all debts and other liabilities, plus the liquidation price of any preferred issues. The sum arrived at is divided by the number of common shares outstanding and the result is book value per common share. Book value of the assets of a company or a security may have little or no significant relationship to market value.

Bottom-Up Manager—Common stock manager who places his or her selection emphasis on recognizing favorable characteristics of individual companies, as opposed to developing the portfolio with an emphasis on the economy and industries.

Brand-Name Drug—A drug protected by a patent issued to the original innovator or marketer. The patent prohibits the manufacture of the drug by other companies as long as the patent remains in effect. See also Generic Equivalent Drugs.

Breach of Fiduciary Duty—A fiduciary's violation of a duty owed to an employee benefit plan or a participant or beneficiary in such a plan.

Breach of Trust—Violation of a duty of a trustee to a beneficiary.

Break in Service—Under ERISA, a calendar year, plan year or other 12 consecutive month period designated by the plan during which a plan participant does not complete more than 500 hours of service. (This general rule has been modified for certain industries, particularly those characterized by seasonal employment patterns.) When a break in service occurs, the participant must again meet the plan's eligibility requirements to participate.

Breakpoint—The dollar level of an investment in a mutual fund at which a purchaser qualifies for a reduction in sales charges on a quantity purchase.

Bridge Benefit (Canada)—A supplemental pension benefit payable from the date of early retirement until the age of entitlement for government pensions.

Broadbanding—In compensation, a strategy for salary structures that consolidates a large number of pay grades into a few broad bands. Broadbanding attempts to overcome a rigid, hierarchical pay structure.

Broker—

  —An insurance solicitor, licensed by the state, who places business with a variety of insurance companies and who represents the buyers of insurance rather than the companies even though he or she is paid commissions by the companies.

  —An agent who handles the public's orders to buy and sell securities, commodities or other property. For this service, a commission is charged that, depending upon the firm dealt with and the amount of the transaction, may or may not be negotiated.

Broker-Dealer—A person or firm that buys and sells securities for others and also for its own account. With some exceptions, broker-dealers must register with the Securities and Exchange Commission and with the securities commissioner in the state where they transact business.

Brokerage Accounts—See Self-Directed Brokerage Account.

Brokerage Fee—A fee charged by a broker for execution of a transaction; an amount per transaction or a percentage of a total value of the transaction; usually referred to as a *commission fee.*

Browser—Software that assists in the retrieval and viewing of documents on the World Wide Web.

Bubble Economy—A time period when stocks rise quickly, usually in a certain sector, but which investors expect to fall when a certain unsustainable level is reached. Also, a period of rising prosperity and increased commercial activity such as in Japan in the late 1980s, resulting from artificially adjusted interest rates.

Building Lien—A builder's charge or encumbrance upon property. See also Mechanic's Lien.

Bull—One who believes the stock market will rise.

Bull Market—An advancing stock market. The opposite of bear market.

Bundled Services—A package of complete administrative and investment services such as investment management, recordkeeping and custody, provided to 401(k) plan sponsors by a single entity or offered to employees by companies. Compare with Unbundled Services.

Bureau of Labor Statistics (BLS)—The U.S. Department of Labor unit that collects and reports labor statistics, including area wage data, national pay data and industry surveys.

Business Associate—Under HIPAA privacy legislation, an individual who, on behalf of a covered entity, performs or assists with a function or activity involving protected health information. Examples include lawyers, consultants, third-party administrators, doctors and health care clearinghouses.

Business Coalition—See Health Care Coalition.

Business Continuation Insurance—When a partner dies or is disabled, the remaining partners are provided with the funds to purchase that partner's interest in the firm. See also Key Employee Insurance.

Business Cycle—Four basic stages of the U.S. economy, as follows:

  • *Expansion*—The economy strengthens as business activity accelerates.
  • *Peak*—The economy overheats, causing inflation and interest rates to rise.
  • *Recession*—Higher interest rates lead to waning business activity and a contracting economy.
  • *Trough*—Declining inflation and interest rates spark the beginnings of an economic rebound.

Business Judgment Rule—A judicial doctrine offering protection to corporate officers and directors from personal liability for their actions, as long as they were taken in good faith and with reasonable care.

Business Life Insurance—See Key Employee Insurance.

Business Representative—Usually a paid union official representing workers in a labor agreement.

Business Travel Accident Insurance—Coverage for an accident while traveling on company business. Generally applies to all accidents occurring while away from home, not just those during actual travel.

Buy-Back Provision—When terminating employees who are no more than 50% vested withdraw their own contributions and the employer cancels the remainder of their benefits, this arrangement allows the employees to buy back the forfeited employer contributions by repaying the withdrawn amounts.

Bylaws—The rules adopted by the members or by the board of directors of a corporation or other organization for its government. Bylaws must not be contrary to the laws of the land, and affect only the members of the given corporation or organization; they do not apply to third parties.

C

C—Quality rating assigned by Standard & Poor's for speculative grade bonds. Reserved for income bonds on which no interest is being paid.

C Corporation—A regular corporation that elects to be taxed at the corporate, rather than individual level. See also S Corporation.

Cafeteria Plan—An employee benefit plan that offers participants a choice between cash and one or more qualified, or tax-favored, benefits. To obtain the benefit of tax-favored treatment, the plan must comply with Internal Revenue Code Section 125. Typical benefits include health insurance, child care, 401(k) contributions, group term life and dental benefits. See also Flexible Benefit Plan; Section 125 Plan.

Calendar Year Deductible—A deductible that applies to any eligible medical expenses incurred by the insured during any one calendar year.

Call Center—A telephone call center used to provide on-demand tracking, routing and reporting of employee benefit questions. Computer telephony integration can instantly provide relevant information about the caller, and speech recognition allows callers to verbalize their requests. The latest developments in call centers include systems for e-mail management. See also Employee Self-Service.

Call Date—The earliest date on which a bond may be redeemed before maturity at the option of the issuer.

Call Option—An option to buy a specified number of shares at a definite price within a specified period of time.

Call Price—The price at which a corporation or other obligor is permitted to redeem securities containing call provisions. To compensate for this privilege, a price above par is usually paid.

Callable—A bond issue all or part of which may be redeemed by the issuing corporation under specific terms before maturity. The term also applies to preferred shares that may be redeemed by the issuing company.

Called Bond—A bond drawn for redemption before maturity.

CalPERS (California Public Employees' Retirement System)—Provides retirement benefits for some 1.4 million current and retired state government employees. The nation's largest pension fund, it has been a crusader for shareholder rights and corporate governance reform.

Canada Customs and Revenue Agency (CCRA)—Formerly known as *Revenue Canada,* this agency promotes compliance with Canadian tax, trade and border legislation and regulations.

Canada Pension Plan (CPP)/Quebec Pension Plan (QPP) (Canada)—The Canada Pension Plan is a contributory, earnings-related social insurance program that ensures a measure of income protection to a contributor and his and her family against the loss of income due to retirement, disability or death. The plan operates throughout Canada; the Quebec Pension Plan (QPP), a similar plan, operates in the province of Quebec.

Canadian Association of Pension Supervisory Authorities (CAPSA)—Consists of senior government officials (provincial and federal) responsible for the administration of pension legislation in each jurisdiction.

Capital—Money and other assets needed by a company to operate a business and provide facilities for production and distribution of a product or service.

Capital Appreciation—A rise in the market prices of shares owned.

Capital Asset Pricing Model (CAPM)—Describes the way prices of individual assets are determined in markets where information is freely available and reflected instantaneously in asset prices—that is, efficient markets. According to this model, prices are determined in such a way that risk premiums are proportional to systematic risk, which is measured by the beta coefficient. As such, the CAPM provides an explicit expression of the expected returns for all assets. Basically, the CAPM holds that, if investors are risk averse, high-risk stocks must have higher expected returns than low-risk stocks.

Capital Assets; Fixed Assets—Relatively permanent assets held for use or income rather than for sale or direct conversion into salable goods or cash. Examples would be plant, equipment and property—also such intangible assets as good will and patents.

Capital Expenditures—Monies appropriated to increase or improve capital assets.

Capital Gain or Capital Loss—Profit or loss from the sale of a capital asset.

Capital Gains Distributions—Payments to mutual fund shareholders that consist of the realized gains on the assets sold by the fund. These gains are usually paid once a year and are usually long term in nature.

Capital Market—That segment of the securities market that deals in instruments with more than one year to maturity, that is, long-term debt and equity securities.

Capital Stock—All shares representing ownership of a business, including preferred and common.

Capital Structure—The division of the capitalization among bonds, preferred stock and common stock. A high common stock ratio to the total is considered conservative, and a low one is considered speculative.

Capital Sum—See Principal Sum.

Capitalization—Describes the value of a company in terms of its size. The aggregate or total amount of the various securities, in all forms, issued by a corporation. Includes bonds, debentures, preferred and common stock, and surplus. Bonds and debentures are usually carried on the books of the issuing company in terms of their par or face value. Preferred and common shares may be carried in terms of par or stated value. Stated value may be an arbitrary figure decided upon by the directors or may represent the amount received by the company from the sale of securities at the time of issuance. Determining a present value of income property by taking either the known or estimated annual net income and discounting by using a rate of return commonly accepted at the time by buyers of similar properties.

Capitation—A capitation benefit program is one in which a provider contracts with the program's sponsor or administrator to provide all or most of the services covered under the program to subscribers in return for payment on a per capita basis. This payment is known as a *capitation fee,* and it is fixed without regard to the actual number or nature of services provided to each person in a set period of time. Capitation is the characteristic payment method in health maintenance organizations.

Captive Insurance Company—An insurance company that is a subsidiary of a noninsurance corporation. The insurer primarily writes insurance on its parent and the parent's other subsidiaries, although nonrelated business may be solicited.

Card Program—Use of a drug benefit identification card which, when presented to a participating pharmacy by employees or their dependents, usually entitles them to receive the medication for a minimal copay.

Career Average Pay Formula/Career Average Plan—A career average pay formula is a defined benefit plan formula that bases benefits on the employee's compensation over the entire period of service with the employer. A career average pay plan is a plan with such a formula.

Carrier—A commercial insurer, a government agency or a Blue Cross or Blue Shield plan that underwrites or administers programs that pay for health, life or other insurance services.

Carryover Deductible—The deductible payable under continuation coverage includes the portion of the deductible satisfied before the qualifying event.

Carryover Provisions—
—(Compensation) An employer policy that lets employees take unused vacation time in a subsequent calendar or fiscal year.

—(Health Care) Provision in major medical plans to avoid two deductibles applied to covered medical expenses when expenses are incurred toward the end of one calendar year, and sickness or injury continues into next year.

Carve-Out—
—A program separate from the primary group health plan designed to provide a specialized type of care, such as a mental health carve-out.
—Also, a method of integrating Medicare with an employer's retiree health plan (making the employer plan excess or secondary) which tends to produce the lowest employer cost.
—(Canada) Used in reference to a plan integrated with OAS, CPP/QPP.

Case Management—A utilization management technique that focuses on coordinating a number of health care and disability services needed by clients. It includes a standardized, objective assessment of client needs and the development of an individualized service or care plan that is based on the needs assessment and is goal oriented. Often used for patients with certain conditions who need extensive medical services; usually overseen by an individual or team of medical practitioners.

Case Mix—The classifications or categories of patients treated by a hospital.

Cash Balance Plan—A defined benefit plan that simulates a defined contribution plan. Benefits are definitely determinable, but account balances are credited with a fixed rate of return and converted to a monthly pension benefit at retirement. See also Target Benefit Plan.

Cash Equivalents—Very short-term investments, coming due in a year or less—the maturity range of money market funds and treasury bills. Similar to cash in liquidity and safety from market volatility.

Cash Flow—The reported net income of a corporation plus amounts charged off for depreciation, depletion, amortization and extraordinary charges to reserves, which are a bookkeeping deduction and not paid out in actual dollars and cents.

Cash or Deferred Arrangement (CODA)—Section 401(k) of the Internal Revenue Code allows employers to offer employees a choice between receiving compensation and having a contribution made on their behalf to a qualified plan. See also 401(k) Plan; Salary Reduction Plan.

Cash Out—A pension plan may provide for the forfeiture of an accrued benefit where the plan provides for a *cash out* of an employee's benefits by making a lump-sum distribution to the employee. The cash out applies only to the employee's nonforfeitable interest upon termination of service prior to retirement.

Cash Refund Annuity—See Refund Annuity.

Cash Surrender Value—See Surrender Value.

Catastrophic Health Care—Health care for life-threatening conditions whose cost can drain an individual's family income.

Catchment Area—The geographic area from which a particular program or facility for health care draws the bulk of its users. See also Service Area.

Catch-Up Contributions—For years beginning after 2001, eligible employees aged 50 or older can make higher tax-deferred annual contributions in the years prior to retirement in 401(k) plans, IRAs, 403(b) plans and 457 plans. These contributions can help to offset the effect of inflation because past service and contributions based on compensation may be inadequate.

CD—See Certificate of Deposit.

CD-ROM—A compact disk on which read-only computer data is stored.

Centers for Disease Control (CDC)—The federal agency that researches and investigates causes of diseases, provides educational and prevention programs, and issues definitions of diseases and the conditions that determine eligibility for state, federal and/or private benefit programs. CDC is part of the Public Health System, a division of the Department of Health and Human Services.

Centers for Medicare and Medicaid Services (CMS)—The agency of the Department of Health and Human Services that administers Medicare, Medicaid and other federal programs established by the Social Security Act of 1935. Formerly the Health Care Financing Administration (HCFA).

Centers of Excellence—Specific providers selected to

perform certain procedures because of their expertise and willingness to provide discounts.

CERES Principles—A ten-point environmental reporting and accountability code previously called the Valdez Principles and now named after the Coalition for Environmentally Responsible Economies (CERES). The ten principles are intended to expand the concept of socially responsible action with an emphasis on environmental issues.

Certificate—The actual piece of paper that is evidence of ownership of stock in a corporation. Watermarked paper is finely engraved with delicate etchings to discourage forgery. Loss of a certificate may at the least cause a great deal of inconvenience—at the worst, financial loss.

Certificate of Creditable Coverage—Notes the amount of previous qualified health coverage; required by HIPAA in certain circumstances.

Certificate of Deposit (CD)—A short-term, interest-bearing debt instrument offered by banks and savings and loan associations. The bank or savings and loan association offers a written certification that a fixed dollar amount has been deposited with it for a certain period of time at a predetermined rate of interest. Early withdrawal of the money is penalized.

Certificate of Insurance—A document that is given to insured members of a group insurance plan and that outlines the plan's coverage and the member's rights.

Certificate of Need (CON)—A certificate issued by a governmental body to an individual or organization proposing to construct or modify a health facility, acquire new medical equipment or offer a new health service. CON is intended to control expansion of facilities and services by preventing their excessive or duplicative development.

Certification—The process by which a governmental or nongovernmental agency or association evaluates and recognizes a person who meets predetermined standards; sometimes used with reference to materials or services. *Certification* is usually applied to individuals and *accreditation* to institutions. See also Accreditation; Licensure.

Certified Employee Benefit Specialist® (CEBS®)—A designation granted jointly by the International Foundation of Employee Benefit Plans and the Wharton School of the University of Pennsylvania to individuals who complete eight college-level courses and examinations in the areas of compensation and design and operation of employee benefit plans and who pledge to a code of ethical standards and continuing education. In Canada, the program is presented jointly by the International Foundation of Employee Benefit Plans and Dalhousie University of Halifax.

Certified Financial Planner (CFP)—A professional designation granted by the International Board of Standards and Practices for Certified Financial Planners, Inc. (IBCFP), to individuals who have passed a series of examinations on investing, tax preparation and management, insurance, retirement and estate planning.

Certified Length of Stay—The period of time approved as necessary and appropriate for a patient to receive inpatient care in a hospital.

Certified Pension Consultant (CPC)—A designation awarded by the American Society of Pension Actuaries. Holders must combine required experience with passing three examinations covering employee benefits fundamentals.

Certified Public Accountant (CPA)—A professional license granted by the various states to persons meeting certain educational, experience and examination requirements. These requirements vary from state to state, but typically they include a college degree with accounting and auditing course work and qualifying experience. The examinations include passing the Uniform CPA Examination, covering accounting theory and practice, auditing and business law.

Channeling—The practice by a plan or medical provider of directing patients or workload away from one source to another, such as to a different plan, physician or hospital.

Chapter 218 Agreement—See Federal-State Agreement.

Charitable Corporations—Such employers are exempt from tax, and their employees enjoy a unique deferment of tax liability in connection with employer-purchased annuities.

Charitable Remainder Trust—A living trust that allows a donor to a charity to receive income from the assets donated, while any remaining assets in the trust transfer to the charity when the donor dies.

Charter—A certificate of incorporation, issued by a state, legally authorizing a corporation to conduct business as stipulated in this charter.

Chartered Financial Analyst (CFA)—Awarded by the Institute of Chartered Financial Analysts. Holders must combine required experience and education with passing three examinations covering ethical and professional standards, securities laws and regulations, financial accounting and so on.

Chartered Financial Consultant (ChFC)—A designation granted by the American College to individuals who complete a ten-course program in the areas of personal financial and retirement planning and who pledge to a code of ethical standards and continuing education.

Chartered Life Underwriter (CLU)—A designation granted by the American College to individuals who complete a ten-course program in the areas of insurance and estate planning and who pledge to a code of ethical standards and continuing education.

Chartered Property and Casualty Underwriter (CPCU)—A designation awarded by the American Institute for Property and Liability Underwriters. Formal application and acceptance is required. Holders must combine required experience with passing ten examinations on various insurance topics.

Chemotherapy—Treatment of internal disease by chemical reagents (including drugs), primarily involved in the treatment of cancer.

Child Tax Benefit (Canada)—A refundable tax credit for low- and middle-income families with children. It is given on a monthly basis.

Chiropractic—A system of medicine based on the theory that disease is caused by malfunction of the nerve system, and that normal function of the nerve system can be achieved by manipulation and other treatment of the structures of the body, primarily the spinal column and pelvis. A practitioner is a chiropractor, Doctor of Chiropractic (DC).

Chronically Ill—A person unable to perform two of six activities of daily living for at least 90 days, or who is severely cognitively impaired is said to be chronically ill. Under this term, qualification for long-term care expenses is determined.

Church Plan—
—A plan established and maintained by a church or convention or association of churches that is tax exempt under Internal Revenue Code Section 501. The following, however, are not church plans: (1) a plan that is primarily for the benefit of employees of an unrelated business (as described in IRC Section 513) and (2) a multi-employer plan that includes one or more employers that are not tax-exempt churches or conventions of churches. For plan years beginning before January 1, 1983, employees covered by a plan (in existence on January 1, 1974) for employees of a tax-exempt agency of a church (or convention or association of churches) are considered employees of the church.
—Although exempt, a church (or convention or association of churches) can make an irrevocable election to be covered by the participation, vesting and funding requirements of ERISA.

Churning—
—A form of code gaming where the same medical procedure is billed more than once, or a provider sees a patient more often than medically necessary.
—Excessive trading in a customer's account. The term suggests that the registered representative ignores the objectives and interests of clients, and seeks only to increase commissions.

Civil Action—A proceeding in a law court or a suit in equity by one person against another for the enforcement or protection of a private right, or the prevention of a wrong. Civil action is in contrast to criminal action, in which the state prosecutes a person for commission of an illegal act or breach of a duty.

Civil Rights Act of 1964—This act, as well as its amendments and other similar legislation, prohibits discrimination on the basis of race, color, sex, national origin, age, religion, handicap status and Vietnam War veteran status.

Civilian Health and Medical Program of the Uniformed Services (CHAMPUS)—Provided coverage for armed forces personnel dependents and retirees receiving care outside a military treatment facility. Replaced by TRICARE. See TRICARE.

Claim—
—An itemized statement of services rendered by a health care provider for a given patient. The claim is submitted to a health benefits plan for payment.
—A request for payment under an employee benefit plan (pension or health and welfare) or insurer by a plan participant or beneficiary for the payment of certain benefits.
—The right to any debts, privileges or other things in possession of another; also, the titles to anything which another should concede to, or confer on the claimant.

Claim Administrator—Any entity that reviews and determines whether to pay claims to enrollees or physicians on behalf of the health benefit plan. Claim administrators may be insurance companies or their designated claims review organizations, self-insured employers, management firms, third-party administrators or other private contractors.

Claim Form—The form used to file for benefits under a health plan.

Claimant—Plan participant who files a claim for benefits. See also Beneficiary.

Claims Experience—The frequency, cost and types of claims insured employees file to receive benefits. One of the primary factors used in calculating insurance premiums.

Claims Procedure—Under ERISA, each plan is required to provide a claims procedure, which must be explained to plan participants and beneficiaries. The denial of a claim made under the claims procedure must be in writing, with an explanation of the reasons for the denial.

Claims Reserve—See Reserve.

Claims Review—
—In health care prepayment, the routine examination by a carrier or intermediary of the claim submitted to it for payment or for predetermination of benefits; may include determination of eligibility, coverage of service and plan liability.
—In quality assurance, examination by organizations of claims as part of a quality review or utilization review process.

Claims Services Only (CSO)—A contract designed for fully self-insured employers that need very little administrative assistance. Under a CSO arrangement, the insurer administers only the claims portion of the plan.

Class Rating—An approach to rate making in which a price per unit of insurance is computed for all applicants with a given set of characteristics. For example, the rate may apply to all persons of a given age and sex, to all buildings of a certain type of construction or to all businesses of a certain type.

Classification Method of Job Evaluation—Job contents are compared to predefined class descriptions established for each job grade.

Clawback (Canada)—The process of taxing government benefits such as Old Age Security (OAS) at a certain income level.

Cliff Vesting—Full 100% vesting after x years of service, with no gradation of vesting before that time. Benefits must be 100% vested after five years. If participants leave the company or are terminated prior to the vesting date, no partial benefits are received. See also Graded Vesting; Vesting.

Clinical Outcomes—Health status changes or effects that individual patients experience resulting from the delivery of health care, usually measured in terms of morbidity, mortality, functional ability and satisfaction with care.

Clinical Outliers—Cases that cannot adequately be assigned to an appropriate diagnostic-related group (DRG) because of unique combinations of diagnoses and surgeries, very rare conditions or for other unique clinical reasons. Such cases will be grouped together into clinical outlier DRGs. See also Outliers.

Closed-End Fund/Closed-End Investment Company—Closed-end funds were established as a way to give investors access to illiquid but profitable investments that could not be bought or sold on an exchange. Closed-end funds are not required to redeem shares from investors, and the investment costs of these funds are higher than for open-end funds. See also Open-End Fund/Open-End Investment Company.

Closed Panel—A closed panel practice is established if patients eligible for health services in a public or private program can receive these services only at

24

specified facilities through a limited number of providers. A staff model HMO is an example.

Closed Shop—A union security arrangement in a labor agreement that requires union membership for employment. Prohibited by the Taft-Harley Act (1947).

Closely Held Corporation—A nonpublic corporation that is owned by a small number of shareholders.

Closing Agreement Program (CAP)—Part of the IRS-administered program for qualified pension plans that allows employers to avoid plan disqualification by remedying certain types of violations and paying a fine. The program enables employers to talk to the IRS anonymously and negotiate fines without risk. See also Employee Plans Compliance Resolution System (EPCRS).

Closing Costs—The numerous expenses buyers and sellers normally incur in the transfer of ownership of real estate.

Closing Price—The price at which the final transaction in a security took place on a particular business day. Stock prices are quoted daily in the financial pages of leading newspapers, where number of shares traded and the opening, high, low and last sale (closing) prices, plus net change from the previous day, are printed from left to right in that order.

Closing Transaction—A transaction in which the seller (writer) of an option terminates his or her obligation. In the case of a listed option, a seller effects a closing transaction by purchasing a listed option having the same terms as the option previously sold.

Coalition—See Health Care Coalition.

COBRA—See Consolidated Omnibus Budget Reconciliation Act of 1985.

Code—
—The Internal Revenue Code of 1986.
—A collection or compilation of the statutes passed by a legislative body.
—A system of characters and syntax rules that can translate human language into computer language.

Code Gaming—The use of incorrect billing codes to increase provider income, or to enable a patient to receive reimbursement for a treatment that would otherwise be nonreimbursable.

Coding—A mechanism for identifying and defining physician services.

Cofiduciary Liability—Plan fiduciaries are obligated under ERISA to guard against breaches of fiduciary responsibilities by other plan fiduciaries, as well as being responsible (and personally liable) for their own fiduciary breaches.

Coinsurance—A policy provision, frequently found in major medical insurance, by which the insured person and the insurer share the hospital and medical expenses resulting from an illness or injury in a specified ratio (e.g., 80%:20%), after the deductible is met. A form of cost sharing.

Collateral—Usually securities or other property pledged by a borrower to secure payment of a loan. However, collateral can also be intangible, such as an interest in future payments. Basically, it is anything considered to have value.

Collateralized Mortgage Obligation (CMO)—A mortgage security with different *tranches* or maturity classes. Such an instrument can fill the predetermined need for maturities by a fund.

Collective Bargaining—The process of good faith negotiation between employer and employee representatives concerning issues of mutual interest.

Collective Bargaining Agreement or Contract—Formal agreement over wages, hours and conditions of employment entered into between an employer or group of employers and one or more unions representing employees of the employers.

Collective Investment Fund—A pool of investments managed by a bank according to a written plan on behalf of several individual fiduciary accounts whose assets are lawfully contributed to the fund. Participation in these funds is available only to fiduciary assets held in trust by a bank or other lawful trustee.

Collective Trust Fund—See Common Trust Fund.

Collectively Bargained Plans—Plans that provide benefits under a collective bargaining agreement between employee representatives and one or more employers.

Combination Plan—The use of two or more types of plans to provide retirement benefits. For example, a defined contribution plan, such as a money purchase plan, may be combined with a defined benefit pension plan or with another defined contribution plan, such as a profit-sharing plan.

Commercial Paper—Short-term corporate promissory notes issued for the purpose of raising capital for a limited period of time. They are usually sold in denominations of $100,000 or more.

Commingled Funds—The collective investment of the assets of a number of small pension funds, usually through a bank-administered plan allowing for broader and more efficient investing.

Commission—The broker's basic fee for purchasing or selling securities or property as an agent. This fee may or may not be negotiated.

Commodity Exchange—An organization of traders who buy and sell contracts for future delivery of such things as grain, cotton, hogs, sugar, coffee, gold and mortgages.

Common Control—Corporations, trades or businesses, including sole proprietorships and partnerships, are under common control when either one entity owns at least 80% of the stock, profit or capital interest in the other organization; or the same five or fewer people own a controlling interest in each entity.

Common Law—That body of law deriving from judicial decisions, as opposed to legislatively enacted statutes and administrative regulations.

Common Law Employee—Individual who performs services for an employer if the employer has the right to control and direct the individual; income and employment taxes are withheld by the employer.

Common Stock—Securities that represent an ownership interest in a corporation. If the company has also issued preferred stock, both common and preferred have ownership rights. The preferred normally is limited to a fixed dividend but has prior claim on dividends and, in the event of liquidation, assets. Claims of both common and preferred stockholders are junior to claims of bondholders and other creditors of the company. Common stockholders assume the greater risk, but generally exercise the greater control and may gain the greater reward in the form of dividends and capital appreciation. The terms *common stock* and *capital stock* are often used interchangeably when the company has no preferred stock.

Common Stock Fund—A mutual fund that primarily invests its assets in common stocks.

Common Trust Fund—A trust fund in which the assets of a number of trusts are commingled. Also referred to as a *collective trust*.

Commonly Controlled Businesses—All employees of corporations that are members of a *controlled group of corporations* are treated as employed by a single employer for purposes of plan qualification. A comparable requirement applies to partnerships, sole proprietorships and other businesses under common control.

Community Health Center (CHC)—A facility that provides care for the needy at the community level as a safety net for other systems that do not provide services. It may or may not receive federal funding.

Community Rating—The process of determining the premium for a group risk on the basis of the average claims experience for the general population instead of a particular employer. This is especially helpful for small groups, whose claims experience over two or three years may not be typical. Community rating is used by most HMOs, which use the plan's entire client population to set premiums. See also Experience Rating.

Comorbidity—A preexisting condition that will, because of its presence with a specific principal diagnosis, cause an increase in length of hospital stay by at least one day in approximately 75% of the cases.

Comparability Pension Plans—Defined contribution pension plans such as profit-sharing or money purchase plans that allow contributions to be higher for one group than for another. These plans are tested under the cross testing rules of IRC Section 401(a)(4) to satisfy nondiscrimination requirements.

Compa-Ratio—A comparison of total actual pay in a pay grade to the midpoint or some other point of that pay grade. The ratio can be expressed as actual pay divided by the applicable salary range. Compa-ratios can be calculated for a group, a department or an entire organization and are used to analyze the relative position of the individual or group to the pay guide.

Comp Time—Compensation time; refers to overtime hours that are worked and then taken later as paid time off.

Comparable Worth—The doctrine that men and women who perform work of the same inherent value should receive comparable compensation.

Compensable Factor—Any factor, such as skill, effort, responsibility and working conditions, used to provide a basis for creating a job worth hierarchy (job evaluation) within an organization. These factors were established by the Equal Pay Act of 1963.

Compensation—An approach to assigning a monetary value to work performed by employees. Compensation may include wages, salary, base pay, overtime pay, profit sharing, vacations and all benefits employees receive in return for their work.

Competency-Based Pay—Connects pay to the depth and scope of abilities needed to perform a job. Includes *skill-based pay* and *pay for knowledge*.

Complementary and Alternative Medicine (CAM)—Includes nontraditional medical practices such as acupuncture, chiropractic, herbal medicine, homeopathy, massage therapy and yoga, that focus on the entire person, not just the physical, and on the innate healing power within. Alternative medicine stresses quality of life, use of natural substances, being healed as opposed to being cured, and energy flow.

Compound Interest—The interest upon principal that is being increased, or augmented, periodically by interest paid on the previous amount of principal. Interest may be compounded daily, monthly, quarterly, semiannually or annually.

Compounding—The arithmetic process of finding the final value of an investment or series of investments when compound interest is applied. That is, interest is earned on the accrued interest as well as on the initial principal.

Comprehensive Major Medical Coverage—This coverage provides protection similar to a combined basic and major medical plan and is often characterized by a low deductible, less than 100% reimbursement and a high maximum benefit. A typical type of comprehensive plan provides that most types of medical expenses are covered, usually after the satisfaction of a relatively low initial deductible (such as $100). After covered expenses exceed this initial deductible, the plan typically pays:
1. 100% of certain kinds of expenses up to a certain limit (such as 100% of the first $2,000 of covered hospital expenses after the deductible)
2. A percentage, such as 80%, of all other covered medical expenses, including the expenses that exceed the limit mentioned in item 1.

Comprehensive Medical Care—A complete package of health care services and benefits, including prevention, early detection and early treatment of conditions.

Compulsory Retirement—When the employee must retire when he or she reaches a given age. Now prohibited under ADEA if based solely on age, except for certain executives or where public safety outweighs individual protection (e.g., airline pilots). Also known as *automatic* or *mandatory retirement.*

Computer Language—A group of symbols, numbers, letters, words or a combination of these that can be used to communicate with the computer and cause it to perform desired operations for processing data.

Computerized Axial Tomography (CAT) Scanner—Uses a minicomputer and highly sensitive X-ray detectors to produce extremely accurate three-dimensional pictures of body and brain tissues.

Concierge Benefits—Any kind of convenience service offered by an employer to employees, such as errand service (drycleaning pickup, shopping, waiting for the cable repair person) or on-site services (banking, medical services, mail room services). The benefits help employees balance work and personal needs and improve morale and productivity.

Concurrent Review—The process by which hospital admissions for elective and emergency treatment are certified for appropriateness at the time of service and by which continued stays are verified for medical necessity and level of care.

Conduit IRA—While retirement funds are being rolled over from one qualified pension plan to another, a conduit IRA is used to temporarily hold the transferring funds.

Confidentiality—In HIPAA privacy concerns, the property that data or information is not made available or disclosed to unauthorized persons or processes.

Conflict of Interest—A situation that provides potential for self-dealing. For example, a trustee has a conflict of interest if he or she has an interest in a construction project to be financed by the plan the trustee represents.

Conglomerate—A corporation that has diversified its operations, usually by acquiring enterprises in widely varied industries.

Congress of Industrial Organizations (CIO)—A federation primarily made up of industrial unions originally established in 1935 as a committee within the AFL (the Committee for Industrial Organization) and later becoming an independent body. In 1955, the Congress of Industrial Organizations merged with AFL to form AFL-CIO, with which most, although not all, major U.S. unions are affiliated. See also American Federation of Labor.

Consideration—One of the elements of a binding contract. Means that each party to a contract has received or been promised something of value from the other party, such as money, property or a promise to perform an act.

Consolidated Omnibus Budget Reconciliation Act of 1985 (COBRA)—Among the provisions of this legislation that deal with health care coverage are the following:
1. Employer-provided medical plans can no longer require Medicare to be the primary payer for participants aged 70 and over.
2. Medicare coverage is extended to state and local government employees.
3. Almost every group health plan must provide each participant and qualified beneficiary under the plan the option to pay for continued coverage for a specified period of time under the plan in the event coverage would otherwise have ceased as a result of one of a number of "qualifying events."

Constructive Receipt—Federal tax law doctrine that maintains compensation becomes taxable when it is made available to the taxpayer, even though it has not actually been received. If an employee can choose between immediate taxable income or a deferred income or benefit, the employee is in constructive receipt of the income. See also Economic Benefit.

Consultant—A person or firm offering expert business, professional or technical advice to an organization for a salary or fee.

Consumer-Driven Health Care—Any type of employer-sponsored health benefits plan or initiative that seeks to give employees greater responsibility for choosing their own health care and provides incentives for them to seek the most cost-effective care. Internet-based plan administration and Internet use by employees for personal health management can be part of these plans. See also Flexible Spending Accounts (FSAs); Health Reimbursement Accounts (HRAs); Health Savings Accounts (HSAs); Medical Savings Account (MSA).

Consumer Price Index (CPI)—The name given in the United States and Canada to the series of numbers whose ratios measure the relative prices at various times of a fixed market basket of goods and services that typify those bought by urban families. The CPI is a measure of inflation.

Contingency Reserve—That portion of contributions or premiums set aside in a special account to cover possible loss resulting from adverse experience with respect to investments, interest earnings, mortality, withdrawals and so on.

Contingent Annuity Option—An option under which an employee may elect to receive, under certain conditions, a reduced amount of annuity with the same income, or a specified fraction, to be paid after his or her death to another person designated as his or her contingent annuitant, for that person's lifetime. The contingent annuitant is usually the husband or wife. See also Automatic Survivor Coverage; Joint and Survivor Annuity.

Contingent Beneficiary—Person(s) named to receive

policy benefits if the primary beneficiary is deceased.

Contingent Employee—Any worker employed on less than a permanent full-time basis and who has no explicit or implicit expectation for continued employment.

Continuation Coverage—Coverage under a health insurance plan paid for by a qualified beneficiary following the occurrence of a qualifying event under COBRA.

Continuation of Benefits—Under COBRA, employers have the obligation to make available to employees and their dependents some continued benefit coverage, even after the employment relationship ceases. Employees or dependents must pay for this coverage.

Continued Stay Review (CSR)—A review and an initial determination by a utilization review committee, during a patient's hospitalization, of the necessity and appropriateness of continuation of the patient's stay at a hospital level of care.

Continuing Care Retirement Community (CCRC)—A residential community which, in exchange for an entrance fee and a monthly charge, guarantees lifetime housing and nursing care as required.

Continuity of Care—The result of a planned treatment program designed to provide the individual patient with the total range of needed services under continuing responsible direction.

Continuous Quality Improvement (CQI)—An approach to quality management that builds on traditional quality assurance methods by emphasizing the organization and systems, the need for objective data with which to analyze and improve processes, and the ideal that systems and performance can always improve even when high standards appear to have been met; similar to total quality management (TQM).

Continuous Service—All creditable service rendered by a member without a break in service including periods of absence for which salary is paid or for military service.

Contract—A promissory agreement between two or more persons that creates, modifies or destroys a legal relation. In general, it must have the following elements: creates an obligation, competent parties, subject matter, legal consideration, mutuality of agreement, mutuality of obligation, must not be so vague or uncertain that terms are not ascertainable, and generally is in writing signed by both parties.

Contract Administrator—See Third-Party Administrator.

Contract Group—See Enrolled Group.

Contract In/Out (International Benefits)—*Contracted out* refers to an employer providing benefits in lieu of the state earnings-related social security pension. If an employer is *contracted* in, the employee participates in the state earnings-related scheme.

Contract Worker—An employee who works under contracts as the employee of a technical service firm. These employees are not independent contractors or contingent workers.

Contrarian—A common stock manager whose style of management places emphasis on stocks currently out of favor.

Contribution—The transfer of funds or property by either an employer or an employee to an employee benefit plan.

Contribution Carryover—This is created whenever annual contributions exceed the maximum allowable deductions. This carryover can be deducted in future years in which contribution payments are less than the maximum deduction.

Contribution Formula—As used under a qualified profit-sharing trust or money purchase pension plan, it is the formula that spells out when and in what amounts the employer will make contributions to the trust.

Contribution Limit—The maximum dollar limit on annual additions (employer contributions, certain employee contributions and forfeitures) for an employee under defined contribution plans of an employer.

Contribution Rate—
  —As to an employee—a factor, such as a percentage of compensation, used in determining the

amounts of payments to be made by the employee under a contributory pension plan.

—As to an employer—a factor, calculated in an actuarial valuation, to be used in determining the employer's annual normal cost contribution under a pension plan. An employer's contribution rate may be either a percentage to be applied to the total compensation paid to covered employees for a particular year, or an amount in dollars to be applied to the total number of covered employees at a particular date.

Contribution Requirement—In profit-sharing plans, a definite predetermined contribution formula is not required, but "substantially recurring" contributions must be made out of profits if the requirements of plan permanency are to be met. Nevertheless, liability must be established within the fiscal year.

Contributory Plan—

—A qualified pension plan that requires employees to make contributions by payroll deduction to qualify for benefits under the plan. May be a defined benefit or defined contribution plan.

—A benefit plan under which employees bear part of the cost. In some contributory plans, employees wishing to be covered must contribute; in other contributory plans, employee contributions are voluntary and result in increased benefits.

Controlled Group—A group of corporations, trades or businesses, each of which is at least 80% owned (either directly or through one or more chains of subsidiary corporations) by a common parent corporation or a group of five or fewer individuals, estates or trusts.

Controller—The officer responsible for the accounting function of the business.

Conventional Loan—A mortgage or deed of trust not obtained under a government-insured program, such as FHA or VA. The most prevalent type of mortgage loan made. These may or may not be insured by a private mortgage insurer.

Conversion—

—(Insurance) Privilege given to participant to convert to individual policies on termination of group coverage without evidence of insurability.

—(Investments) The process of converting a security, such as a bond or preferred stock, into common stock.

—(Pension Plans) Refers to employers changing from one type of plan to another. For example, from a defined benefit plan to a defined contribution plan, or from a traditional pension plan to a cash balance plan.

Conversion Fund—An unallocated fund held either by a corporate trustee or by an insurance company and used for the purpose of buying annuities to supplement the annuities purchased through individual insurance contracts.

Conversion Premium (Convertible Securities)—The percentage difference between the conversion value and the market price of a bond or preferred stock.

Conversion Price—The price for which a convertible bond of a corporation may be exchanged for stock of the same corporation.

Conversion Privilege—The right of an individual to convert a group health or life insurance policy to an individual policy should the individual cease to be a member of the group. Under such a provision, a physical examination is usually not required.

Conversion Ratio (Convertible Securities)—The number of shares of common stock received when one bond or one share of preferred stock is converted.

Convertible Bonds or Debentures—Bonds that are convertible into the common stock of a corporation at a prescribed price or ratio at the option of the holder, who is a creditor of the issuer, and who may share in additional profits over and above the coupon's rate of the bond, if the company prospers.

Convertible Mortgage—A mortgage where the pension fund gains interest and appreciation, based on the increase in rent. In addition, the fund has the option (usually between the seventh and tenth year of the loan) to convert into equity ownership, ranging from 50-80%. Primarily made on commercial properties.

Convertible Preferred Stock—Preferred stock that, in addition to having preference as to dividends and/or assets in the event of liquidation, is convertible into the common stock of the company, thereby enabling the holder to share in additional profits via appreciation and/or dividends. See also Cumulative Preferred Stock; Noncumulative Preferred Stock; Participating Preferred Stock; Preferred Stock.

Convertible Term Insurance—Term insurance under which the policy owner has the right (within the limitations stated in the policy) to exchange for insurance on a permanent plan without evidence of insurability.

Coordination of Benefits (COB)—A group health insurance policy provision designed to eliminate duplicate payments and provide the sequence in which coverage will apply (primary and secondary) when a person is insured under two contracts.

Copayments—Payments made by consumers, in addition to deductibles and coinsurance, to discourage inappropriate utilization and to help finance health benefit plans. See also Coinsurance; Deductible.

Core Alternative—Under a 404(c) plan, a participant's choice from at least three diversified investment options.

Core Benefits—The central components of a health care plan, generally comprehensive major medical and hospitalization benefits. These may be supplemented by additional noncore benefits such as dental and vision benefits.

Core Compensation—The monetary rewards received by employees. Includes base pay, seniority pay, merit pay, incentive pay, cost-of-living adjustments (COLAs) and competency-based pay.

Core Competencies—Integrated skill and knowledge sets that distinguish an organization and deliver value to customers.

Core Management—A method of supervising a portfolio of securities that is relatively passive in nature. Although fundamental analysis is applied to achieve performance in excess of the market indexes over the long pull, turnover ratios are limited in the interest of reducing transaction costs.

Corporate Bond—An instrument written under seal whereby a corporation acknowledges a stated sum is owed, which it will repay at a specified date. It also obligates itself to pay a stipulated amount of interest to the bondholders for the privilege of using their money.

Corporate Governance—The legal and practical system for the exercise and control of power in the conduct of the business of a corporation. Includes relationships among the shareholders, board of directors and committees, and the executive officers.

Corporate Owned Life Insurance (COLI)—A policy covering an executive who is essential to an organization. The organization is the beneficiary; if the executive dies while covered, the organization pays an equivalent noninsured amount to designated survivors. Policy loans on the insurance are available to the organization; the interest is partially deductible. See also Split Dollar Life Insurance.

Corporation—A legal entity composed of one or more individuals and established by law for some specific purpose or purposes whose existence, power and scope of action are determined by its charter. The owners are not personally liable for any debts of the corporation.

Corpus—The principal or property in a trust as opposed to the income from it.

Correction on Audit Program (Audit CAP)—If an uncorrected error is noticed by the IRS on a benefit plan audit, the plan sponsor may correct the error and pay a reasonable sanction, depending on the nature, extent and severity of the error and the extent to which correction occurred before the audit. See also Employee Plans Compliance Resolution System (EPCRS); Self-Correction Program (SCP); Voluntary Correction Program (VCP).

Correlation—A statistical term used to describe the relationship between two variables. Investors use correlation as a measurement tool to tell how well their investments will work together. Combining investments that have low correlations with each other can reduce risk.

Corridor Deductible—A deductible provision separating an underlying basic medical expense plan from a supplementary major medical plan, which represents a margin of covered expenses to be borne by covered persons before the major medical plan provides benefits.

Cost/Benefit Analysis—A comparison of the cost of an action with the economic benefits it produces through elimination of other direct and indirect costs.

Cost Containment (Medical)—Methods and programs designed to contain costs by ensuring appropriateness, medical necessity and relatedness of treatment and procedures. Examples include utilization review and bill review.

Cost of Living—The average cost of the goods and services required by a person or family.

Cost-of-Living Adjustment (COLA)—An across-the-board increase (or decrease) in wages or pension benefits according to the rise (or fall) in the cost of living as measured by some index, often the consumer price index (CPI).

Cost-of-Living Allowance—In expatriate compensation, the amount by which base pay is increased or decreased to adjust for a geographic area's cost of living.

Cost Sharing—Arrangements whereby consumers pay a portion of the cost of health services, sharing costs with employers. Deductibles, copayments, coinsurance and payroll deductions are forms of cost sharing.

Cost Shifting—
—(Employer) Policies designed to shift the relative burden of health care costs borne by one party or market segment to another. For example, many employers are shifting a portion of the costs of care to employees by copayments and increased contributions.
—(Provider) The practice by some providers of redistributing the difference between normal charges and amounts received from certain payers by increasing charges made to other payers.

Counsel—A lawyer or lawyers; also, legal advice.

Coupon—
—The interest an investor receives from a bond. It is expressed in annual percentage terms and is derived by multiplying the face value amount by the interest rate.
—Certificate attached to a bond representing the interest due on the bond. Coupons may be in ticket form so they can be clipped as they become due and presented at a bank for deposit or

cash. The bank is then reimbursed by the issuer of the bond.

Coupon Bond—A negotiable bond, the regular interest of which is payable to the person who clips the coupon and deposits it at his or her bank for collection. Upon maturity, the bearer is paid the face value of the security.

Coupon Rate—The interest rate stated on the face of a bond, note or other fixed income security expressed as percentage of the face value (principal).

Coupon Stripping—The process of separating the interest payments of a bond from the principal amount that is due at maturity. Once separated, each coupon, as well as the principal amount (the corpus), represents a different single payment claim due from the issuer of the security. Each single payment claim, then, becomes tantamount to a zero-coupon bond. By "stripping" a bond, a yield curve of zero-coupon bonds can be created; the maturity of each may be used independently. For example, if $1 million par amount of a 14% bond due in ten years was stripped, the result would be a series of 20 semiannual zero-coupon bonds, each with a par value of $70,000, and one ten-year zero coupon bond, with a par value of $1 million.

Covariance—A measure of the degree to which two variables move together. A positive value means that, on average, they move in the same direction.

Coverage—
—Describes the number or percentage of employees eligible for participation under an employee benefit plan.
—Benefits available to eligible individuals under an employee benefit program.
—With reference to revenue and corporate bonds, it indicates margin of safety for payment of debt service, reflecting the number of times by which earnings for a period of time exceed debt service payable in such period.

Coverdell Education Savings Accounts (ESAs)—Trust or custodial accounts that can be used to pay for qualified education expenses for a designated beneficiary; they are designed to help parents fund their children's education. Contributions to the accounts are taxed, but these accounts grow tax-free. The accounts are transferable among family members, and contributions can be made by anyone on behalf of the beneficiary. The accounts must be used before the beneficiary turns the age of 30; withdrawals after this date or for nonqualified expenses are penalized. The Coverdell Education Savings Account has replaced the Education IRA. See also 529 Plans.

Covered Compensation—The amount of compensation for which old age and survivors insurance benefits would be provided under the Social Security Act computed as though, for each year until the employee reaches the age of 65, his or her annual compensation is at least equal to the taxable wage base.

Covered Employee—A person covered by a pension or welfare plan is one who has fulfilled the eligibility requirements in the plan; for whom benefits have accrued, or are accruing; or who is receiving benefits under the plan.

Covered Entity—Under HIPAA, a health plan, health plan clearing house or health care provider who sends any heath information electronically for a transaction covered by the Privacy Rule.

Covered Expenses—Hospital, medical and related costs incurred by those covered under the insurance policy that qualify for reimbursement according to the terms of the contract. Most commonly used in regard to major medical plans.

Covered Option—A situation in which the writer (seller) of the option owns the underlying stock.

Covered Service—
—Period of employment during which an employee is a participant in an employee benefit plan.
—A benefit provided to either individual beneficiaries or a purchasing group or employer.

CPT Codes—See Current Procedural Terminology.

Crash—
—A decline of 20% or more in the stock market in a single day or a few days. There were only two crashes in the 20th century, in 1929 and 1987.
—The sudden failure of a computer system due to causes such as a power failure or an undetected computer virus.

Credentialing—Obtaining and reviewing the doc-umentation of professional providers. Such documentation includes licensure, certifications, insurance, evidence of malpractice insurance, malpractice history and so forth.

Credit—
—The relative financial standing of one company versus another in terms of what it will be charged to raise funds as regards the amount and interest to be paid.
—An entitlement to a pension or welfare benefit that is payable sometime in the future.

Credit Rating—An assessment of the factors that determine the financial soundness of a borrower. For example, a person or corporation with a strong financial position, good income prospects and a low level of indebtedness in relation to total net worth is given a high credit rating. In contrast, an entity with a weak financial position, poor income prospects and a high level of debt in relation to net worth gets a low credit rating.

Credit Risk—The risk of a company or individual defaulting on its debt obligations. Also called *financial risk*.

Creditable Coverage—Prior group health plan coverage that may be applied to a plan's preexisting exclusion period. Includes health insurance coverage, continuation coverage under COBRA, Medicare, Medicaid, a state heath benefits pool or a public health plan. Group health plans and health insurance issuers must provide documentation certifying this prior coverage.

Credited Earnings—The maximum taxable income for each year that forms the basis for Social Security benefits.

Credited Projected Benefits—See Projected Benefits.

Credited Service—A period of employment before or after the effective date of the plan that is recognized as service for one or more plan purposes, such as determination of benefit amounts, entitlement to benefits and/or vesting.

Critical Care—Health care provided to acutely ill patients during a medical crisis, usually within a critical care area such as an intensive care unit or coronary care unit.

Critical Illness Insurance—A limited form of health insurance that pays for treatment of specified diseases, such as cancer. Also known as *dread disease policy*.

Cross-Testing—Allows a firm to test for nondiscrimination based on either current contributions or future benefits. Provides greater flexibility in plan design. See also Nondiscrimination Rules.

Cross-Trading—Trading that seeks to profit from relationships among different types of securities.

Crown Corporation (Canada)—A corporation that is wholly owned, directly or indirectly, by a provincial government or by the federal government of Canada, such as the Canadian Broadcasting System.

Cumulative Bulletin (CB)—A government publication in which revenue rulings and other pertinent IRS pronouncements are published. The *Cumulative Bulletin* is published semiannually and incorporates the materials that were published weekly by the IRS in its *Internal Revenue Bulletins*.

Cumulative Preferred Stock—Preferred stock having a provision that, if one or more dividends are omitted on the preferred, the omitted dividends must be paid before any dividends may be paid on the common stock. See also Convertible Preferred Stock; Noncumulative Preferred Stock; Participating Preferred Stock; Preferred Stock.

Cumulative Rate of Return—A compounded rate of return covering more than one period or year.

Currency Devaluation—Action by the government or by the marketplace to reduce the value of a currency in relation to the currencies of other nations.

Currency Exchange Rate—See Exchange Rate.

Currency Risk—Changes in the value of one country's currency relative to other currencies that could dramatically affect investment performance. Also called *exchange rate risk*.

Current Assets—Those assets of a company that are reasonably expected to be realized in cash, or sold, or consumed during the normal operating cycle of the business. These include cash, U.S. government bonds, receivables, money due (usually within one year) and inventories.

Current Liability—Money owed and payable by a company, usually within one year.

Current Procedural Terminology (CPT)—A five-digit coding system developed by the American Medical Association to categorize medical procedures for billing purposes.

Current Service Benefit—
—The annuity payable for each year of participation in the plan after its adoption.
—That portion of a participant's retirement benefit that relates to his or her credited service in a contemporary period (usually a year).

Current Value—Fair market value, where available. Otherwise, it is the fair value as determined in good faith by a trustee or a named fiduciary pursuant to the terms of the plan and in accordance with regulations of the secretary of labor, assuming an orderly liquidation at the time of such determination.

Current Yield—Annual bond interest divided by market price per bond.

Currently Insured—As applied to Social Security, a worker must have a minimum of six quarters of coverage that were earned in the most recent 13-quarter period.

Curtailment—A reduction of future benefits or augmenting of eligibility requirements in a qualified plan that causes a partial termination of the plan.

Custodial Care—General assistance in performing the activities of daily living, as well as board, room and other services, generally provided on a long-term basis and that do not include a medical component.

Custodian—
—An organization such as a bank, brokerage firm or mutual fund company that holds the cash and securities of a 401(k), IRA or mutual fund and performs a variety of clerical services like collecting income and reporting on the value of the assets.
—A person responsible for an asset given to a minor under the Uniform Transfers to Minors Act.

Customary Charge—The amount that a physician or other medical provider usually charges the majority of patients for each service. Generally the maximum amount a health insurance plan or Medicare will allow for covered expenses. See also Usual, Customary and Reasonable (UCR) Fees.

Cyclical Stocks—Stocks that move directly with the business cycle; i.e., generally, they advance as business conditions improve and decline when business slackens. Steel, chemical, textile and machinery stocks are included in this category. To offset cyclical factors, many companies today are striving to diversify their operations among other fields and products.

D

Daily Valuation—Occurs when participants' accounts in a defined contribution pension plan, typically a 401(k) plan, are assigned a value on a daily basis. This process can include updating the account transactions.

Damages—The amount claimed or allowed as compensation for injuries sustained or property damaged through the wrongful acts or the negligence of another; an award.

Danger Pay—Compensation provided over and above hardship pay for employees living and working in a foreign country subject to civil war, revolution or terrorism. Set by the State Department, it does not go above 25% of the base pay.

Database—A collection of numeric data or textual information that is processed in computer-readable form and stored electronically in a computer's memory for later electronic publishing or distribution.

Day Care (Adult)—See Adult Day Care.

De Minimis Benefit—Any property or service that an employer provides to an employee, if the value of such property or service is so minimal that accounting for it would be unreasonable or administratively impractical. The employee can exclude from income the value of these benefits.

De Minimis Rule—In the plan termination context, a rule that may reduce or eliminate small amounts of multiemployer withdrawal liability.

Death Benefit—The payment made to designated beneficiaries upon the death of a participating employee. This could be the employee's share in the investment fund, the life insurance purchased for him or her, or both.

Death Rate—The proportion of persons who die within a year, usually expressed as so many per 1,000.

Debenture—An unsecured long-term debt backed only by the integrity of the borrower, not by collateral. An example is an unsecured bond.

Debenture Bonds—Bonds backed by the general credit of the issuer but not secured by a specific lien on property.

Debit Card—In flexible spending accounts (FSAs) a card, similar to a bank debit card, that electronically stores data concerning an employee's contributions to the FSA and includes filters and edits that incorporate benefit design features such as copays and deductibles. When the card is used at a participating vendor like a medical office or pharmacy, the appropriate amount is deducted from the employee's account. See also Flexible Spending Accounts (FSAs).

Debt—Something owed by one person to another. Debt securities are loans at a specified rate of return for a specified period of time.

Debt Limit or Ceiling—The maximum debt that can be legally created by a state or local government.

Debt Service—The sum of money required periodically to make the payments necessary to amortize a debt and interest charges, the principal and interest payments.

Debt-to-Equity Ratio—A measure of the relative amount of funds provided by lenders and owners.

$$\text{Debt/Equity Ratio} = \frac{\text{Long-Term Debt}}{\text{Stockholder's Equity}}$$

Dedicated Bond Portfolio—Portfolio designed to meet a specific set of future benefit payments with the cash flow from the bonds held in a portfolio. The most common application of the dedicated portfolio concept is in funding benefits due to retired employees. Ideally, the cash flow from the portfolio exactly matches each future payment, both in amount and timing. If this exact matching is achieved, the funding of future payments will *not* depend on the level of interest rates in the future. The actuary may then raise the actuarial assumption to a market rate of interest. This reduces the actuarial liability of the plan and could substantially lower its annual funding costs.

Deductible—The amount of out-of-pocket expenses that must be paid for health services by the insured before becoming payable by the carrier. Most common in major medical policies, but also found in basic policies. See also Family Deductible; First Dollar Coverage.

Deductible Carryover—A feature whereby covered charges in the last three months of the year may be carried over to be counted toward the next year's deductible. See also Carryover Deductible.

Deed—A written instrument by which lands, tenants and hereditaments are transferred, which instrument is signed, sealed and delivered by the grantor.

Deed of Trust—Written instrument by which title to land is transferred to a trustee as security for a debt or other obligation. See also Mortgage.

Deemed IRA—Under the Economic Growth and Tax Relief Reconciliation Act of 2001 (EGTRRA), a qualified retirement plan such as a 401(k) plan or a tax-sheltered account may allow employees to make voluntary contributions to an IRA that is a separate account established under the plan. Also known as a *sidecar IRA*. See also Economic Growth and Tax Relief Reconciliation Act of 2001 (EGTRRA); Individual Retirement Account (IRA).

Default—The nonperformance of a duty, whether arising under a contract or otherwise; failure to meet an obligation when due.

Defensive Industry—An industry relatively unaffected by business cycles, such as the food industry or the utility industry.

Defensive Issues—Issues of established companies in industries relatively unaffected by business cycles.

Defensive Medicine—The practice by physicians of authorizing medically unnecessary tests and procedures, increasing hospital admissions and extending lengths of stay in an attempt to limit their exposure to malpractice suits.

Defensive Portfolio—A portfolio consisting mainly of short-maturity bonds, preferred stocks or other securities that are unlikely to fluctuate much in either direction. Compare with Aggressive Portfolio.

Deferred Annuity—Annuity contract providing for the initiation of payments at some designated future date or age. Contrast with Immediate Annuity.

Deferred Benefits—Noncash compensation to which an employee may be entitled at a later date following employment, assuming he or she has enough credited years of service for vesting (e.g., pension plans, 401(k) savings plans, stock options, etc.).

Deferred Compensation Plan—Any plan in which employees can accumulate money on a tax-deferred basis. A qualified plan can have the option of permitting employees to withdraw assets without penalty for certain "emergency" situations specified in the plan, although the normal taxes must be paid on the withdrawn portion. The assets when withdrawn are subject to the favorable ten-year lump-sum tax treatment. Many also give employees the option of taking the benefit in cash. A deferred compensation plan can be combined with other plans such as a profit-sharing plan.

Deferred Payments—Compensation or benefit payments to be made at a future time.

Deferred Premium Plan—A funding arrangement that extends the grace period beyond the normal 31 days, usually to 60 or 90 days.

Deferred Profit-Sharing Plan—
—A plan established and maintained by an employer to provide for participation in its profits by its employees or their beneficiaries. The plan must provide a definite predetermined formula for allocating the contributions made to the plan among the participants and for distributing funds accumulated under the plan after a fixed number of years, the attainment of a stated age, or upon the prior occurrence of some event such as layoff, illness, disability, retirement, death or severance of employment.
—(Canada) An employer-sponsored savings plan registered under the Income Tax Act that al-

lows an employer to set aside a portion of company profits for the benefit of employees. The amount accumulated in these plans can be paid out as a lump sum at retirement or termination of employment, transferred to an RRSP, received in installments or used to purchase an annuity. Payments from the plans received by employees are taxable.

Deferred Retirement—When the employee works past normal retirement age.

Deferred Retirement Option Plan (DROP)—A retirement plan feature that allows an employee to retire from a defined benefit plan (freezing the calculation for years of service and final compensation formulas that determine benefit levels) and accumulate new benefits under a defined contribution plan with interest for a specified period of time. An employee receives benefits through the defined contribution plan as he or she continues to work past normal retirement age. DROPs facilitate phased retirement and help organizations retain experienced personnel.

Deferred Vested Pension—For terminating employees, a plan offering a pension, usually deferred until retirement. Benefits are determined when employment is terminated.

Deferred Vesting—That form of vesting under which rights to vested benefits are acquired by a participant commencing on the fulfillment of specified requirements (usually in terms of attained age, years of service and/or plan membership).

Deferred Wage Concept—The forgoing of a present increase in wages for employee benefits or a pension plan.

Deficit—
- —As a balance sheet item, the amount by which assets fall short of meeting the sum of liabilities plus capital stock.
- —The money a government or business pays out in excess of what it takes in over a given period.

Deficit Reduction Act of 1984 (DEFRA)—One part of this act was the Tax Reform Act of 1984. DEFRA had a major impact on employee benefits in the following areas:
- 501(c)(9) trusts and experience-rated plans—prohibits tax deductions for contributions to trusts or premiums paid to experience-rated

plans if reserves for benefits exceed certain limits
- Flexible benefit plans and flexible spending accounts—excludes most taxable benefits from being offered
- Health care for dependents—requires companies to give employee spouses who are senior citizens the opportunity to enroll in corporate health insurance programs.

Deficit Reduction Contribution—An amount in addition to the required minimum annual contribution if the pension plan is less than 100% funded. It consists of old liabilities (such as benefit increases granted before 1988), which are to be amortized over 18 years, and a share of new liabilities (resulting from benefit increases or plan amendments).

Defined Benefit Formulas—See Flat Benefit Formula; Flat Percentage of Earnings Formula..

Defined Benefit Limitation—The maximum annual benefit allowed by the Internal Revenue Code that a participant may receive from a qualified retirement plan.

Defined Benefit Plan—Both ERISA and the Internal Revenue Code define a *defined benefit plan* as any plan that is not an individual account plan. Under a defined benefit plan, there is a definite formula by which the employee's benefits will be measured. This formula may provide that benefits be a particular percentage of the employee's average compensation over his or her entire service or over a particular number of years; it may provide for a flat monthly payment; or it may provide a definite amount for each year of service, expressed either as a percentage of his or her compensation for each year of service or as a flat dollar amount for each year of service. In plans of this type, the employer's contributions are determined actuarially. No individual accounts are maintained as is done in the defined contribution plans. (Defined benefit plans are subject to regulation by the PBGC and are "pension plans" under the Internal Revenue Code. That is, they are designed primarily for retirement.)

Defined Benefit Pension Plan (Canada)—A pension plan usually calculated on the basis of career average, final average or best average earnings and years of service. Investments in the plans are not taxed and the employer generally makes all contributions to the plan.

Defined Contribution Limit—The maximum contributions and additions an employer may make on behalf of a pension plan participant.

Defined Contribution Plan—A *defined contribution* or *individual account plan* is defined by the Internal Revenue Code and ERISA as a plan that provides for an individual account for each participant and for benefits based solely on (1) the amount contributed to the participant's account plus (2) any income, expenses, gains and losses, and forfeitures of accounts of other participants that may be allocated to the participant's account. 401(k), 403(b) and 457 plans are defined contribution plans. See also Individual Account Plan.

Definitely Determinable Benefits—A mandatory requirement for a service benefit pension plan. For variations, see also Money Purchase Plan; Target Benefit Plan.

Deflation—A phase of the business cycle during which consumer spending is seriously curtailed, bank loans contract and the amount of money in circulation is reduced. (Antonym: *inflation*).

Delayed Retirement—See Deferred Retirement.

Delinquent Contributions—Failure by a participating employer to make promised payments to a multi-employer benefit fund.

Demand—The amount of a given service sought by consumers in response to their perceived need for that service.

Demand Management—The combination of strategies such as preventive health, health promotion, self-care guidelines, patient education programs and company practices that is designed to reduce actual and perceived need for health care services and promote and support informed, appropriate health care decision making, thereby reducing costs.

Demographics—The statistical study of the characteristics of a given population. May include such factors as birth rate, age and sex composition, marital status, income, employment, urban/rural distribution and mobility.

Dental Care Benefits—Dental insurance plans usually cover preventive care and treatment of teeth, gums and the mouth. Some plans may also cover orthodontia, X-rays and cosmetic work. Dental care benefits are considered a part of health care benefits, but insurance plans generally separate the two.

Department of Health and Human Services (DHHS)—See Health and Human Services Department.

Department of Labor (DOL)—The nontax (regulatory and administrative) provisions of ERISA are administered by the Department of Labor. The Department issues opinion letters and other pronouncements, and requires certain information forms to be filed.

Dependent—Generally the spouse or child of a covered individual, as defined in a contract. Can be any person who relies on, or obtains coverage through, a covered individual. See also Working Families Tax Relief Act of 2004.

Dependent Care Assistance Program (DCAP)—A tax-advantaged benefit program permitting employers to pay or reimburse employees for qualified child and dependent care expenses.

Dependent Care Flexible Spending Account—Employer-sponsored flexible benefits plan feature that permits employees to use pretax (tax-free) dollars from their paychecks to pay the cost of care for children or elderly dependents up to a certain legislated limit and within very specific guidelines. See also Flexible Spending Accounts (FSAs).

Depreciation—Normally, charges against earnings to write off the cost, less salvage value, of an asset over its estimated useful life. It is a bookkeeping entry and does not represent any cash outlay nor are any funds earmarked for this purpose.

Depreciation—All Causes—Loss in value from any cause in comparison with a new item or property of like kind resulting from physical deterioration, functional obsolescence and economic obsolescence.

Economic obsolescence—Loss in value caused by unfavorable conditions usually external to the property such as the local economy, economics of the industry, encroachment of objectionable enterprises, loss of material and labor sources, lack of efficient transportation, shifting of business center, passage of new legislation, changes in ordinances, etc.

Functional obsolescence—Loss in value caused by conditions within the property such as changes in design, materials or process resulting in inadequacy, overcapacity, excess construction, lack of utility or excess operating costs.

Physical deterioration—Loss in value caused by physical deterioration resulting from wear and tear in operation and exposure to the elements.

Depreciation Reserve—A sum that reflects the total depreciation value to date and, therefore, the expired portion of the useful life of the assets to which it is applicable. The residual value of the asset may or may not be its true market value.

Depression—A prolonged period of sharply reduced business activity characterized by widespread unemployment, low production, a contraction of credit and a drop in consumer buying.

Derivative—A financial contract to pay or receive money in the future based on the performance of some underlying asset such as a currency of a portfolio of stocks or bonds.

Determination Letter—Issued by the office of a district director of the IRS, the letter states whether or not the submitted plan meets the qualification requirements under the Internal Revenue Code.

Determination Period—The 12-month period used for computing the premium to be charged for continuation coverage under COBRA.

Diagnosis-Related Group (DRG)—A prospective hospital claims reimbursement system first implemented by the Medicare program. The reimbursement amount for an episode of care does not reflect actual cost for that care. Reimbursement is based on a predetermined classification of diagnoses, treatments, age, sex and discharge status of patients. This system is also used by some states for all payers. Also called *diagnostic related group*.

Dialysis—A process by which dissolved substances (waste products) are removed from a patient's body by diffusion from one fluid compartment to another across a semipermeable membrane. Regular treatment for ESRD patients.

Direct Contracting—A cost-containment strategy in-volving an exclusive contractual arrangement between an employer and a provider for health care services, usually obtained at reduced prices for employee groups. This may be accomplished without going through a health plan.

Direct Placement—See Private Placement.

Direct Rollover—A distribution to an employee made in the form of a direct trust-to-trustee transfer of tax-deferred retirement plan money from a qualified retirement plan to an eligible retirement plan, such as an IRA; does not incur any taxes or penalties.

Direct Service Plan—See Prepaid Group Practice.

Directed Trust—A trust under which the trustee has less than full managerial authority. This will be the case whenever someone other than a trustee has the power to control particular actions of the trustee.

ERISA contemplates three different kinds of directed trusts. A plan may call for the shift of authority over assets, to whatever extent is desired, from the trustee to plan participants or beneficiaries in respect of the assets allocated to their own individual accounts; or to a "named fiduciary who is not a trustee"; or to an investment manager.

Director—A person elected by shareholders to establish company policies. The directors appoint the president, vice president and all other operating officers. Directors decide, among other matters, if and when dividends shall be paid.

Disability—A condition that renders an insured person incapable of performing one or more duties of his or her regular occupation. Benefit plan definitions of *disability* vary. The Social Security Act defines *disability* as follows:

> (Total disability is the) inability to engage in any substantial, gainful activity by reason of any medically determinable physical or mental impairment which can be expected to result in death or has lasted or can be expected to last for a continuous period of not less than 12 months (and which precludes the claimant from performing not only his previous work, but considering his age, education and work experience any other kind of substantial gainful work which exists in the national economy regardless of whether such work exists in the immediate area in which

he lives, or whether a specific job vacancy exists for him, or whether he would be hired if he applied for the work).

Disability Benefit—Periodic payments, usually monthly, payable to participants under some retirement plans if such participants are eligible for the benefits and become totally and permanently disabled prior to the normal retirement date. Includes short-term and long-term disability benefits.

Disability Income Insurance—A form of health insurance that provides periodic payments to replace a certain percentage of income lost when the insured is unable to work as a result of illness, injury or disease.

Disability Management—The proactive employer-centered process of coordinating the activities of labor, management, insurance carriers, health care providers and vocational rehabilitation professionals in order to minimize the impact of injury, disability or disease on a worker's capacity to successfully perform his or her job.

Disability Pension—The annuity that is payable in the event that an employee becomes disabled before the age of normal retirement.

Disability Retirement—A termination of employment, generally involving the payment of a retirement allowance, as a result of an accident or sickness occurring before a participant is eligible for normal retirement.

Disbursed Self-Funded Plan—In this type of self-insured or self-funded plan, employees' claims are paid directly out of the company's cash flow as part of the expense of doing business; thus, claims settlements are tax deductible when they are paid, not when they are incurred. The company sets aside no reserves and pays no premiums or expense load to an insurer. Most companies that employ a disbursed self-funded plan buy stop-loss insurance, usually in the range of 120% of expected claims, in order to protect themselves against a significantly poorer-than-expected experience. See also 501(c)(9) Trust; Self-Insurance (Self-Funding).

Discharge Planning—A centralized, coordinated program developed by a hospital to ensure that each patient has a cost-effective program for needed continuing or followup care.

Disclaimer—A statement denying legal responsibility for the accuracy or correctness of the presented facts.

Disclosure—The requirement of plan administrators to distribute or make available to plan participants and/or other beneficiaries materials such as summary plan descriptions and annual reports.

Discount—
—The difference between the original offering price of a security and the price to which it may fall in the "after offering" market.
—The amount by which a security sells below its face value (par value). A $1,000 par value bond selling at 95 (worth $950) would be selling at a $50 or 5% discount. (Antonym: *premium*)

Discount Bond—A bond that may be purchased below par (i.e., 1,000), thereby producing a higher yield to maturity and, in most cases, reducing the risk of call. As a general rule, the greater the discount, the lesser the chances of call and the greater the bond's attraction. Interest is paid upon presentation of the coupon attached to the bond.

Discount Factor—The factor used to calculate the present value of dollars due in the future.

Discount Rate—
—The interest rate the Federal Reserve Bank charges to member banks for loans.
—The percentage rate used to calculate the present value of future cash flows.

Discount Stock Option—Allows executives to purchase company stock in the future at a predetermined price. Functions as a kind of executive deferred compensation.

Discounted Fee-for-Service—A managed care payment structure in which physicians are paid an agreed-upon percentage of their normal fees.

Discretionary Account—An account in which the customer gives the broker or someone else discretion, which may be complete or within specific limits, as to the purchase and sale of securities or commodities, including selection, timing, amount and price to be paid or received.

Discretionary Contributions—Employer contributions to a benefit plan such as a 401(k) or profit-sharing plan that are not mandated by the plan.

Discretionary Formula—A profit-sharing plan contribution arrangement that enables the employer annually to determine or change the amount or the formula for its plan contribution.

Discrimination—

—Occurs when a plan discriminates in favor of highly compensated employees, officers or stockholders; steps must be taken to avoid or rectify such discrimination in order to retain qualified status.

—It is permissible to discriminate by group definition, such as salaried only, union employees only or hourly workers only.

—Artificial, arbitrary and unnecessary barriers that bring about disparate treatment of certain groups, based upon race, sex, religion, national origin, age or other such classification. Discrimination also may include the failure to remedy the effects of past discrimination.

Discrimination Testing—To meet IRS guidelines, all tax-qualified plans must be tested by a series of numerical measurements to determine whether contributions or benefits within a plan are being provided fairly to a wide range of employees; specifically, whether a plan favors highly compensated employees. See also Actual Contribution Percentage (ACP); Actual Deferral Percentage (ADP).

Disease Management—A proactive, integrated systems approach targeting individuals who are or may become at risk for chronic conditions. Uses educational and prevention initiatives, careful monitoring techniques, patient self-care and evidence-based clinical practice guidelines to improve health outcomes and reduce health care costs for chronic disease patients.

Disenrollment—Termination of an employee's health care coverage, whether voluntary or involuntary.

Dismemberment—The loss, or loss of use, of a limb or loss of sight from an injury.

Disparate Impact—The result of an employer action or policy that does not appear unlawful but affects one or more classes of employees differently than other classes of employees.

Disposable Personal Income—Income of individuals after taxes are paid.

Disqualification—Loss of tax-favored, or qualified, status.

Disqualified Benefit—In a welfare benefit fund context, a portion of the fund that reverts to the benefit of the employer or a postretirement medical or life insurance benefit provided either under a discriminatory plan or with respect to a key employee but not made from the mandatory separate account. The employer is subject to an excise tax equal to 100% of the disqualified benefit.

Disqualified Person—The IRC term roughly equivalent to *party in interest*. The term *disqualified person* also includes a highly compensated employee. See also Party in Interest; Prohibited Transaction.

Distress Termination—An underfunded pension plan that is terminated by a company with financial problems.

Distribution—A payment to a participant or beneficiary such as a mutual fund's payment to shareholders of the profits, interest or dividends it has earned on its investments; payments from a pension plan, IRA, etc.

Diversification—The spreading of investment funds among different securities, issuers, maturity dates and localities in order to distribute the risk.

Divestiture—

—A company transaction that disposes of or sells an asset owned by the company or a part of the business. Depending on the circumstances, also may be called a *spinoff.*

—The antitrust remedy that forces a company to get rid of assets acquired through illegal mergers or monopolistic practices.

—The decision to purge a portfolio from holding the stock, or in some cases any securities issued, of corporations that do business in certain countries. The intent is to bring economic pressure to bear ultimately on the government of the country to reverse its policies in the area of human rights. In a broader sense, divestiture can apply to the purging of a portfolio of holdings whose ownership would be in contradiction to the social/political/religious/philosophical convictions of the sponsor(s), or owner(s), of the portfolio.

Dividend—
—The proportion of net earnings a corporation pays to its stockholders.
—A policyholder's share in the divisible surplus funds of an insurance company apportioned for distribution, which take the form of a refund of part of the premium on a participating policy.
—A *regular dividend* is an established dividend rate fixed by a corporation on its stock and usually paid quarterly or semiannually.

Dividend Equivalents—Some incentive plans provide payments equal to the dividends that are paid per share. Most common in phantom stock plans.

Dividend Options—Different ways an insured under a participating policy may elect to receive his or her share of surplus earnings. These are usually (1) cash, (2) reduction of premium, (3) additional paid-up insurance, (4) on deposit at interest, and (5) additional term insurance.

Dividend Reinvestment Plan (DRIP)—A device for automatically reinvesting dividends in additional shares. In the case of mutual funds, capital gains may also be reinvested.

Dividend Yield—Expressed in percent, it is calculated by dividing the dividend by the market price of a stock.

Divisible Surplus—See Dividend.

Dollar Averaging; Dollar Cost Averaging—A policy by which the same dollar amount is placed in one or more common stocks at fixed successive intervals, thereby enabling the investor to average the purchase of his or her shares over a good many years. Assuming that each investment is of the same number of dollars, a greater number of shares are purchased when the price is low and fewer when it is high. Thus, a satisfactory average price is obtained, which precludes the investor from buying all the shares at the high levels of the market.

Dollar Temporary Annuity—See Annuity Certain.

Dollar-Weighted Rate of Return—
—This method of calculating rate of return is affected by the amount and the timing of cash flows during a given time period. This rate is an effective measure of the fund's rate of growth, giving full weight to the impact of cash flows on fund assets. The dollar-weighted rate also is referred to as the *internal, discounted cash flow* or the *real rate of return.*
—Assesses what happened to all money available to a given fund during a given period. As such, it is the best way of assessing the actual condition of the fund at any point, but it may not accurately reflect the skill of the investment manager, since he or she has no control over cash flows (deposits, etc.) as to either timing or amount.

Domestic Partner Coverage—Benefit coverage that recognizes as a family the ongoing, personal, intimate and committed relationship between two unrelated people of the same or opposite sex that is the approximate equivalent of marriage, but does not involve formal marriage. Benefit plans that recognize domestic partnerships treat the partners of participants as if they were spouses. Also known as co-habitants, life partners or spousal equivalents.

Domestic Relations Order (DRO)—See Qualified Domestic Relations Order (QDRO).

Double Dipping—Variously applied to mean:
1. Qualifying for, and obtaining, pension benefits under two or more plans
2. Qualifying for, and obtaining, pension benefits under one plan while remaining employed by another employer
3. Qualifying for, and obtaining, Social Security retirement benefits while also qualifying for and obtaining retirement benefits under a civil service retirement system, particularly a federal plan.

Double Indemnity—A provision under which certain benefits are doubled when accident is due to specified circumstances, such as public conveyance accidents; in a life insurance policy, a provision that the face amount payable on death will be doubled if the death is the result of an accident.

Double Taxation—"Double taxation of dividends." The federal government taxes corporate profits once as corporate income; any part of the remaining profits distributed as dividends to stockholders may be taxed again as income to the recipient stockholders, except dividends paid from an ESOP.

Dow Jones Industrial Average (DJIA)—A popular gauge of the stock market based on the average closing prices of active representative stocks, as published by Dow Jones & Co. since July 3, 1884.

Nine of the original 11 stocks were rails. The DJ Averages currently consist of 30 stocks. They include only high-quality, common stocks listed on the New York Stock Exchange, which are thought by some to be representative of the entire U.S. economy. However, in recent times other wider, more inclusive indexes are also watched.

Dow Theory—A theory of market analysis based upon the performance of the Dow Jones industrial and transportation stock price averages. The theory says that the market is in a basic upward trend if one of these averages advances above a previous important high, accompanied or followed by a similar advance in the other. When the averages both dip below previous important lows, this is regarded as confirmation of a basic downward trend. The theory does not attempt to predict how long either trend will continue, although it is widely misinterpreted as a method of forecasting future action.

Downcoding—A practice of third party payers in which the benefits code has been changed to a less complex and/or lower cost procedure than was reported.

Downloading—Transferring information from the Internet to a computer.

Downsizing—The action taken by an organization in an effort to eliminate inefficient operations; or the reduction of the number of jobs in the organization.

DRG—See Diagnosis-Related Group.

DRG Payment Method—An approach to paying for hospital inpatient acute services that bases the unit of payment on the DRG system of classifying patients.

Drug Formulary—See Prescription Drug Formulary.

Drug-Free Workplace Act—A federal law that requires employers with $25,000 or more in government contracts to certify that they are running a drug-free workplace.

Drug Testing—Tests administered on a pre-employment basis, for probable cause (after accidents), or at random; combinations of these models to comply with the drug-free workplace legislation and to facilitate drug-free workforces. Urine tests may be the most common type.

Drug Utilization Management (DUM)—A set of utilization management techniques for determining whether a prescribed drug therapy is the most appropriate form of therapy and also which drug is both medically appropriate and financially cost-effective for the presenting condition.

Drug Utilization Review (DUR)—A review system to monitor usage of prescriptions by enrollees, to identify potential interactions with other medications, or to identify alternative effective or cost-effective therapies.

Due Diligence—The careful investigation necessary to ensure that all material information pertinent to an issue has been disclosed to the public.

Due Process—Fundamental fairness. Applied to judicial proceedings, it includes adequate notice of a hearing and an opportunity to appear and defend in an orderly tribunal.

Duplication of Benefits—Overlapping or identical coverage of an insured person under two or more health plans, usually the result of contracts with different insurance companies, service organizations or prepayment plans. Synonymous with *multiple coverage*. See also Coordination of Benefits (COB).

Durable Medical Equipment (DME)—Medical equipment that is not disposable (i.e., is used repeatedly) and is only related to care for a medical condition. Examples would include wheelchairs, home hospital beds, and so forth. An area of increasing expense, particularly in conjunction with case management.

Durable Power of Attorney—A legal document in which a person designates another person to act as his or her representative in financial transactions. It continues even if the person becomes incompetent.

Durable Power of Attorney for Health Care—A legal document in which a person designates another to make medical decisions for him or her if the person becomes incompetent. See also Health Care Proxy.

Duration—Measure of the price change of a bond to a change in its yield to maturity. It summarizes, in a single number, the characteristics that cause bond prices to change in response to a change in interest rates. The price of a bond with a duration of three years will rise by approximately 3% for each 1% decrease in its yield to maturity. That price will decrease 3% for each 1% increase in the bond's yield. Price changes for two different bonds can be compared using duration. A bond with a duration of six years will exhibit twice the percentage price change of a bond with a three-year duration. The actual calculation of a bond's duration is somewhat complicated, but the idea behind the calculation is straightforward. The first step is to measure the time interval until receipt for each cash flow (coupon and principal payments) from a bond. The second step is to compute a weighted average of these time intervals. Each time interval is measured by the present value of that cash flow. This weighted average is the duration of the bond measured in years. A table of bond maturities and durations is shown below.

DURATION VS. MATURITY

Coupon	14%
Yield to Maturity	14%

Years to Maturity		Duration	
1	Year(s)	.97	Year(s)
2	''	1.81	''
3	''	2.55	''
5	''	3.76	''
10	''	5.67	''
20	''	7.13	''
30	''	7.51	''
40	''	7.61	''

E

EAFE Index—See Europe, AustralAsia and Far East Index.

Early and Periodic Screening, Diagnosis and Treatment (EPSDT)—Medicaid program for participants under age 21 that pays for screening and diagnostic services to detect physical or mental problems and to provide health care, treatment and other measures needed to correct or ameliorate any defects or chronic conditions discovered.

Early Distribution—An early distribution is a distribution taken from a pension plan prior to age 59½ other than because of death or disability. Early distributions are generally subject to a 10% IRS penalty.

Early Retirement—A termination of employment involving the payment of a retirement allowance before a participant is eligible for normal retirement. The retirement allowance payable in the event of early retirement is often lower than the accrued portion of the normal retirement allowance.

Early Retirement Age—An age, established by the terms of an employee pension benefit plan, that is earlier than normal retirement age, at which a participant may retire and receive benefits (usually reduced) under the plan.

Early Retirement Programs—Designed to reduce the workforce. Most plans are voluntary, waive any early retirement penalties, offer subsidies for choosing early retirement and must be accepted within a specified time. See also Window Plan.

Early Withdrawal Penalty—A 10% penalty, in addition to any income taxes owed, on money withdrawn from a tax-advantaged retirement plan before age 59½. Penalty does not apply in special circumstances.

Earmarked Accounts—Separate accounts established for each participant in a retirement plan trust, with the specific investments for each account selected and controlled by the participant.

Earned Income—Under federal income tax laws, the income of an individual from services he or she has performed, thus excluding, e.g., income from the sale or rental of property and interest income.

Earned Income Tax Credit—A federal tax credit given to working taxpayers who support a dependent, or to low-income workers without any dependents. The amounts of the tax credit are indexed and can change annually.

Earned Premium—That portion of a policy's premium payment for which the protection of the policy has already been given. For example, an insurance company is considered to have earned 75% of an annual premium after a period of nine months of an annual term has elapsed.

Earned Surplus—That part of the excess of the total net worth or stockholders' equity over the total of par or stated value of the capital stock in the amount of proprietorship reserves, which is accounted for by accumulated retained earnings.

Earning Power—That rate of earnings considered to be normal for a company under regular operating conditions. It should take the past record into consideration as well as the probabilities of that record being continued in the future.

Earnings-Based CDs—FDIC- or FSLIC-insured CDs invested in real estate and sold by brokers.

Earnings Limit—The maximum amount of an individual's earnings in a calendar year that will be subject to federal, Social Security or state unemployment taxes.

Earnings Per Share (EPS)—Net income less preferred stock dividends divided by shares of common stock outstanding.

Earnings Record—The information maintained by the Social Security Administration on each individual's Social Security and Medicare covered wages and self-employment income.

Earnings Report—A statement—also called an *income* or *profit and loss statement*—issued by a company showing its earnings or losses over a given period. The earnings report lists the income earned, expenses and the net result.

Earnings Yield—A ratio found by dividing the market price of a stock into its earnings.

Econometrics—Use of computer analysis and modeling techniques to describe in mathematical terms the relationship among key economic forces such as labor, capital, interest rates and government policies; and then test the effects of changes in economic scenarios.

Economic Benefit—The IRS uses this doctrine to determine current tax liability when there is no constructive receipt. An employer's promise to pay an amount in the future has no economic benefit to the employee unless that promise is backed by a funded instrument to which the employee has nonforfeitable rights and there is no risk of forfeiture. If the promise is backed in this way, it has economic value and a tax liability occurs. See also Constructive Receipt.

Economic Growth and Tax Relief Reconciliation Act of 2001 (EGTRRA)—Includes numerous changes to rules for pensions and benefits, such as raising contribution limits on IRAs and qualified retirement plans and liberalizing portability and vesting rules.

Economic Recovery Tax Act of 1981 (ERTA)—Governs specific areas of employee compensation, including incentive stock options, deductible voluntary employee contributions, tax credit ESOPs and withdrawal provisions in savings/thrift plans. Expanded IRAs and Keogh plans.

Economic Value Added (EVA)—A measure of a company's return on investment that exceeds what is predicted by the capital asset pricing model.

Economically Targeted Investments (ETIs)—Investments made by funds within the overall context of social investments that are more specifically targeted toward a vested interest of the fund; i.e., the plan sponsor, participants or beneficiaries. ETIs can enhance the fund's contribution base, protect participants' jobs, and provide affordable housing and infrastructure projects. See also Socially Responsible Investments.

Economies of Scale—Efficiency and cost savings that are the result of mass production.

Educational Assistance Plan—Program under which an employer fully or partially reimburses an employee's expenses for education and training on a predetermined basis (usually pay as you go) and is permitted a business expense deduction whether or not the reimbursement is tax free or taxable to the employee.

Educational Assistance Programs—Permit tax-free payments by an employer of certain educational expenses of its employees. The program must meet the requirements of IRC Section 127.

Education IRA—A special type of IRA created to pay the qualified higher education expenses of the IRA beneficiary. Contributions are nondeductible, and earnings on distributions used to pay education expenses are nontaxable. See also Coverdell Education Savings Accounts (ESAs).

Effective Date—The date on which an insurance policy or retirement plan goes into effect and coverage begins. Also, the date pay increases go into effect.

Efficacy—Level of benefit from a fixed level of input or amount of input costs to achieve a defined level of benefit.

Efficient Market Hypothesis—The assertion that, in a market with numerous investors who prefer high returns over low returns, and low risk over high risk, "information" is of no value. In such a market, an investor can attain no more, or less, than a fair return for the risks undertaken. The three forms of the efficient market hypothesis are (1) weak form: a market in which historical price data cannot be used to predict future price changes (see also Technical Analysis); (2) semistrong form: a market in which all publicly available information is efficiently (i.e., quickly and accurately) impounded on the price of a stock and, hence, a market in which no amount or item of publicly available information can be used to predict future price changes; and (3) strong form: a market in which even those with privileged (nonpublic) information cannot obtain superior investment results.

Efficient Portfolio—A portfolio that is fully diversified. For any given return, no other portfolio has less risk; for a given level of risk, no other portfolio provides superior returns. All efficient portfolios are perfectly correlated with a general market index, except portfolios with beta coefficients above 1.0 and that do not achieve that relatively high risk by levering an efficient portfolio. Such portfolios lie on the curved frontier of portfolios consisting exclusively of risky assets.

EGTRRA—See Economic Growth and Tax Relief Reconciliation Act of 2001.

Elapsed Time Method of Service Counting—A method for determining a worker's time in service by subtracting the hire date from the termination date.

Elder Care—Financial, emotional, physical and referral support to parents and older relatives, including adult day care.

Election Period—The period during which a qualified beneficiary may elect to receive continuation coverage. It must last a minimum of 60 days and begins with the date coverage terminates.

Elective Contributions—The amount of pay an employee chooses to defer from salary that is then invested by the employer in a plan such as a 401(k) plan.

Electronic Data Interchange (EDI)—A generic name for electronic, computer-based networks that transmit health care data between participating organizations. For example, claims can be processed electronically using EDI, and data can be gathered for use in outcomes research, in order to improve efficiency and save costs.

Electronic Media—
—Electronic storage media including memory devices in computers (hard drives) and any removable/transportable digital memory medium, such as magnetic tape or disk, optical disk, or digital memory card.
—Transmission media used to exchange information already in electronic storage media including the Internet, extranet, leased lines, dialup lines, private networks, and the physical movement of removable/transportable electronic storage media.

Electronic Protected Health Information (ePHI)—Individually identifiable health information that is transmitted by electronic media or maintained in electronic media.

Eligibility Date—The date an individual and/or dependents become eligible for benefits under an employee benefit plan.

Eligibility Period—A period of time, usually 31 days, when potential members of a group life or health insurance plan can enroll without evidence of insurability.

Eligibility Requirements—Conditions that an employee must satisfy to participate in a plan or obtain a benefit.

Eligible Employees—Those members of a group who have met the eligibility requirements under a group life insurance, health insurance, pension or other benefit plan.

Eligible Employer—Qualified as a tax-exempt organization under Section 101(6) of the 1939 Internal Revenue Code or Section 501(c)(3) of the 1954 Code.

Eligible Expenses—Medical expenses for which a health insurance policy will provide benefits.

Elimination Period—See Waiting Period; Qualification Period (Canada).

Emergency Child Care Services—A form of direct

employer-supported child-care benefit that involves provisions for sick children, such as helping pay for special sick child infirmaries or family day care homes, or sending health care workers into the child's home.

Emergency Medical Condition—Sudden onset of a medical condition manifesting itself by acute symptoms of sufficient severity that the absence of immediate medical attention could cause serious impairment in bodily functions or cause serious and permanent dysfunction of any bodily organ or part. See also Prudent Layperson Standard.

Emergency Medical Services (EMS)—Treatment of patients suffering from accidents or sudden and serious illness.

Eminent Domain—The right of the people or government to take private property for public use upon payment of compensation.

Employee—An individual who is compensated for services performed and whose duties are under the control of an employer.

Employee Assistance Program (EAP)—An employment-based health service program designed to assist in the identification and resolution of a broad range of employee personal concerns that may affect job performance. These programs deal with situations such as substance abuse, marital problems, family troubles, stress and domestic violence, as well as health education and disease prevention. The assistance may be provided within the organization or by referral to outside resources.

Employee Benefit Plan—Under ERISA, a plan established or maintained by an employer or employee organization, or both. The purpose is to provide employees with a certain benefit such as pension, profit-sharing, stock bonus, thrift, medical, sickness, accident or disability benefits.

Employee Benefit Trust—A trust established to hold the assets of an employee benefit plan.

Employee Benefits—A collection of nonwage compensation elements, including but not limited to, income protection, services and income supplements for employees, provided in whole or in part by employer payments.

Employee Benefits Security Administration (EBSA)—A division of the Department of Labor that oversees compliance with ERISA and the Internal Revenue Code regarding employee benefit matters. Formerly called the Pension and Welfare Benefits Administration (PWBA).

Employee Contributions—Made by an employee into a plan. May or may not be required for participation. See also Contributory Plan; Voluntary Contribution.

Employee-Directed Plan—A plan in which employees are allowed to select investments for their accounts.

Employee Organization—Any labor union, organization, agency, or employee representation committee, association, group or plan, in which employees participate and that exists for the purpose, in whole or in part, of dealing with employers concerning an employee benefit plan, or other matters incidental to employment relationships. The term also includes any employees' beneficiary organization organized for the purpose, in whole or in part, of establishing such a plan.

Employee-Pay-All Plan—One in which employees pay all costs for the plan; the employer does not make any contributions.

Employee Pension Benefit Plan—A plan, fund or program maintained by an employer, an employee organization or both, to the extent that, by its express terms or as a result of surrounding circumstances, such plan, fund or program provides retirement income to employees or results in a deferral of income by employees for periods extending to or beyond the termination of covered employment. The method of calculating employer contributions to or benefits under the plan or the method of distributing benefits is immaterial.

Employee Plans Compliance Resolution System (EPCRS)—An IRS-created system that allows sponsors to correct operational and plan document errors affecting their tax-qualified plans, such as 403(b) plans, SEPs, and SIMPLE IRAs. The system includes three programs: the Self-Correction Program (SCP), the Voluntary Correction Program (VCP) and the Closing Agreement Program (CAP). The system is updated from time to time. See also Correction on Audit Program (Audit CAP); Self-Correction Program (SCP); Voluntary Correction Program (VCP).

Employee Retirement Income Security Act of 1974 (ERISA)—Federal statute that requires persons engaged in the administration, supervision and management of pension monies have a fiduciary responsibility to ensure that all investment-related decisions are made (1) with the care, skill, prudence and diligence that a prudent man familiar with such matters would use and (2) by diversifying the investments so as to minimize risk. This wording mandates two significant changes in traditional investment practice: (1) the age-old "prudent man" rule has been replaced by the notion of a prudent "expert"; (2) the notion of a prudent investment has been replaced by the concept of a prudent portfolio.

ERISA also established the Pension Benefit Guaranty Corporation (PBGC), an insurance program designed to guarantee workers receipt of pension benefits if their defined benefit pension plan should terminate. ERISA includes requirements for funding, bonding, trusts, claims procedures, reporting and disclosure, and prohibited transactions. It regulates the majority of private pension and welfare group benefit plans in the United States.

Employee Self-Service—Automated benefit systems that allow managers and employees to complete processes such as annual benefit enrollment, managing participant-directed accounts like 401(k) plans, changing personal and beneficiary data, tracking vacation and sick days, and referencing the employee handbook online, using company intranets and other Web-based tools. Employee self-service can also include call centers and integrated voice response (IVR). See also Call Centers.

Employee Stock Option Plan—Gives an employee the right to purchase company stock for a certain price during a designated period of time. See also Incentive Stock Option.

Employee Stock Ownership Plan—A qualified defined contribution retirement plan such as a profit-sharing, stock bonus or money purchase pension plan whose assets are invested primarily or exclusively in shares of the sponsoring employer.

Employee Stock Ownership Trust (ESOT)—Holds the ESOP's assets.

Employee Stock Purchase Plan—See Stock Purchase Plan.

Employee Welfare Benefit Plan—A plan, fund or program maintained by an employer or employee organization, or both, for the purpose of providing benefits, other than pension benefits, to its participants or their beneficiaries through the purchase of insurance or otherwise. Benefits provided by such plans include medical, surgical or hospital care benefits, or benefits in the event of sickness, disability, accident, death or unemployment, or vacation benefits, apprenticeship or other training programs, or day-care centers, scholarship funds, or prepaid legal services, or any benefit described in Section 302(c) of the Labor-Management Relations Act of 1947, other than pensions.

Employer—Any person acting directly as an employer, or indirectly in the interest of an employer, in relation to an employee benefit plan. The term also includes a group or association of employers acting for an employer in such capacity.

Employer Mandate—A requirement that employers offer their employees health insurance or other benefits.

Employer Real Property—In connection with the 10% limitation relating to acquisition and holding of employer securities and employer real property by certain plans, real property (and related personal property) that is leased to an employer of employees covered by the plan or to an affiliate of such employer.

Employer-Sponsored IRA—An IRA that is sponsored by the employer for purposes of helping employees make a tax-deductible contribution to an IRA and to invest the funds in a particular type of investment. The employer-sponsored IRA should be distinguished from a simplified employee pension plan, which requires employer contributions and must meet certain requirements with respect to participation, discrimination, withdrawals and contributions.

Employer-Sponsored Medical Center—A medical center, often onsite, provided and paid for by the employer, where employees can go to receive medical treatment. Employer-sponsored medical centers are often costly, but are designed with long-term savings in mind.

Employment-at-Will—A legal doctrine maintaining that it is the right of an employer or employee to terminate the employment relationship at any time and for any reason. The doctrine has been successfully challenged by employees in the courts in recent years.

Employment Cost Index (ECI)—A measure of the change in the cost of labor, free from the influence of employment shifts among occupations and industries.

Employment Insurance (EI) (Canada)—A reemployment system that provides temporary support while unemployed individuals are looking for work, as well as active reemployment benefits and support measures.

Employment Practices—Any policies, procedures, systems, programs or actions by the employer that have a direct impact upon the terms and conditions of the employment relationship.

Encryption—The use of an algorithmic process to transform data into a form in which there is a low probability of assigning meaning without use of a confidential process or key.

End Stage Renal Disease (ESRD)—That stage of renal impairment that is virtually always irreversible and permanent, and that requires dialysis or kidney transplantation to ameliorate uremic systems and maintain life.

Endorsement—
—An alteration to a policy. Can either be attached to the policy or written on a page of the policy itself. See also Rider.
—A writing, usually of the name of the payee, on the back of a negotiable instrument, such as a check or note, whereby the property represented by the instrument is transferred.

Endowment Insurance—Insurance payable to the insured if he or she is living on the maturity date stated in the policy, or to a beneficiary if the insured dies prior to that date.

Enrolled Actuary (EA)—A person who performs actuarial service for a plan and who is enrolled with the federal Joint Board for the Enrollment of Actuaries. An enrolled actuary is granted the right to practice in matters regarding the Internal Revenue Code and ERISA.

Enrolled Group—Persons with the same employer, or with membership in an organization in common, who are enrolled in a health plan. Usually, there are stipulations regarding the minimum size of the group and the minimum percentage of the group that must enroll before the coverage is available.

Enrollee—Any person eligible as either a subscriber or a dependent in accordance with an employee benefit plan.

Enrollment—Any process by which an individual and/or dependents become subscribers to health plan coverage, 401(k) plans, flexible benefit plans, etc. May be done either through an actual "signing up" of the individual, by virtue of a collective bargaining agreement or by conditions of employment.

Entitlement—Employee benefits that have been legislated; perception that longstanding benefits are to some extent a matter of right.

Entry Date—See Eligibility Date.

Epidemiology—The study of the relationships of various factors determining the frequency and distribution of diseases in the human community.

Equal Employment Opportunity—The removal of all illegal discriminatory practices to provide all individuals the same opportunities regardless of their race, sex, religion, national origin, age or other such classification.

Equal Employment Opportunity Commission (EEOC)—The federal agency that enforces Title VII of the Civil Rights Act of 1964, ADEA, ADA and other fair employment practices legislation.

Equal Pay Act of 1963—An amendment to the Fair Labor Standards Act (FLSA) that prohibits gender-related pay differentials for jobs that are equal in terms of skill, effort, responsibility and working conditions.

Equalization Component—As part of expatriate compensation, this term refers to tax equalization, housing allowances, and other allowances and premiums designed to maintain real income or purchasing power of base pay.

Equities—Refers to ownership of property, usually in the form of common stocks, as distinguished from fixed income-bearing securities, such as bonds or mortgages.

Equity—
—Anything of value earned through the provision or investment of something of value.
—(Compensation) Any employee earns equity interest through the provision of labor on a job. Equity often is used as a fairness criterion (i.e., "equal treatment") in compensation. People should be paid according to their contributions.
—(Accounting) On an organization's balance sheet, equity represents the book value of the owners' stake in the firm. Assets minus liabilities; also called *net worth*.
—(Real Estate) The interest or value an owner has in real estate over and above the mortgage against it.

Equity Compensation—Stock options, deferred stock, restricted stock, stock bonuses and other stock awards given as compensation instead of cash.

Equity Theory—A principle proposing that in an employment relationship, job satisfaction or motivation results if the employee ratio of input/outcome is equal to or similar to the input/outcome of a comparable person or group.

Equivalency—A method of crediting employees with service based on working time, periods of employment, compensation or elapsed time.

Ergonomics—The study of human factors in production in order to create and adapt equipment and other technology to more effectively accommodate human needs and abilities.

ERISA—See Employee Retirement Income Security Act of 1974.

ERISA Liability—Statutory liability imposed upon officers or other individuals operating in a fiduciary capacity for the proper handling of pension funds or other employee benefits. It is excluded from most general liability insurance policies.

ERISAfication—A change in a pension plan to bring it in line with amendments to ERISA.

ERISA Preemption—See Preemption of State Law (ERISA).

Errors and Omissions (E&O) Insurance—Professional liability insurance for individuals in professions such as accounting, insurance, law or real estate, where the exposure is primarily a property damage one as opposed to bodily injury. See also Fiduciary Liability Insurance.

Escrow—A deed or something of value delivered to a third person for the grantee to be held by him or her until the fulfillment or performance of some act or condition.

Estate—Generally refers to degree, quantity, nature and extent of the interest a person has in real property.

Estate Planning—The total process of creation, management and conservation of one's assets during life and arranging for their distribution at death to best serve the beneficiaries.

Estate Tax—The tax payable by the estate, after the death of a person.

Euro (International Benefits)—The currency of the European Community introduced in 1999 that replaces the European Community Unit (ECU). The euro replaced currencies like the French franc, German deutsche mark, Irish pound and Italian lira.

Eurodollars—Interest-bearing time deposits, denominated in U.S. dollars, at banks and other financial institutions outside of the United States.

Europe, AustralAsia and Far East Index (EAFE)—This stock index from Morgan Stanley Capital International group serves as a benchmark for international equity portfolio managers.

European Union (International Benefits)—A group of European countries joined together to promote trade and economic and political cooperation. The Treaty of Maastricht of 1993 established new policies for political, social and economic cohesion, including the development of a monetary union. Formerly European Community (EC). With the addition of certain Eastern European countries in 2004, the total number of countries represented is over a dozen.

Evidence of Insurability—Any statement or proof of a person's physical condition, occupation or other factor affecting his or her acceptance for insurance. Usually not required for enrollment in group plans, and prohibited for COBRA continuation coverage.

Evidence of Participation—Usually a certificate given to each participating employee.

Excess Accumulation—During a calendar year, the amount by which an individual's required minimum distribution exceeds the actual amount received. Also called an *underdistribution,* it is subject to a tax penalty of 50% of the difference between the year's minimum payment and the payment actually received.

Excess Aggregate Contributions—The amount by which aggregate contributions of highly compensated employees exceed the maximum amount of such contributions allowed under discrimination (ACP) testing.

Excess Benefit Percentage—The percentage of compensation at which employer-derived benefits are accrued with respect to compensation of participants above the integration level.

Excess Benefit Plan—A nonqualified plan maintained by an employer solely for the purpose of providing benefits for certain employees in excess of those which, because of Internal Revenue Code §415 limitations on contributions and benefits, can be provided by the employer's qualified plan.

Excess Compensation—
—In a plan integrated with Social Security, that portion of compensation, above a specified amount, used for calculating pension benefits.
—In an integrated employment retirement plan, the portion of compensation, above a certain amount, upon which retirement benefits can be calculated.

Excess Contribution—
—Contributions that exceed the deductible limits. Excess amounts are subject to an excise tax.
—Pretax participant contributions that do not satisfy the IRC Section 401(k) discrimination test.
—If the employer contributes more than the maximum amount deductible under the minimum funding rules, the excess will not be currently deductible. However, the excess may be carried over to another year or years and deducted at that time (within the maximum deduction limits).
—The amount by which elective contributions of highly compensated employees exceed the maximum amount of elective contributions allowed under ADP testing.

Excess Deferrals—Pretax participant contribution amounts that exceed the maximum limit for the taxable year.

Excess Distribution—An annual distribution from a qualified plan such as a 403(b) plan, SEP or IRA, that exceeds a certain amount, adjusted for inflation. The IRS imposes a 15% penalty on the participant unless the excess distribution is a result of death, a QDRO, distribution of nontaxable contributions or amounts that are rolled over within 60 days of distribution.

Excess Loss Insurance—See Stop-Loss Insurance.

Excess Plan—
—A plan that provides benefits only with respect to earnings in excess of the maximum earnings base for Social Security benefits.
—A plan that provides benefits to executives whose contributions to 401(k) plans are limited.

Excess Retirement Accumulation—Result of an individual having, at death, interests in qualified plans, tax-sheltered annuities and IRAs exceeding the present value of an annuity with annual payments of a specified amount. The estate may be subject to a 15% penalty tax.

Excess Return—The return derived from a security (during a specified holding period) less the return from holding a riskless security (such as a short-term government obligation) during the same period.

Exchange Rate—
—The price of one currency stated in terms of another currency by bankers, dealers and financial markets.
—(Compensation) The rate of pay at which labor demand and labor supply functions intersect in the external market.

Excise Taxes—
—A variety of taxes imposed as a penalty for failing to perform a required action or as a type of license to perform something. Most of these taxes deal with the administration of benefit programs and taxes.
—An employer that contributes to a qualified plan will be subject to an excise tax liability for failing to contribute the amount determined to be an accumulated funding deficiency (excess of total

charges over total credits in the funding standard account).

Excludable Employees—Employees that do not need to be considered when conducting a nondiscrimination test on a pension plan. Examples include employees who do not meet age and length of service requirements, nonresident aliens with no U.S. source of income, and employees whose retirement benefits are covered under a collective bargaining agreement.

Excluded Plans—Benefit plans exempt from all regulatory provisions of ERISA (reporting and disclosure, participation and vesting, funding and fiduciary responsibility). These plans include the following:
1. A governmental plan
2. A church plan for which no election has been made for coverage under the Internal Revenue Code
3. A plan maintained solely for the purpose of complying with applicable workers' compensation, unemployment compensation or disability insurance laws
4. A plan maintained outside of the United States primarily for the benefit of persons substantially all of whom are nonresident aliens
5. An unfunded plan maintained solely to provide benefits in excess of the limitations imposed on contributions and benefits for tax purposes.

Exclusion Allowance—A method for calculating the amount of compensation that may be excluded from annual income and contributed to a tax-deferred annuity on the employees' behalf, whether by an addition to or reduction of salary.

Exclusion Ratio—Refers to the taxable cost calculation of an annuity plan. It is the ratio of the employee's cost basis to his or her expected return.

Exclusions or Exceptions—Specific conditions or circumstances listed in the policy or employee benefit plan for which the policy or plan will not provide benefit payments.

Exclusive Benefit Rule—A rule under ERISA that says the assets in an employee account may be used only for the exclusive benefit of the employee and beneficiaries. Any transaction that compromises this requirement jeopardizes the plan's tax qualification. Fiduciaries of plans must administer the plans accordingly. See also Fiduciary.

Exclusive Provider Organization (EPO)—A more rigid type of PPO, closely related to an HMO. Provides benefits or levels of benefits only if care is rendered by institutional and professional providers within a specified network (with some exceptions for emergency and out-of-area services).

Executive Compensation—Includes salary, bonuses, perquisites, stock and stock options, and other compensation arrangements. Tax considerations are key in the design of these plans.

Executive Perquisites—See Perquisites (Perks).

Exempt—A term referring to groups of employees that are exempt from the overtime provisions of the Fair Labor Standards Act. Includes executives, administrative employees, professional employees and those engaged in outside sales.

Exempt Jobs—Those jobs in the organization that are exempt from the Fair Labor Standards Act—typically professional and managerial level jobs. Most exempt jobs are paid on a salary basis, not on an hourly basis.

Exemption—The condition of a person or organization that is free or excused from a duty imposed by some rule of law, statutory or otherwise.

Exit Fee—In mutual funds, the sliding scale fee paid by investors who sell shares before a specified time. See also Back End Load.

Expatriate—An employee assigned outside of his or her base country for a year or more. May also be called *foreign-service employee, international assignee* or *international staff.*

Expected Claims—The claims forecast for a group or covered person. The expected claims level becomes the breakeven point with respect to expected premium for a period of coverage.

Expected Rate of Return—The weighted arithmetic average of all possible outcomes for an asset or portfolio; the expected value.

Expense Fund—An operating account providing for the payment of an expense of administering the retirement plan.

Expense Ratio—A statistical way of evaluating how efficiently a mutual fund is operating. It is derived by dividing a fund's operating expenses by its net asset value.

Experience—Usually expressed as a ratio or percentage, it is the relationship of premium to claims, coverage or benefits of a plan for a specified period of time.

Experience-Rated Premium—A premium based on the anticipated claims experience of, or utilization of service by, a contract group according to its age, sex and any other attributes expected to affect its health service utilization. Such a premium is subject to periodic adjustment in line with actual claim or utilization experience.

Experience Rating—The process of determining the premium rate for a group risk, wholly or partially on the basis of that group's experience. See also Community Rating.

Experience Refund—A provision in most group policies for the return of premium to the policyholder because of lower-than-anticipated claims.

Experience Study—An actuarial analysis of the plan's experience in membership age, sex, salary and service giving effect to the assumed rates of mortality, disability, employment turnover, investment earnings and other cost factors.

Experimental Medical Procedures—Health care services or treatments that are not widely accepted as effective by entities such as the Health Care Financing Administration, the American Medical Association, the National Institutes of Health or by American health care professionals; or have not been scientifically proven to be effective. Such services are excluded from most health plans.

Expiration Date—
—The last day on which a stock option may be exercised.
—The date the insurance master contract expires or the date an individual or employee ceases to be eligible for coverage.

Explanation of Benefits (EOB)—A statement from the insurer sent to a group member who files a claim giving specific details about how and why benefit payments were or were not made. It summarizes the charges submitted and processed, the amount allowed, the amount paid, and the subscriber balance, if any.

Exposure—The extent to which members of a retirement plan, in terms of numbers, are exposed to the probability of death, disability or separation from covered employment.

Extended Benefits—
—Comprehensive benefits provided in excess of basic health care plans.
—Extension of benefits for limited periods after termination of plan coverage.
—Extension of unemployment compensation benefits during periods of high unemployment.

Extended Care Facility (ECF)—A health care facility offering skilled nursing care, rehabilitation and convalescent services for patients no longer needing hospital care.

Extended Coverage—Additional insurance at an extra premium for coverage not generally found in the normal insurance contract. For example, a provision in certain health policies that allows the insured to receive benefits for specific losses sustained after termination of coverage; coverage for certain specified risks such as smoke damage, windstorm, vehicle damage and civil disorders.

Extended Medical Expense (Canada)—Same as major medical coverage.

External Evaluation—An evaluation performed by a person or agency not under the direct control of the individual, group or organization being evaluated.

Extra Risk Policy—See Rated Policy.

F

Face Amount—The amount indicated on the face of a life insurance policy that will be paid in the event of death or when the contract matures. Excluded are dividend additions and amounts payable under accidental death or other special provisions.

Face Value—The value of a bond that appears on the face of the bond, unless the value is otherwise specified by the issuing company. Face value is ordinarily the amount the issuing company promises to pay at maturity. Face value is not an indication of market value. Sometimes referred to as *par value*.

Facility—Under HIPAA privacy legislation, the physical premises and the interior and exterior of a building(s).

Fact Finding—An alternative dispute resolution procedure in which a neutral or neutrals—known as a fact finder (or fact finding panel)—conduct a hearing at which the opposing parties define the issues in dispute and propose their resolutions therefor with supporting evidence and argument. Following the hearing, the fact finder(s) issues recommendations for a solution, usually in writing. It is hoped that both parties will accept these recommendations and that the dispute will end. The recommendations are not binding, and the parties are free to accept or reject them, or to use them as a basis for further negotiation. See also Arbitration/Arbitrator.

Facts and Circumstances Test—The test that determines if financial need exists for a hardship withdrawal (loan) from a 401(k) or other pension plan.

Fair Labor Standards Act of 1938 (FLSA)—A federal law, enacted in 1938 and subsequently amended, which governs minimum wage, overtime pay, equal pay for men and women in the same type of jobs, and child labor. See also FairPay Overtime Initiative.

Fair Market Value—The amount a stock is worth on a given date and time; the average value between the highest and lowest price at which a stock trades on the New York Stock Exchange on a given date.

FairPay Overtime Initiative—Amended the Fair Labor Standards Act of 1938 (FLSA) by providing new federal overtime pay regulations. More white-collar workers are eligible for overtime; the maximum annual income below which overtime is guaranteed regardless of job duties is raised; exemption from guaranteed overtime for office and nonmanual workers earning between $23,660 and $99,999 is subject to meeting the job duty requirements under one of five exemption categories: executive, administrative, professional, computer and outside sales. Additionally, a highly compensated test is imposed for workers earning $100,000 or more annually.

Fair Return—A return on the investment, commensurate at least with the prevailing rate of interest at any bank or similar institution.

Fair Value—Used in financial accounting procedure. Fair value does not carry the restrictions of tax-oriented *fair market value*. Rather, it can be defined as whatever is reasonable and fairly represents the relative worth of each asset or class to another.

Family Allowances (International Benefits)—Payments made under social systems for support of one or more children in a family. Frequently funded by the social security system of the country.

Family and Medical Leave Act of 1993 (FMLA)—Requires employers with more than 50 employees to provide eligible workers with up to 12 weeks of unpaid leave each year for birth, adoptions, foster care placements, and illnesses of employees and their families.

Family Deductible—A deductible that is satisfied by the combined expenses of all covered family members. For example, a program with a $100 deductible may limit its application to a maximum of three deductibles ($300) for the family, regardless of the number of family members. An aggregate family deductible may be met by one or more family members. See also Deductible.

Family Practice—Practice of health care directed at the whole family by a family physician, a generalist who cares for patients of all ages with a variety of medical and surgical conditions.

Fannie Mae—See Federal National Mortgage Association. (FNMA or Fannie Mae)

FASB—See Financial Accounting Standards Board (FASB).

Fed Funds Rate—Rate at which banks are willing to lend or borrow immediately available reserves on an overnight basis.

Federal Deposit Insurance Corporation (FDIC)—An agency created by Congress in 1933 to insure repayment of savings and time deposits if a member bank becomes insolvent.

Federal Employees Retirement System (FERS)—Includes Social Security, a federal employee pension plan and a thrift savings plan, which cover federal employees hired after January 1, 1984 and those who joined from July through December 1987.

Federal Home Loan Mortgage Corporation (FHLMC or Freddie Mac)—Created in 1970 to promote the flow of capital into the housing market by establishing an active secondary market for residential mortgages. Freddie Mac is owned by the Federal Home Loan Bank System and is under the direction of the Federal Home Loan Bank Board. It deals only with government-supervised lenders and certain mortgage bankers that meet specified criteria.

Federal Insurance Contributions Act (FICA)—The statute that requires employers and employees to pay Social Security and Medicare taxes.

Federal National Mortgage Association (FNMA or Fannie Mae)—The Federal National Mortgage Association is a government-created corporation established by Congress in 1938, owned entirely by private stockholders to serve as a secondary market for Federal Housing Administration, Veterans Administration or Farmers Home Administration insured or guaranteed mortgages. The association provides liquidity on mortgage investments by buying mortgages from financial institutions, such as savings and loan associations and life insurance companies, when investment funds are in short supply and selling mortgages when funds are plentiful. To finance its operations, it issues debentures, bonds and common stock, the latter being bought by institutions that sell mortgages to Fannie Mae, as well as by private investors. FNMA stock is listed on the New York Stock Exchange. The bonds and debentures are highly liquid investments that enjoy an active secondary market and have varying maturities up to 25 years. Fannie Maes come in bearer form only, in amounts of $10,000 to $500,000. The maturities on these securities vary and interest is paid semiannually by coupon.

Federal Register—The daily publication of the United States government in which federal administrative agencies officially publish their rules (including proposed rules subject to public comment).

Federal Reserve System—The central banking system of the United States, consisting of 12 Federal Reserve Banks and supervised by the Federal Reserve Board of Governors, whose seven members are appointed by the president. It is an independent monetary authority operating outside control of Congress and the president.

Federal Savings and Loan Association—A financial institution that is federally chartered and privately owned either by stockholders or depositors. Federal Savings and Loan Associations' prime functions are twofold: (1) financing homes and, to a more limited degree, commercial properties, through conventional loans and FHA and VA mortgages and (2) providing interest-bearing savings accounts that are government insured to $100,000. All Federal Savings and Loan Associations are required to be members of their regional Federal Home Loan Bank.

Federal-State Agreement (Chapter 218 Agreement)—An agreement between the Social Security Administration and a state to provide Social Security coverage for public employees in accordance with state statutes.

Federal Unemployment Tax Act (FUTA)—An act under which employers must make contributions to finance a federal unemployment insurance program. Some states have similar laws.

Fee (Fee Simple) (Fee Simple Absolute)—These three terms are synonymous and mean that an owner has absolute, good and marketable title to the property conveyed to him or her. It is complete ownership without condition. Can refer to an estate inheritance.

Fee for Service (FFS)—A traditional health benefits plan that pays benefits directly to physicians, hospitals, or other health care providers, or that reimburses the patient for covered medical services. Examples are Blue Cross & Blue Shield and Medicare.

Fee Schedule—A listing of fees or allowances for specified medical procedures, which usually represents the maximum amounts the program will pay for specified procedures. Sometimes called a *table of allowances*.

Fee Schedule Payment Structure—A fee structure used by some HMOs under which the HMO places caps or limits on the dollar amounts that it will reimburse providers for covered medical procedures and services.

Fellow of the Life Management Institute (FLMI)—Awarded by the Life Office Management Association. Holders must pass ten university-level examinations covering various aspects of life and health insurance.

Fellow of the Society of Actuaries (FSA)—Designation awarded by the Society of Actuaries to members who pass ten examinations in mathematics, statistics, insurance, actuarial science, accounting, finance and employee benefits.

Fellow of the Society of Pension Actuaries (FSPA)—To obtain fellowship status, holders must pass two examinations on pensions and actuarial practice.

Fiduciary—
— Indicates the relationship of trust and confidence where one person (the fiduciary) holds or controls property for the benefit of another person. For example, the relationship between a trustee and the beneficiaries of the trust.
— Under ERISA (the Employee Retirement Income Security Act of 1974), any person who (1) exercises any discretionary authority or control over the management of a plan or the management or disposition of its assets, (2) renders investment advice for a fee or other compensation with respect to the funds or property of a plan, or has the authority to do so, or (3) has any discretionary authority or responsibility in the administration of a plan.
— One who acts in a capacity of trust and who is therefore accountable for whatever actions may be construed by the courts as breaching that trust. Under ERISA, fiduciaries must discharge their duties solely in the interest of the participants and beneficiaries of an employee benefit plan. In addition, a fiduciary must act exclusively for the purpose of providing benefits to participants and beneficiaries in defraying reasonable expenses of the plan. See also Prudent Man Rule.

Fiduciary Liability Insurance—Protects fiduciaries who act in good faith from mistakes in violating complex fiduciary rules, including errors and omissions. See also Errors and Omissions (E&O) Insurance.

Fiduciary Responsibility—Under ERISA, a fiduciary must discharge his or her duties solely in the interest of the participants and beneficiaries and for the exclusive purpose of providing benefits, while defraying reasonable expenses of the plan. The conduct of a fiduciary will be governed by the "prudent man" or "prudent person" standard: that is, a fiduciary must act with the same care as a prudent person dealing with similar would exercise. Fiduciaries must also keep abreast of legal developments and be able to respond to the changes necessitated by economic and demographic fluctuations. See also ERISA; Prudent Man Rule.

Final Average Salary—A measure of a participant's level of earnings that is based on his or her average rate of salary for a specified period of time, usually the three, five or ten years immediately preceding retirement. A participant's final average salary may be one of the factors used in determining the amount of his or her benefits.

Final Pay Plan (Final Pay Formula)—A benefit formula that bases benefits on the employee's compensation over a specified number of years near the end of the employee's service period or on the employee's highest compensation periods. For example, a plan might provide annual pension benefits equal to 1% of the employee's average salary for the last five years (or the highest consecutive five years) for each year of service. A final pay plan is a plan with such a formula.

Financial Accounting Standard 87—The statement issued by FASB regarding employers' accounting for pensions.

Financial Accounting Standard 106—Requires employers to record on their balance sheets the future financial liability that they incur by promising health benefits to retirees.

Financial Accounting Standards Board (FASB)—The independent, private (nongovernmental) authority for establishing accounting principles in the United States. Successor to the Accounting Principles Board.

Financial Advisor—An investment professional that assists clients with money management, including asset selection and allocation, goal setting, tax planning, retirement planning and estate planning. Advisors charge clients an ongoing fee for their services as opposed to a single commission charge, resulting in a greater focus on the client's money management, than on performing a transaction. Also called *financial planner, investment consultant* and *wealth advisor.*

Financial Assets—Assets that are intangible in nature, e.g., stocks, bonds, U.S. Treasury bills.

Financial Futures—Exchange-traded contracts on securities, securities indexes or foreign currencies that obligate the holder to take or make future delivery of a specified quantity of those underlying securities or currencies on a predetermined future date.

Financial Planning—Developing, implementing and coordinating a plan to achieve a financial goal such as retirement security. Includes analyzing an individual's sources of present income, net worth and expenditures; projection of finances into the future; budget guidelines; and use of financial investments, such as stocks, bonds, mutual funds, insurance, money market accounts, qualified retirement plans, etc., to achieve financial goals and the eventual transfer of assets to designated heirs.

Financial Planning Education—An ongoing combination of knowledge, strategy and commitment; a learned lifelong process that promotes financial security and the orderly accumulation and disposition of wealth. Includes retirement planning, tax and investment planning, and personal cash and debt management. See also Investment Education; Monte Carlo Simulation.

Financial Risk—See Credit Risk.

Financial Statement—The means by which the information accumulated and processed in financial accounting is communicated; a term for *balance sheet*. For employee benefit plans, ERISA has several special requirements that financial statements must follow.

Financing Method—The method of administering the pension program through group annuities, deposit administration, individual policies by an insurance company or a self-administered trust.

Firewall—Security measure that may be a physical device or software that prevents or restricts access between computer networks.

First Dollar Coverage—A benefit plan that provides reimbursement for incurred health care costs "from the first dollar," with no deductible.

Fiscal Intermediary (FI)—An agency, usually a Blue Cross plan or private insurance company, selected by health care providers to pay claims under Medicare. Sometimes referred to simply as *intermediary*.

Fiscal Policy—Government strategy on taxes, spending and borrowing aimed at stabilizing economic activity.

Fiscal Year (FY)—A corporation's accounting year. Due to the nature of their particular business, some companies do not use the calendar year for their bookkeeping, but rather any 12-month period.

5% Owner—Individual owning more than a 5% interest in an employer in one of the following ways: (1) the stock of a corporate employer, (2) the voting power in stock of a corporate employer or (3) the capital or profits interest of a noncorporate employer. A 5% owner is a key employee under the Tax Code. See also Key Employee; Top-Heavy Plan.

501(c)(9) Trust—
   —Used by employers and jointly administered welfare funds to provide group employee benefits governed by provisions of Section 501(c)(9) of the IRC. Only certain benefits may be provided under a 501(c)(9) program: medical, disability, term life insurance, severance compensation, vacation benefits, recreational facilities and unemployment compensation.
   —A type of self-insured or self-funded plan that is a tax-exempt trust. Under the terms of the trust, both employer and employee contributions are paid into the fund, and claims and expenses paid from it. Excess funds are invested as reserves by the fund's trustees. In a tax-qualified fund, the employer's contributions are immediately tax deductible; the trust's investment income is tax exempt; and employees' contributions are not currently taxed. See also Disbursed Self-Funded Plan; Self-Insurance (Self-Funding); Voluntary Employees' Beneficiary Association (VEBA).

529 Plans—Qualified state-administered tuition programs under IRC Section 529. Developed by state legislatures to encourage savings for postsecondary education, they consist of two specific types: savings plans and prepaid tuition plans. Both plans allow participants to enjoy tax-free earnings on their investments for a child's education. The plans differ in the flexibility and degree of risk they impose on participants. See also Coverdell Education Savings Accounts.

Five-Year Averaging—A method used to determine income tax liability on a lump-sum distribution made from a qualified plan. This method often reduces the amount of income tax due to the IRS. The Tax Reform Act of 1986 generally replaced ten-year averaging with five-year averaging.

Fixed Access Charge—Flat fee charged by a PPO to allow employees and dependents to gain access to network providers.

Fixed Annuity—An annuity contract in which the insurance company makes fixed (or guaranteed) dollar payments to the annuitant for the term of the contract (usually until he or she dies). The interest rate may not fall below a specified amount.

Fixed Assets—Those assets that are acquired for use in the continuing operations of a business over a number of accounting periods rather than for resale to customers. Includes the value of land, leasehold improvements, equipment and fixtures.

Fixed Benefit Retirement Plan—A type of plan providing retirement benefits only on a fixed amount or at a fixed percentage such as 1% of monthly salary times the number of years of credited employment; or 25% of the employee's average pay over the last few years prior to retirement.

Fixed Charges—
—Expenses of a company, such as bond interest, rental expense and amortization of bond discount.
—Fees or expenses assessed as flat amounts, not as a percentage or function of volume.

Fixed Income—Income that remains constant and does not fluctuate, such as income derived from bonds, annuities, preferred stock and royalties.

Fixed Income Fund—A mutual fund that invests in corporate, government or other issuer bonds, for the purpose of providing current income.

Fixed Income Investments—Investments such as public and private bonds, government securities and guaranteed 401(k) accounts that offer specific payments at predetermined times. Guaranteed fixed income accounts offer a guarantee against loss of principal as well as earned interest.

Fixed Rate Mortgage—A loan made on real property that has a constant interest rate over the life of the loan. See also Variable Rate Mortgage.

Flat Benefit Formula (Flat Benefit Plan)—A benefit formula that bases benefits on a fixed amount per year of service, such as $20 of monthly retirement income for each year of credited service. A flat benefit plan is a plan with such a formula.

Flat Dollar and Service Benefit Formula—A retirement benefit formula based on years of service times a specific dollar multiplier, such as $10 per month per year of service.

Flat Dollar Benefit Formula—A retirement benefit formula that calls for a specific pension amount without regard to income or service.

Flat Percentage of Earnings Formula—Some percentage of earnings, usually 20-40%, is selected as the measure of the pension benefit. It may be used with either career average or final average earnings, although it is used most frequently in final pay plans. This type of formula does not take an employee's service into account, except in those plans that require the employee to have completed a minimum period of service by normal retirement date and provide for a proportionately reduced benefit if the employee's service is less than the required number of years.

Flat Schedule—A type of schedule in group insurance under which everyone is insured for the same benefits regardless of salary, position or other circumstances.

Flat Tax (Canada)—A tax applied at the same rate to all income for all individual taxpayers, usually on a broadly defined income base with only a limited number of deductions.

Flexible Benefit Plan—A benefit program under Section 125 of the Internal Revenue Code that offers employees a choice between permissible taxable benefits, including cash, and nontaxable health and welfare benefits such as life and health insurance, vacation pay, retirement plans and child care. Although a common core of benefits may be required, the employee can determine how his or her remaining benefit dollars are to be allocated for each type of benefit from the total amount promised by the employer. Sometimes employee contributions may be made for additional coverage.

Flexible Pension Plan (Canada)—A defined benefit pension plan that allows participants to purchase certain enhanced pension benefits (ancillary benefits). Contributions are tax-deductible and do not affect participants' RRSPs.

Flexible Spending Accounts (FSAs)—Many flexible benefit programs include flexible spending accounts, which give employees the opportunity to set aside pretax funds for the reimbursement of eligible tax-favored welfare benefits. FSAs can be funded through salary reduction, employer contributions or a combination of both. Employees can purchase additional benefits, pay health insurance deductibles and copayments, or pay for child-care benefits with the money in their FSAs. See also Debit Cards; Dependent Care Flexible Spending Account; Health Care Flexible Spending Account.

Flextime—Schedules permitting employees to structure their work hours around their personal responsibilities.

Float—An idle cash balance, such as checks that have been written but not paid, contributions not yet invested, or outstanding distributions. Sometimes put into interest-bearing investment vehicles.

Floating Debt—Temporary or shifting short-term debt that has not been funded on a permanent basis in the longer term maturities.

Floating Interest Rate—An interest rate that fluctuates with changes in an established index, such as the prime rate.

Floating Supply—Indicates the total amount of securities believed to be available for immediate purchase offered by security dealers and other investors.

Floor Offset (Pension) Plan—A defined contribution plan is used as the primary vehicle for providing retirement benefits. Recognizing that many factors might result in the defined contribution plan providing less than adequate benefits in some situations, the employer also maintains a defined benefit floor plan. This floor plan uses a defined benefit formula to establish a minimum benefit. If the defined contribution plan provides a benefit that equals or exceeds this minimum, no benefit is payable from the floor plan. If the defined contribution benefit is less than this minimum, the floor plan makes up the difference. Thus the total benefit from both plans is equal to the minimum described in the floor plan.

Fluctuations—Variations in the market price of a security. If a stock advances or declines three points, it is said to have experienced a three-point fluctuation.

Focus Group—A group of employees brought together to discuss their attitudes and perceptions toward a proposed company initiative.

Foreclosure—The legal procedures involved in enforcing payment of a debt secured by a mortgage by taking title to the applicable property or other assets and selling them. Often associated with a default of principal and interest on a loan involving real estate.

Foreign Affiliate—A non-U.S. company in which the U.S. employer owns at least 10%.

Foreign Exchange Transaction—Purchase or sale of the currency of one nation for that of another.

Foreign (or International) Fund—A mutual fund that invests only in foreign securities (differs from a *global fund,* which invests both in U.S. and foreign securities).

Foreign National—A citizen of another country who is authorized to work in the United States.

Foreign Securities—Investment in the securities issued by a company that is incorporated outside of the United States and generates a major portion of its business outside the United States, or securities issued by governments other than the U.S. government.

Forfeiture—The amount that is lost when a participant terminates employment before being fully vested under the plan's vesting schedule. In a pension plan, such amounts must be applied to reducing future employer contributions. In a profit-sharing plan, such amounts may be allocated to the accounts of remaining participants. Also applicable to flexible spending accounts.

Form 5500—A joint agency financial form developed by the IRS, DOL and PBGC that may be used to satisfy the annual reporting requirements of the IRC and Titles I and IV of ERISA.

Formulary—See Prescription Drug Formulary.

401(h) Account—A separate account of a pension plan that, under provisions of IRC Section 401(h), may be used to fund medical benefits for retirees and dependents.

401(h) Plan—A provision of a pension or annuity plan

that provides for the payment of benefits for sickness, accident, hospitalization and medical expenses, of retired employees, their spouses and their dependents, subject to certain requirements.

401(k) Plan—A plan established by an employer under which employees can elect to defer income by making pretax contributions. The plan may also allow for employer matching contributions. Taxes on contributions to the account are not taxable until the money is withdrawn. A 401(k) plan is a defined contribution plan.

401(k) Wraparound Plan—An unfunded, nonqualified deferred compensation plan to which a highly compensated employee may make pretax contributions. The employer makes matching contributions. By using this procedure, the employee avoids certain IRC limits on deferrals and compensation and is able to maximize his or her 401(k) plan. Also known as *nonqualified 401(k) plan* and *shadow 401(k) plan*.

403(b) Annuity—An annuity that provides retirement income for employees of certain tax-exempt organizations or public schools. Also known as a *tax-sheltered annuity*.

403(b) Plan—A defined contribution plan established by tax-exempt organizations such as public schools, educational or research organizations, and charities in which contributions are used to purchase annuities or mutual fund shares by employers for employees. The plan must be nonforfeitable to the employee, and contributions must not exceed a specified limit. The funds in the plan are nontaxable until they are taken as income in retirement. Similar to 401(k) plans, these plans are also called *tax-sheltered annuities* or *tax-deferred annuities*.

404(c) Plan—An individual account plan, such as a money purchase pension, profit-sharing, 401(k) or 403(b) plan, in which the participant or beneficiary exercises control over the assets in his or her account and chooses from within a broad range of investment alternatives, in such a way that a participant will not be considered a fiduciary and no other fiduciary shall be held liable for losses resulting from that control. See also Participant-Directed Plan; Section 404(c) (ERISA); Self-Directed Investment.

412(i) Plan—A defined benefit retirement plan that allows the owner of a small business that generates

a large and steady cash flow to make a significant annual tax deduction that provides pension benefit payments. The plans are usually funded through life insurance, often mixed with annuities.

415 Limits—See Section 415 Limits.

419(A) Plan—A welfare benefit plan funded through trusts to which many unrelated employers contribute. It is referred to as a *multiple employer plan*. These plans are often structured as nondiscriminatory VEBAs or taxable trusts and offer life insurance or severance benefits.

457 Plan—An elective tax-deferred retirement plan for government employees that allows employees to make tax-deferred contributions from their salaries to the plan. Similar to 401(k) plans and 403(b) plans. See also Section 457.

Fractional Rule—The employee's accrued benefit on any given date is not less than the projected normal retirement benefit prorated for years of plan participation. See also Accrued Benefit.

Fractional Share—A portion of a whole share of stock. Fractional shares may be generated when stock dividends are declared or two corporations merge.

Franchise Insurance—A form of insurance in which individual policies are issued to the employees of a common employer or the members of an association under an arrangement where the employer or association agrees to collect the premiums and remit them to the insurer. Also known as *wholesale insurance*.

Fraternal Insurance—A cooperative type of life or disability insurance some social organizations offer to their members.

Fraud—An intentional misrepresentation of the truth for the purpose of deceiving another person that causes damage of some sort.

Freddie Mac—Trade name for the Federal Home Loan Mortgage Corporation.

Free and Clear—A reference to ownership of property that is free of all indebtedness. Property that never had a mortgage encumbering it or for which the mortgage has been paid in full.

Freestanding Additional Voluntary Contributions (United Kingdom)—Money that can be put into a pension fund outside of the company scheme or plan in order to enhance benefits at a later date.

Freestanding Ambulatory Facility—A medical facility where outpatient surgery and/or renal dialysis procedures are performed. Treatment is provided by or under the supervision of physicians or nurses. The facility does not provide inpatient accommodations, nor is it used as an office or clinic for the private practice of a physician or other professional. See also Ambulatory Surgical Center (ASC).

Freestanding Emergency Medical Center—A facility offering emergency treatment or treatment for minor injuries; unlike traditional facilities, care is available on weekends and evenings. Charges are generally lower than those of hospital emergency rooms.

Fringe Benefits—
—Nontaxable benefits as defined by IRC Section 132. May include employer-operated facilities offering meals for employees at a discount, programs providing employee discounts on property or services offered to customers in the employer's normal course of business, and working condition fringes. Also refers to cafeteria plans and tuition reimbursement programs.
—Generally, refers to both formal and informal benefits other than salary provided by an employer for employees.

Front-End Load—One-time sales charges added to the purchase price of the investment. Charges are mandated by the National Association of Securities Dealers (NASD) to be no more that 8.5% of a fund's public offering price, but most funds limit these charges to 4% or 5%.

Frozen Plan—A qualified retirement plan that has stopped employer contributions and benefit accrual by participants. The plan sponsor continues to distribute plan assets and maintain the trust.

Full Disclosure Act—Another name for the Securities Act of 1933.

Full Funding Limitation—A federal tax law limit that caps the amount an employer maintaining a qualified pension plan subject to the Internal Revenue Code Section 412 Minimum Funding Standard is required or allowed to contribute on a deductible basis for a year. The full funding limitation is the lesser of (1) the accrued liability of the plan for the plan year, less the value of plan assets; or (2) 150% of the current liability over the value of the plan's assets. This limit generally will affect the level of required contributions when a plan's assets are large relative to its benefit liabilities.

Full-Time Employees—Employees of an employer who work for 1,000 or more hours in a 12-month period or employees who usually work 40 hours per week.

Full Vesting—That form of immediate or deferred vesting under which all accrued benefits of a participant become vested benefits.

Fully Funded—
—A specific element of pension cost (for example, past service cost) is said to have been fully funded if the amount of the cost has been paid in full to a funding agency. A pension plan is said by some to be fully funded if regular payments are being made under the plan to a funding agency to cover the normal cost and reasonably rapid amortization of the past service cost.
—If a specific part, or benefit, is fully paid for (such as the past service cost), then this item is fully funded. The total plan is considered fully funded if there are sufficient assets to make all payments due at particular times. This can apply to either level funding or entry age calculations, provided that both the normal costs and the conservative amount of amortization costs for the past services have been paid.

Fully Insured—Having enough quarters of coverage to qualify for Social Security benefits.

Fully Insured Plan—
—A group insurance plan in which an insurer pays all claims and assumes all risks for an employer in exchange for payment of a regular premium.
—Under a fully insured retirement plan, the policy cash value at retirement must be sufficient to provide the full benefit since no other source of funds is contemplated under the plan. Retirement income or retirement annuity contracts must be used since they are specifically designed to provide the proper ratio of insurance to income and to generate the cash value needed.
—Separate contracts are issued on the life of every employee.

Fund—Used as a verb, *fund* means to pay over to a funding agency (as, to fund future pension benefits, to fund pension cost). Used as a noun, *fund* refers to assets accumulated for the purpose of paying benefits as they become due.

Fund Earnings—Earnings that return to the pension trust fund for reinvestment or payment of benefits.

Fund Family—A group of mutual funds with different objectives but the same manager.

Funded Debt—All long-term financing of a corporation; that is, all outstanding bonds maturing in five years or longer.

Funded Plan—A funded plan under ERISA is a plan paying benefits in any manner other than through an employer's or employee organization's general assets, including an insured plan and a plan paying benefits or premiums from a trust.

Funded Ratio—Ratio of the assets of a pension plan to its liabilities.

Funded Retirement Plan—A plan under which funds are set aside in advance to provide expected benefits. The plan is not necessarily insured. In contrast to unfunded or pay-as-you-go plan.

Funding—Setting aside monies in a trust account, with an insurance company or with another third party in advance of the date when benefits are payable.

Funding Agency—An organization or individual, such as a specific corporate or individual trustee or an insurance company, that provides facilities for the accumulation of assets to be used for the payment of benefits under a pension plan; an organization, such as a specific life insurance company, that provides facilities for the purchase of such benefits.

Funding Deficiency—See Accumulated Funding Deficiency.

Funding Instrument—A contract or an agreement describing and controlling the terms of a retirement program and the action of the funding agent. Allocated funding instruments include: individual insurance and annuity contracts, group permanent contracts and group deferred annuity contracts. Unallocated funding instruments are deposit administration contracts, immediate participation guarantee contracts and trust fund plans.

Funding Method—Any of the several techniques actuaries use in determining the amounts of employer contributions to provide for pension costs. An actuarial cost method.

Funding Policy—The program regarding the amounts and timing of contributions by the employer(s), participants and any other sources (for example, state subsidies or federal grants) to provide the benefits a pension plan specifies.

Funding Standard Account (FSA)—A requirement under ERISA. Basically, a bookkeeping account in which credits and debits are used to determine a positive or negative balance. The numbers to be used in the account originate in the actuarial valuation or the plan's actual experience for the period. The purpose of the funding standard account is to determine whether or not an accumulated funding deficiency exists. This will occur whenever the negative entries exceed the positive entries to the account.

Funding Waiver—See Waived Funding Deficiency.

Future Purchase Option Benefit—A supplemental benefit that is provided by some disability income policies and that allows the insured the right to increase the disability income benefit amount provided under the policy in accordance with increases in the insured's earnings.

Future Service—The portion of the participant's retirement benefit that relates to the period of creditable service after the effective date of the plan or after a plan change.

Futures Contract—A transferable agreement or contract to make or take delivery of a commodity such as agricultural products, metals or financial instruments, during a certain time in the future at a specified price. Used by businesses as a hedge against price changes and by speculators to make a profit from price changes.

G

Gain—See Actuarial Gain or Loss.

Gainsharing—A form of incentive under which both employees and the organization share the financial gains according to a predetermined formula that reflects improved productivity and profitability.

Gaming—See Code Gaming.

Garnishment—A court order to an employer to withhold all or part of an employee's wages and send the money to the court or to a person who has won a lawsuit against the employee.

GASB Statement No. 2—Governmental Accounting Standards Board standard for reporting Section 457 deferred compensation assets on governmental financial statements.

Gatekeeper—The primary care provider responsible for managing medical treatment rendered to an enrollee of a health plan. Alternatively, this term has been used to describe third-party monitoring of care to avoid excessive costs by allowing only appropriate and necessary care to be rendered.

GATT—See General Agreement on Tariffs and Trade (GATT).

General Accounting Office (GAO)—An arm of Congress that serves as the watchdog for government cost efficiency and that conducts financial studies.

General Agreement on Tariffs and Trade (GATT)—A multilateral trade agreement reached in 1947 by 23 nations that set out reciprocal rights and duties aimed at liberalizing and expanding world trade. GATT has been superseded by the World Trade Organization, to which almost 100 nations now belong. See also Retirement Protection Act of 1994 (RPA); Uruguay Round Agreements Act of 1994; World Trade Organization (WTO).

General Asset Plan—A type of self-funding arrangement in which benefit claims from nonqualified plans are paid from current operating revenues. Supporting assets are commingled with the employer's other assets. Fiduciary standards and reporting and disclosure requirements apply. See also Pay As You Go.

General Assets—Assets owned by an employer or employee organization. They do not include employee contributions or other plan assets.

General Death Benefit—A benefit payable under a group term life insurance plan on the death of an employee, without special conditions. This type of benefit can qualify for special tax treatment under an IRC Section 79 group life insurance policy.

General Obligation (GO) Bond—A type of municipal bond that is backed by the full faith, credit and taxing power of the issuer for payment of interest and principal. Its sale finances public improvements; it is repaid by taxes.

General Partner—A person who usually is actively engaged in the trade or business of partnership and has unlimited personal liability in the partnership. See also Limited Partner.

General Partnership—A form of business whose partners include only general partners. Profits, losses and deductions are passed through to the individual partners involved in the business. See also Limited Partnership.

Generally Accepted Accounting Principles (GAAP)—Uniform minimum standards of and guidelines to financial accounting and reporting, which govern form and content of financial statements. GAAP encompass principles necessary to define accepted accounting practice at a particular time and include detailed procedures as well as broad guidelines.

Generally Accepted Auditing Standards (GAAS)—Measure the quality of the performance of auditing procedures and the objectives to be obtained through their use. Concerned with the auditors' professional qualities and judgment exercised in the performance of an audit.

Generation X—Individuals born between 1965 and 1980.

Generic Equivalent Drugs—Prescription drugs that are equal in therapeutic power to the brand-name originals because they contain identical active ingredients at the same doses.

Genetic Counseling—A clinical service with informational, educational and psychological components to provide individuals and families as to the likelihood of their offspring having genetic (hereditary) conditions, defects or diseases.

Ginnie Mae—See Government National Mortgage Association (GNMA). Ginnie Mae is the colloquial term.

Ginnie Mae Pass-Through Securities—Under this program, principal and interest payments collected on mortgages in specified pools are "passed through" to holders of GNMA-guaranteed certificates after deduction of servicing and guaranty fees. Actual maturity of these certificates is 40 years, but the average life is approximately 12 years because of prepayments. The minimum denomination of certificates is $25,000 and issuance is in registered form only. Ginnie Maes offer investors an opportunity to participate in "pools" of government-guaranteed or -insured mortgages without having to be concerned with extensive documentation and paperwork normally associated with mortgage-type investments. Colloquial for Government National Mortgage Association (GNMA).

Glass Ceiling—Discriminatory practices that have prevented women and other protected class members from advancing to executive-level jobs.

Global Budget—A government cost-containment strategy that sets a total expenditure ceiling or cap for all of the nation's health care expenditures, versus regulating the price of individual fee elements. Under a global budget, providers do not receive any additional funding if costs exceed budgeted payments.

Global Charge—The sum of the professional and technical components of a service when both are provided by the same physician.

Global Fee—A single fee charged for certain medical services that would otherwise be broken down into a number of separate fees. For example, office visits before and after a complex surgery are included in one single fee. Global fees are often developed by managed care plans for specialty procedures to protect against unbundling of claims.

Global Fund—A mutual fund that invests in stocks and bonds all over the world, including the United States. By contrast, an international fund invests all over the world except in the United States.

Globalization—An investment approach that encompasses world markets and views those markets as separate subsegments of the entire world or global market setting.

Going Concern Value—Implies that a company is actively and profitably in business and, therefore, should be valued on that basis rather than on the liquidation of its assets.

Golden Handcuffs—A method of retaining executives—locking them to the corporation—through use of restricted pay devices such as deferred compensation plans.

Golden Handshakes—Additional benefits paid to employees to induce early retirement.

Golden Parachute—A substantial payment made to corporate executives who are terminated upon change or threatened change of ownership or corporate control. Such a provision in an employment contract discourages hostile takeovers and protects executives of potential target companies with monumental lump-sum bailout benefits, if they are fired.

Good Faith—Honesty in fact in the conduct or transaction concerned.

Good Will—An intangible asset on the balance sheet such as a brand name, overall corporate standing or famous association with, say, a celebrity or an event, that is carried on the books of the company at a nominal value (e.g., $1) but which is expected to generate substantial future profits.

Goods and Services Tax (GST) (Canada)—A federal excise tax imposed on the provision of most goods and services.

Government National Mortgage Association (GNMA)—A wholly owned government corporation within the Department of Housing and Urban Development (HUD) that issues government-backed securities typically yielding one or two percentage points more than a ten-year Treasury bond. "Ginnie Mae," as it is known, helps to ensure that mortgage funds are available throughout the country and assures mortgage capital for government housing programs.

Governmental Accounting Standards Board—An organization similar to the Financial Accounting Standards Board (FASB) that was created to improve and establish standards of accounting and financial reporting for state and local government entities.

Governmental Plan—A benefit plan established or maintained for its employees by the government of the United States, by the government of any state or political subdivision thereof, or by any agency or instrumentality of the foregoing.

Grace Period—
—A specified period after a premium payment is due, in which the policyholder may make such payment, and during which the protection of the policy continues.
—A period when a mortgage payment or other debt becomes past due, and before it goes into default. Most mortgages provide for a specified period of time when it can be paid without penalty or default (commonly 30 days).

Graded Vesting—A vesting schedule under which an employee is partially vested, typically 25%, after a certain number of years of service, with the vesting schedule increasing until full vesting is achieved. See also Cliff Vesting.

Gradual Retirement—A program permitting workers to phase themselves out of a company over a number of years by gradually reducing their workweek, rather than going directly from full-time work into full retirement. Also known as *flexible retirement*. See also Phased Retirement.

Graduated Benefits—Health care or other employee benefits plans in which the amount contributed by the employer is determined by the number of years the worker has been employed by the company, so shorter-term workers pay more for their coverage than those who have been with the company for many years.

Graduated Vesting—See Graded Vesting.

Grandfather Clause—An exception to a restriction that allows all those already doing something to continue doing it even if they would be stopped by the new restriction.

Green Card—Registration card issued to a foreign national as evidence of status as a permanent resident of the United States.

Greenmail—Substantial investor's practice of threatening a takeover until the investor subsequently accepts a premium price for his or her stock in return for a promise to walk away; a variation on blackmail.

Grievance Procedure—
—A formal process for the resolution of member or provider complaints, generally mandated by state law or federal qualification standards for HMOs.
—A formal procedure that provides for the union to represent members and nonmembers in processing a complaint.

Gross Domestic Product (GDP)—The market value of a nation's total output of goods and services in a given year.

Gross Eligible Charges—The cost of providing the postretirement health care benefits covered by a plan to a plan participant, before adjusting for expected reimbursements from Medicare and other providers of health care benefits and for the effects of the cost-sharing provisions of the plan.

Gross Income—The total of money received from income property or a business before operating expenses, taxes, depreciation, commissions, salaries, fees and so on are deducted.

Gross National Product (GNP)—The total value of a nation's output of goods and services in a given year, plus net income from foreign investments.

Gross Revenue; Gross Sales—Used to identify the total business done by a company without any deductions of cost or expenses.

Gross-Up—The practice of increasing the amount of a cash payment to offset for the tax impact to the individual resulting from the cash payment.

Gross Yield—The percentage return on a security which is determined by dividing the dollar price into the annual interest payment and calculating the yield to maturity.

Group Annuity Contract—
—A contract issued by a life insurance company that may be used as the funding instrument for benefits to be made in accordance with a pension plan. A single master contract provides that the group of persons participating in the plan will receive annuities during retirement. Individual certificates stating coverage may be issued to members of the group. Forms of group annuity contracts include deposit administration, immediate participation guarantee, pension investment, deferred annuity and group permanent.
—A funding instrument wherein the insurance company, for a stipulated fee for each partici-

pant's benefit, will guarantee the purchase rates of the future annuity and will administer the plan. Also known as *group deferred annuity plan.*

Group Annuity Plan—A pension program underwritten and administered by an insurance company. Normally uses the unit benefit method of funding. Plan participants are covered under one contract; the employer pays premiums on their behalf.

Group Contract—A contract of insurance made with an employer or other entity that covers a group of persons identified by reference to their relationship to the entity buying the contract: e.g., members of a trade association, employees of a common employer, members of a labor union; or members of some other group or association not formed for the purpose of buying insurance.

Group Deferred Annuity Plan—See Group Annuity Contract.

Group Enrollment Period—An annual period of at least ten working days during which employees must be given the option of enrolling in one or more HMOs or switching from an HMO to another health plan option offered by the employer.

Group Health Plan—Under ERISA, an employee welfare benefit plan providing medical care to participants and beneficiaries, directly or indirectly. Under the Internal Revenue Code, a plan maintained by an employer to provide medical care, directly or indirectly, to employees, ex-employees and their families.

Group Incentive Plans—See Gainsharing.

Group Insurance—Any insurance plan under which a number of employees and their dependents are insured under a single policy, issued to their employer, with individual certificates given to each insured employee; the most commonly written lines are life and accident and health.

Group Model HMO—An HMO that contracts with a single multispecialty medical group to provide care to the HMO's membership. The group practice may work exclusively with the HMO, or it may provide services to non-HMO patients as well. The HMO pays the medical group a negotiated, per capita rate, which the group distributes among its physicians, usually on a salaried basis.

Group of Eight (G-8) (International Benefits)—The Group of Seven plus Russia.

Group of Seven (G-7) (International Benefits)—An economic and financial alliance of the world's seven largest industrial market economies: Japan, Germany, France, the United Kingdom, Italy, Canada and the United States.

Group Pension Plan—A program, usually offered by an insurance company, wherein the provisions of the plan are contained in the group contract itself. Such a program will not normally employ a trust agreement.

Group Permanent Plan—
  —A group insurance contract between the employer and the insurance company that usually combines life insurance with retirement benefits and uses the level premium method. Contains both cash and paid-up values.
  —A program in which a policy is purchased for each participant under a group contract negotiated between an insurance company and an employer. Usually provides life insurance as well as a retirement annuity.

Group Practice—A group of persons licensed to practice medicine in a state. As a principal professional activity and as a group responsibility, it engages, or undertakes to engage in, the coordinated practice of medicine in one or more group practice facilities. In this connection, members share common overhead expenses (if and to the extent that such expenses are paid by members of the group), medical and other records and substantial portions of equipment and professional, technical and administrative staffs. In some cases, income is also shared.

Group Practice Prepayment Plan—In general, members of group practice prepayment plans pay regular premiums to the plan. In return, the members receive the health services the plan provides, whenever needed, without additional charges. Many prepayment plans have made arrangements with Medicare to receive direct payments for services they furnish that are covered by Part B (SMI).

Group Registered Retirement Savings Plans (RRSPs) (Canada)—A collection of individual RRSP contracts in a single trust. Employee contributions to group RRSPs are deducted directly from an employee's pay cheque and are not considered income. Employees have a convenient and disciplined method of saving for retirement, administrative costs are reduced and more investment opportunities are generated. See also Registered Retirement Savings Plan (RRSP) (Canada).

Group Term Life Insurance Plan—A plan qualifying under Code Section 79 to provide employees with employer-paid life insurance coverage at little or no tax cost.

Group Universal Life Plan (GULP)—A form of group life insurance that combines term protection for designated beneficiaries with an investment element for the policyholder, which can be used to create nontaxable permanent insurance or to accumulate tax-deferred capital. Participation is entirely voluntary and all premiums are paid by the employee.

Growth Fund—A type of diversified common stock fund that has capital appreciation as its primary goal. It invests in companies that reinvest most of their earnings for expansion, research or development. The term also refers to growth income funds that invest in common stocks for both current income and long-term growth of both capital and income.

Growth Income Fund—A mutual fund that seeks both capital growth and current income. The assets of these funds may be balanced (consist of both equities and bonds) or stock funds whose assets are invested in high-yielding common stocks.

Growth Managers—Focus on the growth of a company and consistently increase their earnings year after year. Growth managers focus on the earnings of a company, and are sometimes seen as more aggressive investors. Contrast with *value managers*. The purpose of these classifications is to aid comparative review of investment performance. See also Value Managers.

Growth Stock—The stock of a corporation, the earnings of which have increased consistently over a number of years and show every indication of considerable further expansion. Most growth stocks provide a relatively low dividend yield. They are primarily attractive for price appreciation potential, especially from a long-range standpoint. Growth companies should have the following characteristics:
1. A young and aggressive management team
2. Strong emphasis on research and development
3. A favorable record of sales and earnings

4. A line of essential products that seems destined to increase in popularity over the years, while new ones are constantly introduced.

Guaranteed Annual Income (Canada)—Aid provided by the majority of provinces to low-income retirees. Money is in addition to what is received from other sources, up to a guaranteed level of income.

Guaranteed Annuity (Canada)—An annuity that will be paid for the lifetime of a person, but in any event for a minimum period; e.g., if annuity is guaranteed for five years and the annuitant dies after three years, payments will be continued to a beneficiary or the estate for two more years.

Guaranteed Benefit Policy—An insurance policy or contract to the extent that such policy or contract provides for benefits the amount of which is guaranteed by the insurer. It also includes any surplus in a separate account, but excludes any other portion of a separate account.

Guaranteed Certificate of Deposit—Certificate of deposit issued by banks having flexible terms, guaranteed principal and reinvestment rate similar to the guaranteed investment contracts issued by insurance companies.

Guaranteed Income Supplement (GIS) (Canada)—A nontaxable monthly benefit paid to lower-income OAS recipients on the basis of family income.

Guaranteed Investment Certificate (Canada)—Evidences a deposit made with a financial institution. Pays a predetermined rate of interest for a specified term.

Guaranteed Investment Contract (GIC)—A contract between an insurance company, bank or mutual fund and a qualified retirement plan such as a 401(k) that guarantees a specific rate of return over a certain period of time on invested capital. GICs, or *stable value funds,* are a conservative way of guaranteeing a certain rate of return on an investment. The rate of return, not the principal, is guaranteed. There is a penalty for early withdrawal. See also Bank Investment Contract (BIC); Stable Value Funds.

Guaranteed Issue Underwriting—The insurer will issue up to some stipulated amount of insurance for each individual employee without evidence of insurability. The requirements are usually based on size of group and distribution by ages, and amounts are decided on by individual insurers.

Guaranteed Renewable Contract—A contract that the insured has the right to continue in force by the timely payment of premiums to a specified age, during which time the insurer has no right to unilaterally make any change in any provision of the policy while the policy is in force, but may make changes in premium rates by policyholder class.

Guaranteed Stock—Generally, a preferred stock that has dividend payments guaranteed by a corporation other than the issuing corporation but remains the stock of the issuing corporation. Guaranteed stock is considered a dual security.

Guardian—A person appointed by the court to look after the property rights and person of minors, the insane and other incompetents or legally incapacitated persons.

Guardian Ad Litem—A special guardian appointed for the sole purpose of carrying on litigation and preserving the interests of a ward. Exercises no control or power over property. Guardianship can be shared with several people.

GUST—An acronym for the following laws: GATT (General Agreement on Tariffs and Trade), USERRA (Uniformed Services Employment and Reemployment Rights Act of 1994), SBJPA (Small Business Job Protection Act of 1996) and TRA '97 (Taxpayer Relief Act of 1997).

H

Hacker—An individual who attempts to exploit vulnerabilities and penetrate or gain unauthorized access to computer systems.

Hard Assets—Assets that are tangible in nature, e.g., real estate, gold, antiques and precious metals.

Hard Dollars—Goods or services purchased with cash are said to be purchased with hard dollars. Purchases made with brokerage commissions are said to be purchases made with soft dollars.

Hardship Withdrawal—A withdrawal of an employee's contributions to a 401(k) plan prior to retirement at the age of 55 or attainment of age 59½.

A hardship withdrawal may be made only in cases of financial emergency provided there are no other sources available to meet the need; the withdrawal is taxable as an early distribution and subject to a 10% excise tax.

Hazardous Duty Pay—Above-normal rate compensation for employees exposed to high-risk working conditions.

Health Alliance (HA)—An organization whose basic functions are to bargain with and purchase health insurance from accountable health plans (AHPs) or other sources of health care in behalf of consumers, and to furnish information to consumers on the services provided, evaluation of their quality of care, participant satisfaction and price. Includes Health Insurance Purchasing Corporation (HIPC) and Health Plan Purchasing Cooperative (HPPC).

Health and Human Services Department (HHS)—Federal Cabinet level department responsible for Social Security, welfare and health programs (formerly HEW—Health, Education, and Welfare).

Health and Welfare Fund—See Welfare Fund.

Health Care Coalition—An organization working on broad health care concerns, including group purchasing, controlling costs and enhancing quality. Participants can be providers, business, third-party payers and consumers; often there is government participation as well.

Health Care Cost Trend Rate—An assumption about the annual rate of change in the cost of health care benefits currently provided by the postretirement benefit plan, due to factors other than changes in the composition of the plan population by age and dependency status, for each year from the measurement date until the end of the period in which benefits are expected to be paid. Considers estimated health care inflation, changes in utilization and delivery patterns, advances in technology and changes in health status of plan participants. Different health care services may have different trend rates.

Health Care Financing Administration (HCFA)—The former name for the current Centers for Medicare and Medicaid Services (CMS).

Health Care Flexible Spending Account—Allows employees to set aside pretax funds for eligible health

68

care benefits such as physical exams, vision care and dental care, including deductibles and copayments. See also Flexible Spending Accounts (FSAs).

Health Care Fraud—As defined by the National Health Care Anti-Fraud Association, a deception or misrepresentation that is intentionally made by an individual entity, knowing that the misrepresentation could result in some unauthorized benefit to the individual or to some other party.

Health Care Provider—An individual or institution that provides medical services (e.g., a physician, hospital, laboratory, etc.). This term should not be confused with an insurance company which "provides" insurance.

Health Care Proxy—A legal document that an individual provides to another person directing him or her to make medical decisions in the event the individual is incompetent to do so. See also Durable Power of Attorney for Health Care.

Health Care Reform—The changes to the health care delivery system, how it is structured, how it is financed, and how people will obtain insurance and services as opposed to the current system. The term is applied to the efforts on the federal, state and local levels to make changes in the health care delivery system so that costs are reduced or contained; the uninsured population is covered; all citizens have access to health care; financing is assured; and quality of care is maintained or improved. Management options range from highly centralized, federal controls; through the setting of certain requirements at the federal or state level but allowing local innovation as to implementation; through local solutions, even if nothing is done at the state or national level.

Health Care Reimbursement Account—See Health Care Flexible Spending Account.

Health Fair—Type of wellness program conducted to prevent disease, increase employee awareness about unhealthy habits such as smoking or overeating, promote healthful activities such as physical fitness programs and increase community good will. Can also be a marketing tool for medical providers.

Health Insurance—Protection that provides payment of benefits for covered sickness or injury. Included under this heading are various types of insurance, such as accident insurance, disability income insurance, medical expense insurance, and accidental death and dismemberment insurance.

Health Insurance Portability and Accountability Act of 1996 (HIPAA)—Federal legislation that improves access to health insurance when changing jobs by restricting certain preexisting condition limitations, and guarantees availability and renewability of health insurance coverage for all employers regardless of claims experience or business size. The law also increases the health insurance deduction for the self-employed; provides tax incentives for purchase of long-term care insurance; and establishes medical saving accounts (MSAs), which provide for tax-deductible contributions to accounts to cover medical expenses.

Health Insurance Purchasing Cooperative/Corporation (HIPC)—A managed competition reform plan for nonprofit organizations set up as collective buying agents of medical services. Also known as *health alliance.*

Health Maintenance Organization (HMO)—A prepaid medical group practice plan that provides a comprehensive predetermined medical care benefit package. HMOs emphasize preventive care, early diagnosis and outpatient treatment. The HMO can be sponsored by the government, medical schools, hospitals, employers, labor unions, consumer groups, insurance companies and hospital-medical plans. HMOs are both insurers and providers of health care. See also Group Model HMO; IPA Model HMO; Network Model HMO; Staff Model HMO.

Health Plan Employer Data and Information Set (HEDIS)—A core of performance measures designed by participating managed health plans and employers to meet employees' needs to understand the value of their health care, to hold plans accountable for performance and to ensure quality. HEDIS is offered under the sponsorship of the National Committee for Quality Assurance (NCQA).

Health Plan Purchasing Cooperative—See Health Alliance.

Health Promotion—See Wellness (Health Promotion) Programs.

Health Reimbursement Accounts (HRAs)—A tax-exempt arrangement established and funded by employers for employees and retirees to use for qualified medical expenses such as physical exams, vision care and dental care, including deductibles and copayments. Money remaining in the account at year-end can roll over and be used to cover future medical costs ("use it or lose it" does not apply), but the account is not portable. An HRA does not need to correspond with a specific health plan. HRAs are a way to encourage patients to shop wisely for health care.

Health Risk Assessment—A wellness program instrument that can evaluate the health status of an individual and the relative risk of disease, injury or death associated with a specific set of lifestyle behaviors when combined with specific information about the individual involved.

Health Savings Accounts (HSAs)—Introduced by the Medicare Prescription Drug, Improvement, and Modernization Act of 2003, these are tax-exempt trusts or custodial accounts created for employees, retirees and the self-employed who are covered under a high-deductible health plan. Funds can be used for medical expenses, including prescription drugs, qualified long-term care and insurance premiums, and COBRA coverage. Contributions can be made by the employer or the employee. Amounts not distributed can be carried forward. Like an IRA, the individual who is the account beneficiary owns the HSA, making the plan portable. An HSA can be offered under a cafeteria plan. These accounts are designed to empower employees to take more responsibility for their own health care and help employers control health care costs. See also Cafeteria Plan; High-Deductible Health Plans.

Health Stock Ownership Plan (HSOP)—The combination of an employee stock ownership plan and 401(h) account. HSOPs allow the sponsoring employer to provide for retiree medical benefits for its current employees without having to accrue such future liabilities currently for financial accounting purposes as would be required if such benefits were provided outside the qualified plan context.

Hedging—
—(Investment) The temporary purchase and sale of a contract calling for future delivery of a specific quantity of a particular commodity at an agreed-upon price to offset a present (or anticipated) position in the cash market. An opera-

tion intended to protect against loss in another operation.
—(Agriculture) The sale of a commodity by entering a contract for future delivery at an agreed price and a specific time by a farmer who has or is producing the commodity.

HEDIS—See Health Plan Employer Data and Information Set.

Heir—A person who inherits real property; to be distinguished from next of kin and from a distributee.

High-Deductible Health Plans—Health benefit plans that have a minimum deductible of $1,000 for individuals and $2,000 for families, which applies to all health care benefits except preventive care. Out-of-pocket expense requirement cannot be more than $5,000 for single coverage or $10,000 for family coverage. These plans can aid in medical cost control for employers while providing preventive care for employees. These plans may be offered in conjunction with an HSA.

High Self-Insured Deductible (HSID)—Also known as shared funding, HSID is a way for employers to improve cash flow by self-funding the first tier of any employee's health care expenses. Employers can thus retain funds that would normally be paid to the insurance company to cover current and future claims.

High-Risk Pools—State-created insurance pools of individuals with extensive current or anticipated health care needs. These pools spread the risk for those individuals among the health insurance companies doing business in that state. The pools have been used by a number of states in an attempt to extend coverage to their medically uninsurable citizens.

People with a chronic disease or illness, such as diabetes or multiple sclerosis, can purchase health care insurance. Additional funds for these high-risk pools are typically taxes on health insurance premiums.

High-Yield Bond Fund—As defined by the Investment Company Institute, a fund in which two-thirds or more of the portfolio will be invested at all times in lower rated corporate bonds.

Highly Compensated Employee (HCE)—Either a 5% owner or a person who earned more than $80,000 during the current or preceding year (indexed annually). Repeals rule treating highest paid officer as an HCE, the top-100 rule, and family aggregation rules in both the HCE definition and the $150,000 compensation cap. Discrimination in favor of this group is prohibited.

HIPAA—See Health Insurance Portability and Accountability Act of 1996.

Hiring Bonus—An extra sum of money provided at time of hire to entice an applicant to accept a job offer or to make up for compensation forfeited at the previous company.

Hiring Rate—Entry-level wage or salary.

Hold Harmless Clause—
—A contract provision in which one party to the contract promises to be responsible for liability incurred by the other party.
—In health care contracts, a contractual provision under which the provider agrees not to sue or assert any claims against a plan member for services covered under the contract, even if the plan becomes insolvent or fails to meet its obligations.

Holding Company—A corporation that owns the securities of another, in most cases with voting control.

Home Buyers Plan (HBP) (Canada)—Program introduced by the federal government in 1992 allowing individuals to borrow from their RRSPs to buy or build a home. The amount withdrawn must be repaid within 15 years.

Home Country—See Base Country (International Compensation).

Home Equity Conversion Mortgage—See Reverse Mortgage.

Home Health Agency (HHA)—A licensed facility providing skilled nursing and other therapeutic services in the patient's home.

Home Health Care—Items and services provided as needed in patients' homes by a home health agency or by others. Can range from skilled nursing care and physical therapy to personal care and help with household chores.

Home Office—An office located in an employee's home where, for the convenience of the employer, the employee works. If certain requirements are met, the employee may be allowed to deduct home office expenses.

Homeopathy—An alternative medical system that treats the symptoms of a disease with minute doses of a drug that produce the same symptoms in a healthy person as are present in the disease. This is thought to stimulate physiological defenses against the symptoms of the disease. Homeopathy as a formal system of medicine is no longer practiced in the United States. However, it may be informally practiced as an alternative therapy.

Horizontal Integration—Combination of two or more similar health care components into one system to achieve cost savings and/or increased contract leverage. For example, two or more hospitals may form an alliance resulting in elimination of duplicate functions. Can also refer to coordination of similar benefits, such as workers' compensation, short-term disability and group health coverage. Horizontal integration is also called *specialty integration*. See also Vertical Integration.

Hospice—Health care facility or program providing medical care and support services, such as counseling, to terminally ill persons and their families.

Hospital—A legally constituted institution having organized facilities for the care and treatment of sick and injured persons on a resident or inpatient basis, including facilities for diagnosis and surgery under the supervision of a staff of one or more licensed physicians and which provides 24-hour nursing services by a registered nurse on duty or call. It does not mean convalescent, nursing, rest or extended care facilities or a facility operated exclusively for the treatment of the aged, drug addict or alcoholic, whether or not such facilities are operated as a separate institution by a hospital.

Hospital Benefit Plan—A plan that makes cash payments or reimburses employees for hospital charges up to a certain amount or assumes the costs for certain specified hospital charges such as room and board, services, drugs and supplies.

Hospital Confinement Policy—See Hospital Indemnity Policy.

Hospital Indemnity Policy—A form of health insurance that provides a stipulated daily, weekly or monthly indemnity during hospital confinement. The indemnity is payable on an unallocated basis without regard to the actual expense of hospital confinement.

Hospital Insurance (HI)—Medicare Part A, which covers the cost of hospital charges to seniors and the disabled.

Host Country National—A citizen of a country who is employed in a branch or plant of a company that is located in that person's country but the company is headquartered in another country. Also called a *local national*.

Hour Bank—
—A method of banking or crediting the hours worked by a worker to his or her individual account and then drawing out the required hours at each determination date, to establish or maintain the worker's eligibility for health insurance benefits.
—A variation of the system puts only the hours (or some portion of the hours) worked in excess of those required to maintain current eligibility in the hour bank account. Hour bank provisions usually specify the maximum number of hours that can be held in the account.

Hour of Service—An hour for which an employee is paid, or is entitled to payment, for the performance of services for the employer. Includes vacation, sick time and other paid leaves of absence. Measurement of time for determining a year of service.

Hours Worked—Standard hours worked in a year is 2,080 (52 weeks × 40 hours per week).

HR 10 Plan—See Keogh Plan.

HTML—An acronym for *hypertext markup language*, HTML is the computer language used to create hypertext documents. HTML uses a list of tags that describes the general structure of various kinds of documents linked together on the World Wide Web.

Human Resource Information System (HRIS)—A computer-based system for gathering, storing, manipulating, analyzing, retrieving and distributing relevant timely and accurate data and information regarding the staff of an organization, for both organizational effectiveness and legal compliance.

Hybrid HMO—A type of HMO which includes service features of indemnity insurance, such as co-insurance, deductibles, experience rating, open panel of providers, in addition to the various utilization, cost, and access controls and structures of prepaid HMO-type health plans. Sometimes called a mixed model managed care plan.

Hybrid Pension Plan—A qualified retirement-type plan that has characteristics typical of both defined benefit and defined contribution plans. Examples are cash balance plans, pension equity plans and age-weighted profit-sharing plans.

Hypothetical Tax (International Benefits)—The amount deducted from an expatriate's salary that is the equivalent of what an expatriate would pay for income tax if at home. The amounts deducted are used by employers to satisfy expatriate tax obligations worldwide.

I

ICD-9 Codes—See *International Classification of Diseases*.

Immature—An actuarial concept referring to newly established companies, or growing organizations, wherein all employees as yet are active and no one has retired. See also Deferred Annuity; Mature.

Immediate Annuity—An annuity under which income payments begin one annuity period (e.g., one month or one year) after the annuity is purchased.

Immediate Participation Guarantee (IPG) Contract—
—A group insurance contract under which the employer's unallocated account is credited with its share of actual investment income for the year. There is generally no guarantee of principal or a minimum rate of interest. Annuity payments are charged directly against the account as they are paid.
—A funding instrument offered by insurance companies wherein all dollars paid by the employer and dividends credited are immediately participating in the investment program.
See also Investment-Only (IO) Contract.

Immediate Vesting—That form of vesting under which rights to vested benefits are acquired by a participant, commencing immediately upon his or her entry into the plan.

Immunization (Bonds)—The design of a bond portfolio to achieve a target level of return in the face of changing reinvestment rates and price levels. It is the combining of short- and long-term bonds in the same portfolio to produce a predictable rate of return regardless of movements in interest rates. See also Dedicated Bond Portfolio.

Improshare—Gainsharing program incentive in which bonuses are based on the overall productivity of the work team. See also Gainsharing.

Incentive Compensation—Rewarding the performance of an individual in an institution with added compensation, typically in the form of bonuses or percentage increments above the base salary.

Incentive Fees—See Performance-Based Fees.

Incentive Pay Plan—Pay plans that reward the accomplishment of specific results. Awards are usually tied to expected results identified at the beginning of the performance cycle. The plans can be individual, group, companywide or a combination.

Incentive Stock Option—A form of deferred compensation designed to influence long-term performance that gives employees the right to purchase company stock usually at a predetermined, bargain price. The option qualifies for preferential tax treatment provided the employee holds the stock for a certain period of time. The employee pays no taxes until the option is sold.

Incidents of Ownership—Rights that will result in the inclusion of life insurance policy proceeds in the policyholder's estate for federal estate tax purposes.

Income Account—See Profit and Loss Statement.

Income and Service Benefit Formula—A retirement benefit formula based on income and credited service, such as 1% of average annual income multiplied by the years of service.

Income Averaging—A method of determining how much tax is owed on a lump-sum distribution from a qualified pension plan. An individual who receives such a distribution and includes it in taxable income may be eligible to treat the tax liability as if the distribution had been received over a five- or ten-year period. Certain requirements must be met.

Income-Based Benefit Formula—A retirement formula based solely on income, such as 50% of the final yearly salary.

Income Investment—An investment whose main objective is to generate income in the form of interest or dividend payments, rather than to grow principal. For example, a bond fund is an income investment.

Income Manager—A common stock manager whose style places emphasis on the receipt of dividend yield.

Income Protection Insurance Policy—A disability income policy which specifies that an insured is disabled if he or she suffers an income loss caused by a disability, therefore qualifying him or her for benefits under the policy.

Income Replacement Ratio—The percentage of current income that will be needed in each year of retirement to maintain the current standard of living.

Income Statement—See Profit and Loss Statement.

Incurred but Not Reported (IBNR)—Claims that have been incurred but have not been reported to the insurer as of some specific date. Often a disputed figure since carriers must estimate this liability for accounting purposes based on their experience with claims lags.

Incurred Claims—Incurred claims equal the claims paid during the policy year plus the claim reserves as of the end of the policy year, minus the corresponding reserves as of the beginning of the policy year. The difference between the year-end and beginning of the year claim reserves is called the *increase in reserves* and may be added directly to the paid claims to produce the incurred claims.

Incurred Losses—The losses occurring within a fixed period, whether or not they were reported or adjusted during that period.

Indemnify—Literally, "to save harmless." Thus, one person or organization agrees to protect another against loss.

Indemnity—A benefit paid by an insurer for a loss insured under a policy.

Indemnity Plans—In these traditional fee-for-service group health insurance plans, the patient chooses whichever doctor and hospital he or she wants to use. The employer pays premiums to the health insurance company to cover the costs of providing benefits and administering claims. The employee may pay a portion of the monthly insurance premiums, an annual deductible and/or copayments per medical visit. These plans are usually experience rated, and health care providers are paid on a cost-plus, retroactive reimbursement system. The insurance carrier uses the premiums to pay claims and for retention fees, including state premium taxes, administrative expenses, commissions, risk charges and claims processing. The employer has no liability for a deficit.

Indenture (Deed of Trust)—A legal document prepared in connection with a bond issue describing the terms of the issue such as security, maturity date, interest rate and remedies in case of default, etc.

Independent Contractor—As distinguished from an employee by the IRS, a person who works for another whose labor and how it is performed is largely determined by the worker, not the employer. Independent contractors pay their own taxes; the employer does not, for example, pay Social Security or unemployment taxes for the worker.

Independent Practice Association (IPA)—A type of managed care organization composed of a group of independent physicians who have formed an association as a separate legal entity for contracting purposes. IPA physician providers retain their individual practices, work in separate offices, continue to see their nonmanaged care patients and have the option to contract directly with managed care plans. Also referred to as *independent physician association* and *individual practice association*. See also IPA Model HMO.

Index—A statistical model expressed in terms of percentages of a base year or years that serves as a reference in judging investment performance. The index most often used for stock market performance is the Standard & Poor's 500 Index, which measures the average performance of 500 widely held common stocks. Other frequently used indexes are the Dow Jones Industrial Average; the NASDAQ and the Russell 2000, used for smaller company stocks; the Toronto Stock Exchange 300 Composite Index (TSE 300), used in Canada; and the Morgan Stanley Capital International Europe, AustralAsia, Far East Index (EAFE), which is used as a benchmark for foreign company stocks.

Index Fund—An investment fund (or account) composed of securities the characteristics of which will produce a return that will duplicate (or substantially duplicate) a designated securities index.

Index Option—An option based on the market value of a particular group of stocks. Unlike stock options, index options—when exercised—are settled in cash.

Individual Account Plan—A defined contribution plan or profit-sharing plan that provides an individual account for each participant; allows participants to choose, from a broad range of investment options, how their accounts will be invested; and whose benefits are based solely on the amount contributed to the participant's account, including income, expenses, gains and losses. Defined contribution retirement plans such as 401(k) plans are examples of individual account plans. See also Defined Contribution Plan.

Individual Annuity—A contract by which an insurance company undertakes to pay an individual a specified annuity. Two main types are the retirement annuity policy and the retirement income policy. When used for pension plans, the policies are usually held in trust until the employee retires. Generally used when the number of covered employees is too small to permit the use of group annuities.

Individual Life Insurance and Annuity Contracts—Individual life insurance contracts generally provide for paying the face amount in a lump sum upon the death of the insured while the insurance is in force. The insurance may be continuous throughout the lifetime of the insured, for a specified number of years or to a specified age. A medical examination is generally required for insurance under individual contracts, but if the amount of insurance is not large, a statement by the applicant as to his or her physical condition and medical history may be accepted by the insurer.

Individual Mandate—A health care financing option that would require individuals to buy their own insurance if employers do not provide it.

Individual Practice Association (IPA)—See Independent Practice Association (IPA); IPA Model HMO.

Individual Retirement Account (IRA)—A personal, qualified retirement account in which an individual may accumulate contributions up to a certain sum each year for retirement income. Funds accumulate on a tax-deferred basis. Although money can be withdrawn, a 10% penalty has been placed on those assets withdrawn prior to the individual turning 59½, in addition to the normal taxes, which must be paid upon withdrawal. An individual can set up his own plan with a bank, insurance company, brokerage house or mutual fund. A company can also deduct an agreed-upon amount from employees' paychecks and send it along to a designated agent, or set up its own plan where managers are selected to manage the assets. See also Education IRA; Roth IRA.

Infertility Benefits—Insurance coverage for treatments to enable human reproduction where that capacity is reduced or absent. Can range from diagnostic tests, to treatment of underlying causes of infertility to in vitro procedures.

Inflation—A phase of the business cycle characterized by abnormally high prices, a decrease in the purchasing power of money, and spiraling costs and wage rates. Inflation may occur when purchasing power is in excess of goods and services for sale, and/or buyers stampede to convert money into commodities; or when production costs and prices advance to consecutively higher levels. The opposite of *deflation*.

Inflation-Indexed Bonds—Financial instruments designed to fully protect investors against that erosion of principal and interest due to inflation. When held to maturity, the bonds eliminate the variability in real yield associated with long-term investments. See also Treasury Inflation-Protected Securities (TIPS).

Information System—An interconnected set of information resources under the same direct management control that shares common functionality. A system normally includes hardware, software, information, data, applications, communications and people.

Infusion Therapy—A type of home health care involving the self-administering of intravenous drugs. Allows the patient greater quality of life and can be a less expensive alternative to inpatient admission.

Initial Public Offering (IPO)—The first sale of a company's stock to the public. Because there are usually not enough shares to meet the demand, the price increases quickly or sells at a premium.

Injunction—A writ of judicial process by which a party is required to do a particular thing or to refrain from doing a particular thing. Imposed when the complaining party will suffer irreparable injury as a result of unlawful actions by the other party.

Inpatient—A person who occupies a hospital bed, crib or bassinet while under observation, care, diagnosis or treatment for at least 24 hours. (Antonym: *outpatient*)

In-Service Distribution—401(k) and profit-sharing plans may allow a plan participant to take a distribution from the plan prior to the time the participant incurs a traditional triggering event.

In-Service Withdrawal—A withdrawal of plan benefits prior to separation from service with an employer. No in-service withdrawals are permitted from a defined benefit pension plan.

Insider—A stockholder who owns 10% or more of a company, a member of the board of directors or an elected officer of a corporation, or anyone else who possesses information that is not publicly known about the company, but which is important in valuing its stock. Securities and Exchange Commission (SEC) regulations place restrictions on stock purchases and sales by insiders.

Insider Trading—Trading of stock by insiders who use unpublished information to make a profit on the sale or purchase of stocks.

Institutional Investor—An organization the primary purpose of which is to invest its own assets or those held in trust by it for others. Includes pension funds, investment companies, universities and banks.

Insurance—A means of providing or purchasing protection against some of the economic consequences of loss. Risk of loss is transferred to a third party in exchange for a "consideration" or premium. This exchange creates an insurance contract. See also Insurance Contract.

Insurance Contract—An irrevocable contract in which the insurance company unconditionally undertakes a legal obligation to provide benefits in return for a premium, thereby transferring risk from the employer (or the plan) to the insurance company.

Insured—In life insurance, the person on whose life an insurance policy is issued; in property and liability insurance, the person to whom or on whose behalf benefits are payable under the policy.

Insured Event—An occurrence that causes the PBGC to assume responsibility for benefit payments. Termination of a single employer plan or an insolvent multiemployer plan are insured events.

Insured Pension Plan—A plan funded through contracts with a life insurance company, which guarantees payment of the annuities.

Insurer—An organization, insurance company or other, that assumes the risk and provides the policy to the insured.

Intangible Assets—Capital assets carried on the balance sheet that are not physical or financial in character and that often are shown at cost or having nominal value assigned to them which usually does not reflect their substantial contribution to earning power. Examples would be patents, good will, trademarks, copyrights, franchises and unamortized discounts.

Integrated Delivery System—A group of hospitals, physicians, other providers, and insurers and/or community agencies that work together to coordinate and deliver a broad spectrum of cost-effective services to their community. Also known as *integrated service network*.

Integrated Disability Management (IDM)—Single management systems for occupational (workers' compensation) and nonoccupational (short-term and long-term) disability. Aspects of an IDM program include a single claims intake and notification process, a single claims management system, a common medical case management process, a common return-to-work program and a single database. See also 24-Hour Coverage.

Integrated Plan—A plan that makes adjustments in contributions or benefits for amounts available through Social Security. See also Permitted Disparity.

Integration Level—The compensation level below which, under a plan's benefit formula, compensation is excluded in the computation of benefits or contributions.

Integration With OAS, CPP/QPP (Canada)—The usual option provides a larger pension from the plan from retirement until eligibility for these government benefits, reducing at that age by the amount of the government benefits; it thus provides a level total pension throughout retirement.

Integration With Social Security—
—Pension benefits are coordinated with Social Security benefits. For example, a person's monthly pension amount is reduced by a percentage of the amount of money received through Social Security.
—The basic concept of integration is that the benefits of the employer's plan must be dovetailed with Social Security benefits in such a manner that employees earning more than the taxable wage base will not receive combined benefits under the two programs that are proportionately greater than the benefits for employees earning less than the taxable wage base. See also Permitted Disparity.
—(Canada) See Offset Integration.

Integrity—In relation to HIPAA privacy requirements, the property that data or information has not been altered or destroyed in an unauthorized manner.

Interactive Benefits Communication—Use of technologies for communicating employee benefits such as touch-tone phones; personal computers, including use of intranets and the Internet; and multimedia kiosks. Forms of interactive communication include interactive voice response (IVR) systems, desktop personal computers, multimedia personal computers and public kiosks. See also Call Centers; Employee Self-Service.

Interest—
—The return earned or to be earned on funds invested or to be invested to provide for future pension benefits. In calling the return *interest,* it is recognized that, in addition to interest on debt securities, the earnings of a pension fund may include dividends on equity securities, rentals on real estate and gains or (as offsets) losses on fund investments.
—The amount a borrower pays to a lender for the

use of its money. Interest is paid by a corporation to its bondholders for the use of their money.

—Regular interest is a rate of interest to be used in accumulating contributions under the retirement plan and in making actuarial computations.

Interest Rate Risk—When interest rates rise, the market value of fixed income contracts (such as bonds) declines. Similarly, when interest rates decline, the market value of fixed income contracts increases. Interest rate risk is the risk associated with these fluctuations.

Interest Table—A listing of the present or accumulated value of $1 at compound interest or of periodic payments of $1 at intervals of one year or other specified periods.

Interest Yield—The uniform rate of interest on investments computed on the basis of the price at which the investment was purchased, giving effect to the periodic amortization of any premiums paid or the periodic accrual of discounts received.

Intergenerational Care—Programs in which children and elderly relatives are cared for at the same facility.

Intermediate Care Facility (ICF)—An institution licensed under state law to provide, on a regular basis, health care and services to individuals who do not require the degree of care and treatment that a hospital or a skilled nursing facility is designed to provide. The individuals must, however, require care and services above the level of room and board. Federal payment for intermediate care facility services is limited to Medicaid.

Intermediate-Term Bonds—Bonds with between five and 12 years to maturity.

Internal Revenue Code (IRC)—As amended, this code is the basic federal tax law.

Internal Revenue Service (IRS)—Part of the Treasury Department, the IRS is the government agency charged with the collection of taxes, including those related to employee benefit plans. The IRS is also responsible for administering the requirements for qualified pension plans as well as other retirement and welfare plans. It assesses penalties for failure to comply with certain reporting and disclosure requirements.

***International Classification of Diseases,* Ninth Revision, Clinical Modification (ICD-9-CM)**—The classification used for coding of diagnoses and operations, for compiling hospital statistics, and for submitting bills. The ICD-10-CM will use alphanumeric codes. The *International Classification* is a publication of the World Health Organization (WHO).

International Compensation—Pay practices covering employees who move across national borders, including headquarters expatriates, third country nationals and inpatriates. The definition sometimes is extended to include domestic pay practices in foreign countries.

International Fund—As defined by the Investment Company Institute, an international fund has two-thirds or more of the portfolio invested at all times in equity securities of companies located outside the United States.

Internet—A worldwide network of computer networks that can share information because a common set of language protocols is used by all. The Internet was created by the U.S. government in the late '60s to link defense researchers and contractors. Now computer systems at universities, libraries, government agencies, schools, businesses and homes with personal computers with Internet access are all connected.

Intervention—A formal process where the counselor (and often with a team consisting of supervisor, co-workers and family members) confronts an individual, breaks through denial and convinces him or her to enter treatment.

Intervivos Trust—See Living Trust.

Intestate—Dies without a will.

Intranet—An internal computer network accessible to employees only.

These private networks combine text, graphics, audio and video to distribute news, answer employee questions, update personnel records and connect workers in remote locations.

Inventory—

—Current assets representing the present stock of finished merchandise, goods in process of manufacture, raw materials used in manufacture and sometimes miscellaneous supplies such as packing and shipping materials. These are usually stated at cost or market value, whichever is lower.

—Those tangible assets on the balance sheet valued at cost or market, whichever is lower, consisting of raw materials, semifinished and finished goods, and expected to be disposed of within a year, from which a company hopes to derive a profit.

Invested Capital—The sum of a company's long-term debt, capital stock and all surplus.

Investment—The process by which money is transferred from one owner to another for the purpose of making more money in the form of capital gains or additional income or a combination of both.

Investment Advisers Act of 1940—As amended in 1960, a law that established a pattern of regulation of investment advisors and is similar in many respects to Securities Exchange Act provisions governing the conduct of brokers and dealers. It requires, with certain exceptions, that persons or firms engaging for compensation in the business of advising others with respect to their securities transactions shall register with the commission and conform their activities to statutory standards designed to protect the interests of investors.

Investment Advisor—A person generally required to register with the SEC who provides advice to the public concerning the purchase or sale of securities.

Investment Banker—Also known as an *underwriter*. He or she is the intermediary between the corporation issuing new securities and the public. The usual practice is for one or more investment bankers to buy outright from a corporation a new issue of stocks or bonds. The groups form a syndicate to sell securities to individuals and institutions. Investment bankers also distribute very large blocks of stocks or bonds, perhaps held by an estate. Thereafter, the market in the security may be over the counter, on a regional stock exchange, the American Exchange or the New York Stock Exchange.

Investment Company or Trust—A company or trust managed by investment professionals that invests its capital in other companies for purposes of diversification, the two principal types of which are the *closed-end* and *open-end* or *mutual fund*. *Closed-end funds* have a fixed capitalization, and are usually listed and traded on the New York Stock Exchange like any other security, and may sell at a premium or discount to net asset value. *Open-end funds* whose shares are not listed stand ready to sell new shares continuously to investors and to redeem them when called upon to do so. See also Mutual Fund.

Investment Consultant—An individual or firm that provides—for a fixed fee based on a percentage of assets or a fee derived from brokerage commissions—investment advice. Such advice generally includes analyzing portfolio constraints, setting performance objectives, counseling on allocation of assets and selecting and monitoring services. It may or may not include performance measurement services.

Investment Earnings—Investment income on contributions, which is not normally subject to federal income tax for employee benefit plans.

Investment Education—The provision of educational materials and information to assist plan participants in planning for their retirement. Topics can include specific plan information; general financial and investment information such as risk and return, diversification and compound return; hypothetical asset allocation models using different time horizons and risk profiles; and interactive investment material such as questionnaires, worksheets and computer programs for estimating retirement needs, and the impact of asset allocation. Care must be taken to leave decision making in the hands of participants; giving actual investment advice places the employer under ERISA fiduciary liability. See also Financial Planning Education; Investment Consultant.

Investment Gain/Loss—The realized or unrealized increase (decrease) in market value of a portfolio at the end of a time period as compared to its market value at the beginning of that period.

Investment Manager—An individual or organization that provides investment management services, for a fee, on a fully discretionary or nondiscretionary basis. Broadly used to include insurance companies, independent counsel firms, mutual fund organizations, trust departments of banks, and individuals.

Investment Objectives—Long-term, risk-return targets developed principally from careful consideration of plan sponsor factors, investment factors and a forecast of the future. Critical in the adoption of investment objectives is the asset allocation decision.

Investment-Only (IO) Contract—A modification of an IPG contract. The benefit payments are not guaranteed by the insurance company past the current year and investments may be made in the insurance company's general account or in its various separate accounts. See also Immediate Participation Guarantee (IPG) Contract.

Investment Policy—Commonly used to describe how contributions to an employee benefit plan are utilized from the time they are received until benefits are paid. Under ERISA, a written investment policy is required.

Investment Policy Statement—The statement of policy is the communication of a *risk policy* to the fund's investment manager(s). It states unambiguously the degree of investment risk that fiduciaries are willing to undertake with pension trust assets. A statement of investment policy differs importantly from a statement of investment objectives. An investment *policy* prescribes acceptable course of action; a policy can be acted upon, implemented. An investment *objective* (such as a performance standard) is a desired result. A manager cannot implement an objective; a manager can only pursue a course of action, consistent with investment policy, which the manager believes offers a reasonable likelihood of realizing the objective. Therefore, in drafting instructions for an investment manager, primary emphasis should be on stating the investment, or risk, policy clearly.

Investment Portfolio—
—An individual's assets that are not used for everyday living expenses or short-term expenditures. A portfolio may contain both taxable and tax-deferred investments.
—A list of a company's or mutual fund's securities.

Investment Return—See Yield.

Investment-Sensitive Life Insurance—See Variable Life Insurance.

Investor—Someone whose principal purpose is to invest money prudently and productively over the longer, as opposed to the shorter, run with the investment objective being protection of principal, obtaining a reasonable return and capital apprecia-

tion to preserve purchasing power. Compare with Trader.

IPA Model HMO—A type of HMO that contracts with individual physicians or small physician groups to provide services to HMO enrollees at a negotiated per capita or fee-for-service rate. Physicians maintain their own offices and can contract with other HMOs and see other fee-for-service patients. See also Health Maintenance Organization.

IRA—See Individual Retirement Account.

Irrevocable Beneficiary—An unalterable beneficiary. The owner gives up the right to change the beneficiary designation without the beneficiary's consent.

J

January Effect—The observed tendency for stock returns to be higher in January than would be expected.

Job Analysis—A systematic, formal study of the duties and responsibilities a job entails. Includes the requirements necessary to complete a job, considering mainly the order of operation, material and machinery needed, and the necessary qualifications of workers. The process seeks to obtain important and relevant information about the nature and level of the work performed and specifications for a worker to perform the job competently.

Job Creation and Worker Assistance Act of 2002 (JCWAA)—This act changed the funding rules for defined benefit plans and made a number of technical corrections to certain provisions of the Economic Growth and Tax Relief Reconciliation Act of 2001 (EGTRRA) relating to qualified retirement plans. See also Economic Growth and Tax Relief Reconciliation Act of 2001 (EGTRRA).

Job Cluster—A series of jobs considered together for job evaluation and wage and salary administration purposes, based on common skills, occupational qualifications, technology, licensing, working conditions, union jurisdictions, workplace, career paths and organizational tradition.

Job Description—A summary of a job's purpose, listing its tasks, duties, responsibilities, and the skills, knowledge and abilities needed to perform the job competently. A job description describes and focuses on the job itself, not on any specific individual who might fill the job.

Job Evaluation—A systematic procedure to create a job worth hierarchy and pay differential within an organization. Two basic approaches are the market data approach and the job content approach.

Job Family—Jobs of the same nature but requiring different skill and responsibility levels or working conditions.

Job Grade—A class, level or group into which jobs of the same or similar value are grouped for compensation purposes. Usually, all jobs in a grade have the same pay range: minimum, midpoint and maximum. However, sometimes different jobs in the same pay grade have different pay ranges, due to market conditions for some of the jobs.

Job Lock—Remaining in a particular job for fear of losing one's health insurance coverage. This is caused by waiting periods for preexisting conditions, high rates and outright denials of coverage. HIPAA was passed to alleviate job lock.

Job Sharing—Two people, typically in career-oriented professional positions, performing the tasks of one full-time position in order to enjoy more flexibility in their personal schedules, typically for child or dependent care. Salary and benefits are prorated.

Job Specifications—A description of the worker characteristics required to perform a given job competently. These characteristics must be bona fide occupational qualifications (BFOQs), as opposed to requirements that are artificially inflated and not actually required for competent job performance (e.g., requiring a college degree for all exempt jobs). Specifications, commonly referred to as hiring or background requirements, should be written before advertising or interviewing candidates for an open position. They should support the essential functions identified during job analysis to reduce potential liabilities under the Americans with Disabilities Act.

Job Worth Hierarchy—The perceived internal value of jobs in relationship to each other within an organization. Forms the basis for grouping similar jobs together and establishing salary ranges.

Joint and Several Liability—Used when compensation for liability may be obtained from one or more parties either individually or jointly, whichever may be most advantageous. Example: Partners are responsible for their own and the others' actions in business.

Joint and Survivor Annuity—A contract that provides income periodically, payable during the longer of the lifetimes of the two persons. The benefit payable may be adjusted to account for the extended life expectancy of the couple, and the benefit amount may decrease when one or the other dies. The contingent annuitant is usually the spouse. See also Automatic Survivor Coverage; Contingent Annuity Option.

Joint and Survivor Option—A pension plan provision in which, based on the age of a designated survivor (usually one's spouse), a reduced pension is paid as long as one of the two parties is living.

Joint Commission on Accreditation of Healthcare Organizations (JCAHO)—An accrediting body that periodically evaluates and awards accreditation status to facilities such as hospitals, skilled nursing facilities and health maintenance organizations in recognition of satisfactory performance. Most managed care plans and some state and federal programs require JCAHO certification.

Joint Tenancy Estate—The ownership of property by two or more persons in equal shares with the rights of survivorship.

Joint Venture—The joining of two or more people to carry out a specific business venture, often real estate. A joint venture may be a partnership, tenancy in common or corporation.

Jointly Trusteed Single Employer Plan—An employee benefit plan of one employer that is administered by a board of trustees consisting of an equal number of employee and employer representatives.

Junk Bonds—Bonds that are initially issued as low-quality securities, often in conjunction with takeovers, leveraged buyouts and restructurings. They offer high interest and high risk. These securities generally lack the characteristics of a desirable investment. The rights of the bondholder are subordinated to senior debtholders. Assurance of interest and principal payments in the future is limited. Repayment often depends on asset sales rather than on the ongoing profitability of the business. Euphemistically called *high-yield securities.*

Jury Duty Pay—Pay to employees to supplement the small stipend provided by local governments for jury duty service. Jury duty pay, whether provided by the government or employer, is taxable income to the employee.

Just-in-Time (JIT) System—A system of inventory control in which a manufacturer coordinates production with suppliers so that raw materials and components arrive just as they are needed in the production process.

Juvenile Insurance Policy—An insurance policy that is issued on the life of a child but is owned and paid for by an adult.

K

Keogh Plan—A qualified retirement plan for self-employed persons and their employees to which yearly tax-deductible contributions up to a specified limit can be made, if the plan meets certain requirements of the Internal Revenue Code. Keogh plans, also known as HR 10 plans, include defined benefit and defined contribution plans.

Key Employee—A criterion used to describe highly compensated officers or owners of companies and to establish whether a defined benefit pension plan is top-heavy; if it is, special requirements for vesting, contributions and benefits must be met to retain tax qualification. Before 2002, a key employee was a participant who, at any time during the plan year: (1) earned at least 50% of the dollar limitation for defined benefit plans (adjusted annually) and was an officer; (2) earned more than the dollar limitation for defined contribution plans (adjusted annually) and was one of the ten employees owning the largest interest in the employer; (3) owned more than 5% of the employer; or (4) earned more than $150,000 and owned less than 1% of the employer. After 2001, a key employee is a participant who at any time during the preceding year is described in (3) and (4) above or who is an officer and earns more than $130,000 (as indexed).

Key Employee Insurance—Protection of a business firm against the financial loss caused by death or disability of a vital member of the firm; a means of protecting the business from the adverse results of the loss of an individual possessing special skills or experience. See also Business Continuation Insurance.

Key Job—See Benchmark Job.

Kiddie Tax—Minors are taxed on income to savings accounts that exceeds a specific threshold. See also Uniform Gifts to Minors Act (UGMA) Account; Uniform Transfers to Minors Act (UTMA).

Kiosk—A computer-based interactive system installed in high-traffic employee areas to perform a range of functions such as accessing general information about benefits, checking the status of savings plans, making calculations of benefits coverage and changing the mix of benefits in a flexible benefit program. Employees can access the kiosk in passing and interact through a touch screen or mouse. See also Employee Self-Service.

Knowledge-Based Pay—A system of salary differentiation based on the formal education, related experience or specialized training a professional employee has that qualifies the individual to deal with specific subject matter or work effectively in a specific field. Salary level may not be dependent on whether the employee utilizes the knowledge. See also Skill-Based Pay.

L

Labor Force—All persons at least 16 years of age employed as civilians, the unemployed and those in the armed forces. Does not include people not looking for work, those engaged in housework in their own homes, full-time students and unpaid family workers laboring fewer than 15 hours a week.

Labor Grade—Salary classification of a specific job title.

Labor Law—Dictates the rules and regulations that govern the relationship between labor and management, defining the rights, privileges, duties and responsibilities of each.

Labor-Management Relations Act of 1947 (Taft-Hartley Act)—See Taft-Hartley Act.

Labor-Management Reporting and Disclosure Act of 1959—Required the reporting and disclosure of union financial records and administrative acts, to prevent union officials from failing to fulfill their proper roles; also established procedures for the orderly conduct of union elections.

Lag—
—The period of time between the incurring of a claim and the payment of that claim.
—To change after the economy has changed; for example, to lag the market.

Large Cap Funds—*Capitalization,* or *cap,* describes the value of a company in terms of its size. The figure is calculated by multiplying the current stock price of a company by the number of shares available for trading. For example, a company that currently trades its stock at $52 per share and has five million shares to sell has a market capitalization of $260 million. A large cap fund is one valued at over $10 billion. See also Mid Cap Funds; Small Cap Funds.

Lease—A contract between landlord and tenant setting forth the rights and obligations of both parties.

Leaseback—A transaction in which a seller remains in possession as a tenant after completing the sale and delivering the deed.

Leased Employee—An individual employed by a leasing organization that provides contract services for the company for a period of more than one year. The individual's services are directed or controlled by the recipient.

Legal Reserve—The minimum amount of funds that a company must keep to meet future claims and obligations.

Legal Services Plan—A group benefit plan that provides convenient and affordable legal assistance in exchange for a contribution, usually from the employee. The plan can be part of an EAP. Examples of covered services are legal advice, drafting of wills and house closings.

Legally Required Benefits—Benefits that are required by statutory law. In the United States, for example, workers' compensation, Social Security and unemployment insurance are required; benefits vary among countries. Companies operating in foreign countries must comply with host country compensation and benefits mandates. Also called *statutory benefits.*

Length of Stay (LOS)—The number of days that elapse between admission and discharge from a hospital or health care facility.

Lessee—The person, corporation or other legal entity to whom or to which property is leased; tenant.

Lessor—The person, corporation or other legal entity that leases property to a lessee; landlord.

Letter Ruling—A private ruling issued by the IRS in response to a request from a taxpayer about the tax consequences of a proposed or completed transaction. Private Letter Rulings are published informally by several publishers. They are not considered to be precedents for use by taxpayers other than the one who requested the ruling, but they do give an indication of the current attitude of the IRS toward a particular type of transaction.

Level Annual Premium Funding Method—
—The cost of providing a pension where the contributions for any employee remain constant until normal retirement age.
—A method of accumulating money for payment of future pensions under which the level annual charge for a particular benefit is determined by the actuary for each age of entry and is payable each year until retirement, at which time the benefit is fully funded.

Level Premium—A life insurance premium that remains unchanged throughout the life of a policy. In a level premium plan, reserves accumulate in the early years of the policy because the actual cost of coverage is less than the premium charged.

Leverage—
—A strategy that uses borrowed monies to purchase financial assets with the objective of increasing returns.
—Means of enhancing return or value without increasing investment, e.g., buying securities on margin.
—A condition where wide changes in earnings and market value of a company's common stock may be expected because of a heavy preponderance of debt and/or preferred stock in a company's capitalization, which necessitates substantial interest and preferred dividend payments be absorbed before anything is left for

the common. Works to the advantage of common shareholders when earnings are good, and to their disadvantage when earnings are bad. Where a company has no outstanding debts or preferred stock, as in the case of most insurance companies, no leverage exists as earnings flow to the common stockholders.

Leveraged Buyout (LBO)—The purchase of assets or stock of a privately owned company, a public company, or a subsidiary or division of a private or publicly held company in which the purchaser uses a significant amount of debt and very little or no equity capital. This is accomplished primarily by utilizing the purchased assets for collateral and the acquired earnings stream to amortize the debt.

Leveraged ESOP—An ESOP in which money is borrowed by the ESOP trust for the purpose of buying stock of the employer. The stock is normally held as security by the lender and released for allocation to participant accounts as the loan is paid off.

Liabilities—The amount of money that a business, government or individual owes to others. Includes amounts owed for mortgages, supplies, wages, salaries, accrued taxes and other debts. Also includes future obligations.

Liability Insurance—A type of insurance that provides a benefit payable on behalf of a covered party who is held legally responsible (liable) for harming others or their property.

Licensure—The process by which an agency of government—usually state government—grants permission to an individual or organization to engage in a given occupation or business upon finding that the applicant has attained the competency necessary to ensure that the public health, safety and welfare will be reasonably well protected. See also Accreditation; Certification.

Lien—The right in law of one person, usually a creditor, to keep possession of, or control, the property of another for the purpose of satisfying a debt. See also Mechanic's Lien.

Life Care—A long-term care arrangement in which all care required for the lifetime of the participant is provided. A retirement home that agrees to provide not only facilities for independent living, but also nursing care and hospitalization to residents as needed is a *life care community* or a *continuing care retirement community*.

Life Cycle Benefits—Benefits designed to meet the needs of employees throughout the stages of life: when they are single, married, with the birth or adoption of a child, as the child grows, when they are responsible for elderly parents, before they retire, after they retire and at death.

Life Cycle Pension Plan—A defined benefit plan that expresses benefits as a lump-sum benefit rather than as an annuity. There are no account balances for the plan participants. In addition, this plan recognizes final average salary in the benefit calculation. Under the life cycle plan, a participant earns credits for each year of service. Age is not directly a factor, except as it pertains to how much service an individual could accrue. The total of these credits is considered a percentage, which is multiplied by the annual final average salary of the participant to determine what lump sum will be paid at retirement. Also known as *retirement bonus plan* and *lump-sum plan*.

Life Expectancy—Length of time a person of a given age is expected to live. The period is a statistical average, based on mortality tables showing rate of death at each age. It does not seek to predict the life span of any particular individual. See also Mortality Rate.

Life Income Fund (LIF) (Canada)—A personal retirement income plan offered by financial institutions. A life income fund (LIF) receives funds from a locked-in registered retirement savings plan. The owner must withdraw a minimum amount prescribed by pension legislation. The Federal Pension Benefits Act and provincial legislation also restrict the maximum that may be withdrawn. The owner must then use the rest of the funds at the age of 80 to purchase a life annuity.

Life Insurance—A type of insurance that provides a sum of money if the person who is insured dies while the policy is in effect.

Lifestyle Fund—A well-diversified, professionally managed portfolio designed to meet the investor's objectives throughout various life stages via a single, convenient investment vehicle. A lifestyle fund may own stocks, bonds and cash investments at weights within predetermined ranges. Also known as *lifecycle fund*, *balanced fund* and *asset allocation fund*.

Limited Benefits Health Plans—Also referred to as *mini medical plans* or *mini med coverage,* limited benefits health plans are inexpensive health insurance plans that provide significantly lower benefits than the typical comprehensive major medical plan, but cover basic and preventive care. They can provide basic coverage for low-to-moderate income employees. Many such plans also grant access to a PPO.

Limited Liability—The creditors of the corporation have a claim against the assets of the corporation but not against the personal property of the stockholders.

Limited Liability Company (LLC)—A corporation designed to be taxed as a partnership. It provides for partnership agreements and liability protection of the owners. For 401(k) plan purposes, the members of an LLC are treated like partners and the nonmembers are treated like partnership employees. In a medical setting, an LLC is an excellent way to share risk and equity between hospital systems and physician practices.

Limited Partner—An investor who has limited personal liability in a partnership. See also General Partner.

Limited Partnership—An unincorporated business owned both by general partners, having unlimited liability; and by limited partners, whose liability is limited to their investment in the firm. The amount of profit is also limited.

Limiting Charge—The basis for Medicare Part B payments to physicians who do not accept Medicare assignment.

Line Managers—Individuals who have direct responsibility for other employees, including employees' work and duties.

Link—Highlighted words or phrases in a hypertext document that let the user go to another section of the same document or to another Web document. See also HTML.

Liquid Assets—Those assets shown on the left side of the balance sheet that are most susceptible to being turned promptly into cash or the equivalent, usually within the course of a year.

Liquid Market—A market where selling and buying can be accomplished with ease, due to the presence of a large number of interested buyers and sellers willing and able to trade substantial quantities at small price differences.

Liquidated—A claim is liquidated when it has been made fixed and certain by the parties concerned.

Liquidated Damages—A fixed sum agreed upon between the parties to a contract, to be paid as ascertained damages by the party who breaches the contract.

Liquidation—
—The dissolution of a company, with all cash remaining after the sale of its assets and payment of all indebtedness being distributed to the shareholders.
—The process of converting securities or other property into cash.

Liquidity—
—The measure of how quickly an investment can be turned into cash. Mutual funds and Treasury notes are liquid investments, while real estate is illiquid. See also Marketability.
—An actuarial concept that prescribes that sufficient cash, or cash-like securities, be available at times of disbursement for retirement, disability or separation.
—The capacity of the marketplace to accommodate a given supply of and/or demand for a security without unreasonable price changes resulting. Liquidity is a vital requirement of a healthy capital market. Also refers to maintenance of short-term reserves held for special purposes.

Liquidity Risk—The risk that the liquidity of an investment will significantly affect its value and/or restrict the investor from cashing out the investment without major cost. Applies especially to small cap stocks.

Living Benefits—Permit life insurance policyholders to access the face amounts of their policies before death under certain circumstances, such as diagnosis of a terminal illness or confinement to a nursing home. See also Viatical Settlement.

Living Trust—A trust that becomes effective during the life of the owner. Property is placed in the hands of a trustee, who manages the trust for the benefit of one or more individuals. It is not included in probate when the owner of the trust dies.

Living Will—A document that allows a person to state in advance his or her wishes regarding the use or removal of life-sustaining or death-delaying procedures in the event of a terminal illness or injury.

Load—
—A sales charge paid when purchasing or selling fund shares. A front end load, assessed when money is initially invested, effectively reduces the amount invested by 2-8.5%. A back end load, sometimes referred to as a *redemption* or *exit fee,* is a charge for withdrawing money and may be levied as a percentage of the redemption amount or at a flat rate. Loads may also be charged when dividends are reinvested.
—The amount added to the net or pure premium for any type of insurance or pension program for administrative expenses, taxes, contingency reserves and profits.

Loan Broker—See Mortgage Broker.

Local Area Network (LAN)—The hardware and software allowing two or more computers to be connected together over a small geographic area (typically an office or one building).

Local Nationals—Employees hired by a local subsidiary or branch in the country of operation. Usually nationals of that country but may be citizens of any country.

Lockbox Plan—A procedure used to speed up collections through the use of post office boxes in payers' local areas. Insurance or other customer payments are received at a post office box, to which the bank has access. The bank deposits the premiums and sends receipts of transactions to the insurer or other company.

Locked In—
—A situation where, because of the capital gains tax liability, an investor elects not to sell a long-term stock position, thereby substantially reducing both the efficient movement of capital and market liquidity. Often called a *retrogressive tax.*
—A term used to describe the situation of members of a health plan who are restricted to certain doctors, hospitals or other health care providers. A nonplan provider will not be covered by the plan.
—(Canada) Rules that restrict access to money transferred from a pension plan to a personal account to ensure funds provide lifetime income. Money from a company retirement account cannot be transferred to an ordinary RRSP or RRIF; rather, it can be transferred to a locked-in RRSP or locked-in retirement account.

Lockout—Strategy by which the employer denies employees the opportunity to work by closing its operations.

Long-Term Care (LTC)—Includes all forms of services, both institutional and noninstitutional, that are required by all people with chronic health conditions, the elderly or those with physical disabilities who need help with activities of daily living. Long-term care is palliative only—relieving symptoms, but not effecting a cure.

Long-Term Care Benefit—An accelerated death benefit provided by some individual life insurance policies under which the insurer agrees to pay a monthly benefit to an insured who requires constant care for a medical condition.

Long-Term Care Insurance—A type of health insurance available through private insurers that covers long-term care nursing home care and long-term custodial care at home. Designed to prevent depletion of the policyholder's assets.

Long-Term Disability (LTD)—A disability that prevents a person from continuing in the occupation for which he or she was trained, lasting two years or more.

Long-Term Disability Income Insurance—Insurance issued to an employer (group) or individual to provide a reasonable replacement of a portion of an employee's earned income lost through serious and prolonged illness or injury during the normal work career.

Loss—See Actuarial Gain or Loss.

Loss of Benefits—An employee's right to accrued benefits from personal contributions is not subject to forfeiture under any circumstances. However, a plan may provide for the forfeiture of vested benefits derived from employer contributions in the event of the employee's death before retirement.

This forfeiture rule does not apply if the employee continued to work after retirement eligibility and if a joint or survivor annuity was to be provided. A limited forfeiture may take place if a retiree returns to work for his or her employer (or returns to work in the same industry, in the case of a multiemployer plan).

Loss-of-Income Benefits—Payments made to an insured person to help replace income lost through inability to work because of an insured disability.

Loss Ratio—The ratio of paid and incurred claims plus expenses to premium.

Loss Reserve—As stated on a financial statement, an amount representing the estimated liability for unpaid insurance claims (losses) that have occurred as of a given date. Includes losses incurred but not yet reported (IBNR), claims being adjusted and amounts known to be payable in the future (e.g., long-term disability). On an individual basis, loss reserve represents an estimate of the total amount ultimately to be paid out on that claim.

Lost Participants—Former employees who have vested benefits, but whose whereabouts are unknown.

Lump Sum—The capital accumulation in a plan, with or without interest, that may or may not be paid to the plan member on resignation or retirement. Most plans do not allow full cash payment on retirement but permit a small portion to be paid as a lump sum.

Lump-Sum Compensation—Refers to a lump-sum payment to employees negotiated by an employer and a union; often in lieu of general pay increases.

Lump-Sum Distribution—
—In a qualified retirement plan, the distribution of a participant's entire account balance (defined contribution plans) or of the entire amount of the participant's accrued benefit (defined benefit plan) as a single cash payment. Tax restrictions apply.
—A distribution that qualifies for the forward averaging method of computing income tax. The basic requirements are that the distribution be made within one taxable year; include the entire balance of the credit of the employee; and be made on account of the employee's death, attainment of the age of 59½, separation from service (except for the self-employed) or disability (self-employed persons only).

Lump-Sum Plan—See Lifestyle Fund.

M

Magnetic Resonance Imaging (MRI)—A noninvasive diagnostic procedure of imaging soft tissues using a powerful magnet and radio waves to produce computer-processed images of the inner body.

Mail-Order Drug Program—A method of dispensing medication directly to the patient through the mail by means of a mail-order drug distribution company. Offers greatly reduced costs for prescriptions, especially for long-term therapy.

Major Diagnostic Categories (MDCs)—Broad classifications of diagnoses that apply to DRGs.

Major Medical Insurance—Supplementary insurance coverage (beyond basic medical) intended to cover the costs associated with a major illness or injury. Although characterized by large maximum limits, some limitations apply. The term can also refer to the catch-all portion of a medical plan that picks up payment for miscellaneous charges. See also Basic Medical Benefits; Comprehensive Major Medical Coverage; Supplemental Major Medical Coverage.

Malicious Software—Software such as computer viruses, Trojan Horses and worms designed to damage or disrupt a computer system.

Malpractice—A dereliction from professional duty or failure of professional skill or learning that results in death, injury, loss or damage to the patient.

Managed Care—An approach to health care cost-containment whose goal is to deliver cost-effective care without sacrificing quality or access. The techniques used by managed care programs include case management; primary physicians; provider networks; and components of utilization review such as preadmission certification, continued stay review, discharge planning and mandatory second-opinion programs. Managed care can be provided by HMOs, PPOs, exclusive provider organizations (EPOs) or managed indemnity plans.

Managed Care Network—National or regional organization of health care providers (owned by commercial insurance companies or other sponsors) offered to employers either as an alternative to or total replacement for traditional indemnity insurance.

Managed Competition—A health care reform strategy that blends government regulation with competition among health care organizations on quality and cost. The basic idea is to band employers and individuals into large health plan purchasing groups and require health care providers to compete through price and health outcomes to win consumers.

Management—In corporate language, the operating officers of a company appointed by the directors themselves who are elected by the stockholders.

Management Fees (Investments)—An ongoing expense that fund companies charge investors for actively managing their fund. It is represented as a percentage of a fund's average daily assets and is typically the largest component of a fund's operating expense. See also 12(b)-1 Fees.

Management Services Organization (MSO)—Provides administrative and practice management services to medical groups, which are typically owned by physicians; it is usually a subsidiary of the group. It owns all business assets, but the clinic assets stay with the medical group.

Manager—With reference to mutual funds, the entity responsible for investment advisory services.

Managerial Accounting—The segment of accounting concerned with the needs of users who are internal to the firm. (Antonym: *financial accounting*)

Mandated Benefits—A specific set of benefits required by law to be provided by all insurance carriers and reimbursed under all insurance policies.

Mandatory Employee Contribution—A contribution that is made by employees in order to participate in the plan, share in employer contributions or in some way receive more favorable treatment than those not contributing.

Mandatory Retirement—See Compulsory Retirement.

Manipulation—The illegal act or effort designed to artificially influence, either up or down, the price action of a security for the personal benefit or aggrandizement of a few insiders at the expense of the other shareholders and the public at large.

Manual Rate—Premium rate for group insurance coverage from the company's standard rate tables; based on the experience of an average group, not any particular group. It is used to determine the premium for a small group.

Margin—The difference between the current market value of a stock and the amount of a loan. Allows investors to buy stocks by borrowing money from a broker: buying "on margin."

Margin Account—A securities account that a buyer opens by depositing with the broker securities equal to a portion of the price of the security (the margin) and the broker advancing the balance.

Margin Call—A call from a clearinghouse to a clearing member, or from a brokerage firm to a customer, to bring margin deposits up to a required minimum level.

Margin of Profit—Calculated by dividing the operating income by the sales. Nonoperating income received and interest paid are excluded when arriving at operating income.

Marital Deduction—In retirement planning, a tax deduction that lets spouses transfer unlimited amounts of property to one another.

Market Excess Return—Forecast of annual expected return (%) in excess of risk-free rate of return derived from predicted market return.

Market Letter—Any publication that comments on securities and is prepared for distribution to the organization's clients or to the public.

Market Order—An order to buy or sell a security at the most advantageous price available after the order reaches the trading floor.

Market Price—With reference to a security, the last reported price at which the stock or bond sold. The highest price a buyer, willing but not compelled to buy, would pay; and the lowest a seller, willing but not compelled to sell, would accept.

Market Pricing—With reference to compensation, the technique of creating a job worth hierarchy based on the usual rate for benchmark jobs in relevant labor market(s). Under this method, job content is considered secondarily to ensure internal equity after a preliminary hierarchy is established based on market pay levels for benchmark jobs.

Market Rates—The employer's best estimate of prevailing wage rates in the external labor market for a given job or occupation.

Market Risk—Risk engendered by the day-to-day fluctuations in prices at which a security can be bought or sold.

Market Timing—An investment strategy based on predicting market trends. The goal is to buy before the market goes up and sell before the market goes down.

Market Value—The price an investor will pay for each share of common stock at any given time. Market value is determined by the laws of supply and demand.

Market Value per Share—The current price at which a stock is trading in the open market.

Marketability—Term synonymous with *salability* and meaning the degree of investment or speculative interest that underlies any security; the ease with which it can be sold. See also Liquidity.

Marketable Securities—Securities for which there is always a ready market, such as active, listed securities.

Marketplace Reform—A health care reform strategy based on marketplace dynamics of competition and price rather than government regulation, government management or price rate setting.

Mass Withdrawal—The withdrawal of substantially all employers from a multiemployer plan within a specified period.

Master Contract—A life insurance policy that insures a number of people under a single insurance contract; a contract between an insurance company and a group policyholder in which the individuals insured are not parties to the contract.

Master Plan—A defined benefit or defined contribution plan that has been prepared by a sponsoring organization and that provides a single trust account in which all adopting employers must invest their plan contributions; the sponsoring organization must have the plan approved by the Internal Revenue Service. See also Prototype Plan.

Master Trust—A pooling of directed and/or discretionary trusts (a *discretionary trust* is one in which the bank is trustee and also has investment responsibility for all or part of the assets). The "pure" definition is pooling of one sponsor's assets which include multiple managers and multiple plans under one trust agreement.

Matching Contributions—Made by an employer to a plan on an employee's behalf when the employee makes elective or nonelective contributions.

Material Information—Anything of material fact that could affect an investor's decision to buy certain securities. See also Insider.

Material Modification—A change in information required to be in an SPD or the terms of the plan considered important to plan participants.

Material Safety Data Sheets (MSDS)—Documents that contain vital information about hazardous substances.

Materiality Concept—Judgment decision by an auditor about the relative importance of an item for disclosure in financial statements.

Mature—An employee group is said to be mature if the age distribution of the employees, including the ages of employees who have retired and are drawing pensions, is stable and is expected to be duplicated year after year through the effect of new entries and dropouts (deaths and withdrawals). This condition is typical of a company whose pension plan has long been in effect and whose workforce is neither increasing nor decreasing. Newly established companies and growing companies ordinarily have immature employee groups. Employee groups covered by pension plans recently adopted also tend to be immature.

Maturity—The date on which a loan, bond, mortgage or other debt/security becomes due and is to be paid off.

Maturity Value—The amount that the holder of note is entitled to receive at the due date, including the principal plus any accrued interest.

Maximum Age—A company that maintains a defined benefit plan may be discouraged from hiring older employees because of the cost of funding benefits for them. Consequently, ERISA permits a defined benefit plan to exclude an employee who is within five years of normal retirement age at the time when service begins. However, the plan must comply with coverage and antidiscrimination rules.

Maximum Allowable Cost (MAC) List—A list health plans distribute to their participating pharmacies describing the maximum amount the plan will pay for specific medications.

Maximum Benefit—
—The highest annual or lifetime benefit that can be paid by a qualified defined benefit plan.
—(Canada) The highest amount an individual may receive under an insurance contract.

Maximum Fee Schedule—A compensation arrangement in which a participating physician agrees to accept a prescribed sum as the total fee for one or more covered services.

Maximum Out-of-Pocket Payment—The maximum amount of money a person will pay in addition to premium payments. The out-of-pocket payment is usually the sum of the deductible and coinsurance payments.

Mean—The *mean* average is a measure of central tendency; it gives a value around which observations tend to cluster. The average is always between the extreme values.

Means Test—
—A regulation that eligibility for aid and the amount of aid provided do not depend, for example, on past employment or earnings but on specified levels of income and/or assets of those requesting aid.
—(International Benefits) Provides for a reduction in social security disability benefits if other income exceeds minimum levels. Also applies in other forms to other benefits, e.g., surviving spouse benefits. See also Needs Test (Canada).

Mechanic's Lien—A lien created under statute to assist laborers and suppliers in collecting their accounts and wages. It subjects the real property of the owner to a lien in the event of nonpayment for contracted improvements. State laws vary as to procedures and the degree of protection accorded. See also Building Lien.

Median—The value (rate of return, market sensitivity, etc.) that exceeds one-half of the values in the population and that is exceeded by one-half of the values. The median has a percent rank of 50.

Mediation—Arises when a third party, called the *mediator,* comes in to help the adversaries with their negotiations. He or she may either be designated by the government or selected by the parties themselves. In seeking to narrow the differences between the parties, the mediator may meet with them jointly and/or separately. He or she continues to function only as long as the parties both agree to his or her presence. The mediator will remove himself or herself from a case when (1) agreement is reached; (2) one of the parties requests his or her departure; (3) the agreed-upon time comes for appeal to the next step in the procedure; or (4) he or she feels his or her acceptability or effectiveness is exhausted. The mediator can make proposals for settlement and operates without any authority to compel an agreement, depending instead upon his or her ability to persuade the parties to come together and upon the parties' own overriding need to do so.

Medicaid (Title XIX)—A medical benefits program administered by the states and subsidized by the federal government that pays certain medical expenses for those who meet income and other guidelines. See also Title XIX.

Medical Care—Under the IRC definition, diagnosis, cure, mitigation, treatment or prevention of disease or affecting any structure or function of the body; also travel for or incidental to medical care. Insurance for medical care is treated as medical care; so is the cost of prescription drugs and insulin.

Medical Child Support Order—See Qualified Medical Child Support Order (QMCSO).

Medical Insurance—Protection that provides benefits for the cost of any or all of the numerous health care services normally covered under various health care plans.

Medical Loss Ratio (MLR)—An index which compares the costs of delivering health benefits with the revenues received by the plan.

Medical Practice Guidelines—Recommended, codified procedures and techniques for the treatment of specific illnesses and medical conditions, based on the best scientific evidence and expert opinion; designed to serve as educational support for physicians and as quality assurance and accountability measures for managed care plans. Also known as *practice policies* and *treatment protocols*.

Medical Reimbursement Plan—An employer plan that reimburses employees for medical expenses directly from employer funds, and not through a policy of health or accident insurance.

Medical Savings Account (MSA)—A savings account that can be used to pay medical expenses not covered by insurance for employees of small businesses or self-employed individuals who are covered under health plans with high deductibles. Employers with small group MSAs may make contributions on behalf of employees, or employees may make the entire contribution.

Medical Spending Account—See Flexible Spending Accounts.

Medically Indigent (MI)—Unable to pay—either directly or through an insurance program—the full cost of his or her own health care and not eligible for Medicare or Medicaid. This term is used to describe people who do not have health insurance; it is not related to income, employment or housing.

Medically Necessary—Describes services required to prevent harm to the patient or an adverse effect on the patient's quality of life, as judged against generally accepted standards of medical practice. The term is usually used to determine whether or not a procedure or service is covered by insurance. The reasonable and appropriate diagnosis, treatment and followup care as determined and prescribed by qualified, appropriate health care providers in treating any condition, illness, disease or injury.

Medically Needy Program—States receive federal funds to provide care for blind or disabled individuals or families and children who are otherwise eligible for Medicaid except that their income is too high.

Medicare—

—Administered by the Social Security Administration, Medicare is the U.S. federal government plan for paying certain hospital and medical expenses for those who qualify, primarily those over 65. Benefits are provided regardless of income level. The program is government subsidized and government operated. Part A, Hospital Insurance (HI), provides for inpatient hospital services and posthospital care. Part B, Supplementary Medical Insurance (SMI), pays for medically necessary doctors' services, outpatient hospital services and a number of other medical services and supplies not covered by Part A. Enrollment in Part B is voluntary and available for a small premium. See also Medicare Prescription Drug, Improvement Act of 2003; Title XVIII.

—(Canada) Provincial government plans that cover hospital care and services, as well as physician fees.

Medicare Advantage—Formerly called Medicare+Choice, this program offers prescription drug coverage as well as other preventive care benefits to employers and retirees. As part of the Medicare Prescription Drug, Improvement, and Modernization Act of 2003, Medicare reimbursement rates to Medicare managed care planes rose as much as 10%. The payment increases are designed to lower premiums and provide better benefits and to stabilize the Medicare Advantage system by offering more options for insurers offering qualified Medicare coverage to retirees through HMO networks. See also Medicare Prescription Drug, Improvement, and Modernization Act of 2003.

Medicare Prescription Drug, Improvement, and Modernization Act of 2003—This legislation creates a new prescription drug benefit for retirees; raises Medicare payments to the Medicare Advantage program (formerly Medicare+Choice); provides a means-tested Part B premium that increases costs to high-income beneficiaries; increases the Part B deductible from $100 to $110; creates health savings accounts (HSAs), a new tax-favored vehicle for individuals to prefund health care costs; and makes significant changes in Medicare fee-for-service and managed care administration that may affect future employer costs for Medicare HMOs. See also Health Savings Accounts (HSAs); Medicare Advantage.

Medicare Secondary Payer Program—The law now provides that Medicare is the secondary payer for three categories of beneficiaries, if these beneficiaries are also covered by their employer's group health plan. The three categories are (1) individuals with end-stage renal disease (up to the first 18 months); (2) those over age 65 and currently employed (including the spouse of an employed individual); and (3) those who are disabled but active (including disabled dependents of active individuals).

Medicare Supplement Policy—A voluntary, contributory private insurance plan available to Medicare eligibles to cover the costs of deductibles, coinsurance, physicians' services and other medical and health services not covered by Medicare. Also called *Medigap*. See also Carve-Out.

Medigap Policy—See Medicare Supplement Policy.

Member—See Plan Participant.

Member, Society of Pension Actuaries (MSPA)—Holder must pass seven examinations on general mathematics, probability and statistics, employee benefits, regulations and so forth.

Mental Health Parity Act of 1996—Key provision: Plans that offer mental health benefits are prohibited from imposing aggregate lifetime or annual dollar limits for mental health benefits that are less than those imposed on medical/surgical benefits. Substance abuse treatment is excluded.

Merger—A combining of two or more companies or corporations. Called an *amalgamation* in Canada.

Merger of Plans—In the case of a merger or consolidation of plans, each participant must be entitled to receive a benefit after the merger at least equal to the value of the benefit he or she would have been entitled to receive before the merger. The before and after merger benefits are determined as if the plan had been terminated. If a multiemployer plan is involved, this rule will apply only to the extent that the Pension Benefit Guaranty Corporation determines that this provision is necessary for the protection of the participants.

Mid Cap Funds—*Capitalization,* or *cap,* describes the value of a company in terms of its size. The figure is calculated by multiplying the current stock price of a company by the number of shares available for trading. For example, a company that currently trades its stock at $52 per share and has five million shares to sell has a market capitalization of $260 million. A mid cap fund is one valued at between $3 billion and $10 billion. See also Large Cap Funds; Small Cap Funds.

Minimum Benefits—Some plans provide that a minimum amount of annuity will be paid if the regular benefit formula produces less. This minimum is usually payable only if certain service requirements are met at retirement.

Minimum Compensation Level—The amount of compensation an employee must earn before being eligible to participate in a plan.

Minimum Contribution Requirement—Under the Multiemployer Pension Plan Amendments Act of 1980, the sum of the vested benefits charge and the increase in normal cost for the plan year determined under the entry age normal funding method that is attributable to plan amendments adopted while the plan was in reorganization, less the amount of overburden credit.

Minimum Distribution Rules—Distributions from a qualified plan must generally begin by April 1 of the year following the later of: the calendar year in which the employee reaches the age of 70½, or when the employee actually retires. Distributions must usually be paid over a period not to exceed the life expectancy of the retiree. Amounts are determined by the amount in the employee's account and the employee's life expectancy.

Minimum Funding—The minimum amount that must be contributed by an employer that has a defined benefit, money purchase or target benefit pension plan. If the employer fails to meet these minimum standards, in the absence of a waiver from the IRS, an excise tax will be imposed on the amount of the deficiency.

Minimum Funding Standard—See Accumulated Funding Deficiency; Funding Standard Account (FSA).

Minimum Group—The least number of employees permitted under a state law to effect a group for insurance purposes; the purpose is to minimize risk and maintain some sort of proper division between individual policy insurance and the group forms.

Minimum Participation Rules—IRS rules prescribing numbers of employees to participate in most retirement plans. Usually at least 50 employees or 40% of the total number of employees enrolled.

Minimum Participation Standards—In general, the maximum amount of time a qualified retirement plan can require an employee to work before becoming eligible to participate is one year of service and the highest age a plan may require a participant to have attained before being admitted is 21. There are exceptions made for plans maintained by tax-exempt educational institutions and for plans that have an immediate-vesting-upon-participation feature.

Minimum Premium Plan (MPP)—Under this approach, the employer and the insurance company or the service plan agree that the employer will be responsible for paying all claims up to an agreed-upon aggregate level, with the carrier responsible for the excess. This level is usually based on the amount of claims paid in the past two or three years, adjusted by projected increases in claims due to inflation and greater utilization. The carrier usually is also responsible for processing claims and administrative services.

Miscellaneous Hospital Expenses—A provision for the payment on a blanket basis or schedule basis of hospital services (other than room and board, special nursing care and doctor fees) up to a stipulated maximum amount. Also called *ancillary charges*.

Model Plans—Plans prepared by the Internal Revenue Service for small employers. Model plans are easy and inexpensive to implement due to the simple IRS procedure required for qualification. See also Prototype Plan.

Modem—Modulator/demodulator. Modems convert digital (binary) data into an analog signal and back again so that information can be transmitted over the phone. This process allows computers to communicate with other computers via the Internet.

Modern Portfolio Theory (MPT)—The theoretical constructs that enable investment managers to classify, estimate and control the sources of risk and return. In popular usage, the term is not limited to portfolio theory. Instead, MPT encompasses all notions of both modern investment theory and portfolio theory. Also known as *new investment technology (NIT)* and *modern investment theory (MIT)*.

Modification—An amendment to the federal-state agreement relative to Social Security coverage for public employees, entered into between the state and the Social Security Administration pursuant to authority granted under the state Social Security enabling law. Whenever an additional governmental unit adopts Social Security for its employees, a modification in the federal-state agreement must be made to effect coverage for these employees. Such modification is proposed by the state agency administering the Social Security enabling law and must be approved by the Social Security Administration. The term *modification* is also used in connection with any revision of a retirement plan.

Modifications—Changes to a job to accommodate an employee or to make a job safer. See also Accommodation.

Modular Plan—A type of flexible benefits plan that offers a choice of benefits packages rather than a selection of individual levels of coverage. Benefit packages can be structured to meet employee life cycle needs, such as plans for single employees with no dependents; single parents; married workers with dependents; and employees approaching retirement.

Monetary Policy—The policies of the Federal Reserve Board that determine the size of the money supply and the level of interest rates. Meant to improve employment, economic growth and price stability.

Money Follows the Man—See Reciprocal Agreement; Reciprocity.

Money Market—That segment of the securities market that deals in short-term (less than three years) debt and equity issues.

Money Market Fund—A mutual fund that seeks maximum current income through investment in securities whose maturities are less than three years, and allows investors to write checks against their accounts. Such securities may include bank CDs, bankers acceptances, T-bills, repurchase agreements (repos) and commercial paper.

Money Market Instruments—Fixed income securities that mature in less than one year. Also known as cash equivalents since their marketability and characteristics provide easy liquidity access to ready cash, as needed. Included in this category are U.S. government securities, negotiable certificates of deposit, commercial paper, short-term investment fund accounts, bankers acceptances and mutual funds.

Money Purchase Plan—A type of defined contribution plan in which the employer's contributions are determined for, and allocated with respect to, specific individuals, usually as a percentage of compensation. The benefits for each employee are the amounts that can be provided by the sums contributed to his or her account. Unlike a profit-sharing plan, however, forfeitures are currently not added to participants' accounts; they are used to reduce the employer's contributions.

An individual account plan, as defined in Section 3(34) of ERISA, other than a profit-sharing plan or a stock bonus plan, in which the employer's contributions are fixed or determinable.

Money Purchase Plan (Canada)—A defined contribution plan whose amount is determined by employee and employer contributions and the income earned on those invested funds. It operates like a group RRSP. See also Group Registered Retirement Savings Plans (RRSPs).

Money Supply—A measure of the amount of money in circulation.

Monte Carlo Simulation—A mathematical tool and analytical technique that simulates random quantities for uncertain variables and looks at the distribution results to infer which values are most likely. Used in retirement planning to evaluate whether retirement income will last as long as needed. Computer software can simulate thousands of market-condition scenarios to estimate the probability of funds lasting a lifetime. Named for the city of Monte Carlo, known for its casinos. See also Financial Planning Education.

Morbidity—The relative incidence (number of cases) and severity of disease, usually used with respect to specific disease conditions; e.g., tuberculosis morbidity refers to the number of cases of tuberculosis.

Morbidity Table—Shows the average number of illnesses befalling a large group of persons. It indicates the incidence of sickness the way a mortality table shows the incidence of death.

Morgan Stanley Capital International Index (MSCI World Index)—Measures the total return (with dividends reinvested) of stocks available in developed markets worldwide. Serves as an investment benchmark.

Mortality—For health care outcomes measurement purposes, the number of deaths resulting from each specific type of illness or disease.

Mortality Experience—The rate at which participants in a pension or insurance plan actually die. Also the financial effect of such deaths upon the operation of the plan.

Mortality Rate—Number of persons out of a large group (usually 100,000) who, experience shows, will live to reach each age up to the death of the last survivor; inferentially establishing the expectancy of life of the average person of each age. See also Life Expectancy.

Mortality Table—Shows how many members of a group, starting at a certain age, will be alive at each succeeding age. It is used to calculate the probability of dying in, or surviving through, any period, and the value of an annuity benefit. To be appropriate for a specific group, it should be based on the experience of individuals having common characteristics, such as sex or occupational group.

Mortgage—An instrument by which the borrower (mortgagor) gives the lender (mortgagee) a lien on property (commonly real property) as security for the payment of an obligation. The borrower continues to use the property; when the obligation is fully extinguished, the lien is removed. If the subject matter of the lien is personal property other than securities (such as machinery, tools or equipment), the mortgage is known as a chattel mortgage. Investors may buy whole loans, participating interests in a loan or a security representing a participating interest in a pool of loans. The seller of a loan typically services the loan for a fee, relieving the buyer of the paperwork burden. Mortgage loans are used in connection with single family structures, condominiums, multifamily structures, office buildings, large commercial centers and industrial plants or even undeveloped land.

Mortgage Banker—A firm that furnishes its own funds for mortgage loans, which are normally sold later to permanent investors. Usually, they continue to service the loans at a specified fee.

Mortgage Bonds—A debt obligation secured by a property pledge. These are liens or mortgages against the issuing corporation's properties and real estate assets.

Mortgage Broker—An individual or company that obtains mortgage loans for others by finding lending institutions, insurance companies or private sources that will lend the money.

Mortgage Correspondent—An agent of a lending institution authorized to handle and process loans.

Mortgage Pass-Through Securities—A security consisting of a pool of residential mortgage loans with monthly distribution of 100% of the interest and principal "passed through" to the investor. There are non-government-sponsored issues of these securities, as well as the government versions, Freddie Macs and Ginnie Maes.

Mortgage Redemption Insurance—Decreasing term life insurance that provides a death benefit amount corresponding to the decreasing amount owed on a mortgage.

Mortgage REIT—A real estate investment trust formed for the purpose of purchasing mortgages and lending money on real estate. See also Real Estate Investment Trust (REITs).

Mortgagee—The one to whom a mortgage is given—the lender.

Mortgagor—An owner who conveys his or her property as security for a loan—the debtor.

Multiemployer Pension Plan Amendments Act of 1980 (MPPAA)—A federal law that amended ERISA by strengthening the funding requirements for multiemployer pension plans; removing multiemployer plans from ERISA's plan termination insurance system governing multiple and single employer plans; and substituting a system imposing liability for certain unfunded vested benefits when an employer partially or totally withdraws from a multiemployer plan.

Multiemployer Plan—Under ERISA, a multiemployer plan is one that requires contributions from more than one employer and is maintained pursuant to a collective bargaining agreement. They are also known as jointly administered or Taft-Hartley plans. The Multiemployer Pension Plan Amendments Act of 1980 (MPPAA) made substantial changes to ERISA and the Internal Revenue Code which had the effect of enhancing the funding requirements for multiemployer pension plans, providing new rules for multiemployer plans and revising the termination insurance provisions applicable to these plans.

Multinational Corporation—A firm with independent business units operating in multiple countries.

Multinational Pooling—Arrangement that links together the worldwide insured benefit plans of a multinational company to secure cost savings, improved financial information, and improved service and facilities.

Multiple Coverage—See Duplication of Benefits.

Multiple Employer Group—A group of two or more employers that are not financially related.

Multiple Employer Plan—A pension benefit plan maintained by more than one employer allowing them to pool their plan assets for investment purposes and to reduce the cost of plan administration. A multiple employer plan maintains separate accounts for each employer so that contributions provide benefits only for employees of the contributing employer. There are no collective bargaining agreements requiring contributions in a multiple employer plan.

Multiple Employer Trust (MET)—Self-funded or insured corporate group benefit plan that covers medical and dental insurance and pensions, generally geared toward small employers (sole proprietorships and partnerships with several principals and few employees). Not a jointly administered, union-management multiemployer plan.

Multiple Employer Welfare Arrangement (MEWA)—A noncollectively bargained arrangement or plan maintained to benefit employees of two or more employers that are not under common control. ERISA generally does not preempt state law with regard to MEWAs. Small employers participating in MEWAs may be exempt from COBRA's continuation coverage requirement, and other special rules apply under COBRA.

Multiple Funding—See Conversion Fund.

Municipal Bond Fund—A mutual fund that seeks to provide shareholders tax-free income through investment in bonds issued by state and local governments.

Municipal Bonds—
—Long-term promissory notes issued by state and local governments and public agencies. In general, interest paid on municipal bonds is exempt from federal income taxes and state and local income taxes within the state of issue. See also Revenue Bonds; Special Assessment Bonds; Tax-Exempt Securities.
—(Canada) Bonds backed by city governments and sold in the municipal markets.

Mutual Fund—A company that collects funds of thousands of small investors who share similar investment objectives and then uses the funds to purchase a variety of investments such as stocks and bonds. These pooled assets lower transaction costs and allow small investors to invest more as a group. Mutual funds can be categorized according to investment objectives, such as growth mutual fund or income mutual fund. See also Open-End Funds/Open-End Investment Companies.

Mutual Fund Custodian—Usually a national bank, trust company or other qualified institution that physically safeguards securities. It does not act in a managerial capacity; its function is solely clerical.

Mutual Insurance Company—Has no capital stock structure. Members contribute premiums to a common fund, from which each is entitled to indemnity in case of loss. Its policyholders constitute its membership, who elect a board of directors or trustees through whom business is conducted. Earnings belong to the policyholders as a group and are distributed to them as dividends. In years when the loss experience is unfavorable, assessments, in addition to their normal premiums, may be made against the policyholders.

N

Named Fiduciary—A fiduciary who is named in the plan instrument or who, pursuant to a procedure specified in the plan, is identified by an employer and/or employee organization with respect to the plan and is given the express authority to control plan operations.

National Association of Insurance Commissioners (NAIC)—An organization that assists state insurance departments in promoting national uniformity in the regulation of insurance. A major function is the drafting of model laws.

National Association of Securities Dealers Automated Quotation System (NASDAQ)—An organization that facilitates the trading of financial instruments among investors via a computerized system for both over-the-counter and listed stocks. It transmits real-time quote and trade data to more than a million users in over 80 countries.

National Committee for Quality Assurance (NCQA)—An independent, private sector group that reviews care quality and other procedures of managed care organizations to render an accreditation. It has developed the Health Plan Employer Data and Information Set (HEDIS), which contains eight broad criteria focused on outcomes and used as part of the accreditation process. NCQA membership includes health care quality experts, employers, labor union officials and consumer representatives.

National Health Insurance—Any system of socialized health insurance benefits, covering all or nearly all citizens, established by federal law, administered by the federal government and supported or subsidized by taxation.

National Labor Relations Act of 1935 (NLRA) (Wagner Act)—A federal law giving employees the right to self-organize, form or assist labor organizations, bargain collectively through representatives of their own choosing, engage in other concerted activities and refrain from any or all such activities except for requiring membership in a labor organization as a condition of employment.

National Labor Relations Board (NLRB)—The board of five members administering the Wagner Act and the Taft-Hartley Act. The board conducts elections to determine bargaining agents, determines bargaining units and adjudicates unfair labor practice charges. The board seeks enforcement of its orders through the court system.

Needs Test (Canada)—Method of assessing a person's or family's expenditure requirements in relation to other income or means to determine amount of income support to be provided under a government program.

Negative Election—See Automatic Enrollment.

Negotiable—A stock or bond certificate, or other evidence of debt, the title to which is freely transferable at delivery, i.e., coupon bonds, bankers acceptances and so on.

Negotiable Certificate of Deposit (CD)—A negotiable certificate that evidences a time deposit of funds with a bank. It is an unsecured promissory note normally issued in $100,000 denominations.

Negotiable Instrument—Property that includes cash, checks, coupon bonds, stock certificates with stock powers attached, promissory notes and so on, where title passes at delivery and is not subject to challenge when owned by a holder in due course and in good faith.

Negotiated Plan—See Collectively Bargained Plans.

Negotiation—In the labor context, refers to the practice of adversarial parties meeting together for the purpose of reaching agreement on the items that are in dispute between them. This format of face-to-face discussion is usually carried on between the parties without any third-party presence. It is normally the first step in collective bargaining but will probably recur at such other times in the impasse procedure as the parties feel will be helpful to settle all or a portion of their differences.

Net Asset Value (NAV)—The value of a mutual fund share determined by deducting the fund's liabilities from the total assets of the portfolio and dividing this amount by the number of shares outstanding. This is calculated once a day, based on the closing market price for each security in the fund's portfolio.

Net Assets Available for Benefits—The difference between a plan's assets and its liabilities. For purposes of this definition, a plan's liabilities do not include participants' accumulated plan benefits.

Net Income—The money remaining after all expenses are subtracted from the gross income. The profit.

Net Incurred Claims Cost—The employer's share, net of retiree contributions, of the cost of providing postretirement health care benefits, after adjusting for reimbursements from Medicare and other providers of health care benefits and for the effects of cost-sharing provisions such as deductibles and coinsurance.

Net Return—Yield after taxes.

Net Worth (NW)—
—The amount by which actual assets are greater than actual liabilities.
—The amount of equity available for stockholders as shown on the company's books, which consists of common stock, capital surplus, earned surplus and accumulative retained earnings as well as intangible assets. Intangibles are excluded in calculating book value.

Network Model HMO—An HMO model that contracts with multiple physician groups to provide services to HMO members; may involve large single and multispecialty groups.

New York Stock Exchange (NYSE)—Since 1792, a marketplace where members of the exchange, acting as agents for clients, meet in an auction-like setting to trade securities. Buy and sell orders meet directly on the trading floor, in assigned locations, where prices are determined by the interplay of supply and demand. Exchange members trade almost 3,000 listed stocks. Membership on the exchange is obtained by purchasing a seat from a retiring, deceased or expelled member.

New York Stock Exchange Composite Index—A capitalization-weighted index of all stocks listed on the New York Stock Exchange. The value of the index varies with the aggregate value of the common equity of all companies with common stock listed on the NYSE.

Newborns' and Mothers' Health Protection Act of 1996—Federal law that mandates that group health plans (as defined in HIPAA) may not restrict the length of any hospital stay in connection with childbirth for either the mother or the newborn child to less than 48 hours for a normal vaginal delivery or 96 hours for a Caesarean delivery. Plans may not offer incentives to mothers to accept less time, nor may they penalize providers for adherence to the law.

No-Fault Insurance—A type of insurance that will pay benefits whether or not the insured is at fault.

No-Load Fund—A mutual fund that charges little or no commission (load charge) to the buyer of its shares. No sales organization is involved. The shares are sold directly to the public by the sponsoring firm.

Nominal Interest—The actual interest rate paid or received, or the yield to maturity (not adjusted for inflation). This is commonly understood when one says "the interest rate."

Nominal Return—The rate of return on an asset expressed in monetary terms; i.e., unadjusted for any change in the price level. The nominal return is contrasted with the real return, which is adjusted for changes in the price level.

Nominal Yield—The interest rate stated on the face of a bond not including any paid discount or premium.

Noncancelable; Noncancelable and Guaranteed Renewable Policy—A policy that the insured has the right to continue in force to a specified age—such as to age 65—and at a guaranteed rate by the timely payment of premiums. During the specified period, the insurer has no right to unilaterally make any change in any provision of the policy while it is in force.

Noncompliance Period—Under COBRA, the period beginning on the date a violation first occurs. The period is used to compute the penalty excise tax imposed on employers that violate COBRA rules.

Noncontributory Provision—A term applied to employee benefit plans under which the employer bears the full cost of the benefits for the employees; employees need not contribute.

Noncore Coverage—Dental, vision and other types of benefits, as opposed to core coverage, which usually means medical benefits.

Noncumulative Preferred Stock—A type of preferred stock that does not have to pay any dividends in arrears to the holders. See also Convertible Preferred Stock; Cumulative Preferred Stock; Participating Preferred Stock; Preferred Stock.

Nondetachable Warrant—See Warrant.

Nondisabling Injury—An injury that may require medical care but does not result in loss of working time or income.

Nondiscrimination Rules—The requirements in Section 105(h) of the IRC that self-funded employee benefit plans not provide significantly greater benefits to higher paid employees and owners than to lower paid employees. Although some disparity is permitted, there are limits which, if crossed, result in the benefits being deemed taxable income to the beneficiaries. Similar rules apply to 401(k) plans, flex plans and pension plans.

Nonduplication of Benefits Provision—A type of coordination-of-benefits provision under which the benefits payable by an insured's secondary insurance plan are limited to the difference, if any, between the amount paid by the primary plan and the amount that would have been payable by the secondary plan had that plan been primary.

Nonelective Contribution—Any employer contribution (other than a matching contribution) for which (1) the employee may not elect to have the contribution paid to the employee in cash instead of being contributed to the plan and (2) the contributions are nonforfeitable when made and are ineligible for withdrawal prior to the attainment of certain conditions.

Nonexempt Employees—Employees who are subject to the minimum wage and overtime pay provisions of the Fair Labor Standards Act. Most are paid on an hourly basis.

Nonforfeitable; Nonforfeitability—The condition wherein contributions are vested as of the moment they are made into the plan. Under ERISA, all employee contributions are nonforfeitable. See also Vest; Vesting.

Nonforfeitable Pension Benefit—A claim obtained by a pension plan participant or beneficiary to that part of an immediate or deferred benefit arising from the participant's service, which is unconditional and which is legally enforceable against the plan.

Nonguaranteed Life Insurance—See Variable Life Insurance.

Nonhighly Compensated Employees (NHCE)—Employees eligible to participate in the plan who do not meet the definition of *highly compensated employees.*

Noninsured Plan—See Self-Insurance (Self-Funding).

Nonmarket Risk—Volatility of returns from portfolio securities, not related to the movement of the market in general.

Nonoccupational Death Benefit—A benefit payable upon the death of an employee, resulting from any cause other than that occasioned by the performance of an act or acts of duty. See also Death Benefit.

Nonoccupational Disability Benefit—A benefit payable on account of the disability of an employee incurred from any cause other than that occasioned by the performance of an act or acts of duty. See also Disability Benefit.

Nonoccupational Policy—A contract that insures a person against off-the-job accident or sickness. It does not cover disability resulting from injury or sickness covered by workers' compensation. Group accident and sickness policies are frequently nonoccupational.

Nonprofit Insurers—Persons organized under special state or provincial laws to provide hospital, medical or dental insurance on a nonprofit basis. The laws exempt them from certain types of taxes.

Nonprofit Organization—An organization formed for charitable, educational, humanitarian or other limited purposes and not as a profit-making business. Such organizations are exempt from income taxes, but they are liable for other taxes to the extent the organization or corporation owns property. May include churches, foundations and trade associations. See also Church Plan.

Nonqualified Deferred Compensation Plan—An agreement whereby one person (or legal entity) promises to compensate another for services rendered currently with actual payment for those services delayed until sometime in the future. Such agreements are almost invariably reduced to writing, and are mutually supported by the employer's promise to pay deferred benefits and the employee's promise to render services in exchange therefor. Such plans do not receive tax advantages.

Nonqualified Plan—An employer-sponsored plan that does not meet the requirements of Section 401(a) of the 1986 Internal Revenue Code and that, as a result, suffers distinct disadvantages from a tax standpoint.

Nonresident Alien—A foreign national who does not meet the U.S. lawful permanent resident (green card) test or the substantial presence (days of physical presence in the United States) test, and is therefore considered an alien for federal tax purposes.

Normal Form of Benefit—A distribution from a qualified plan that for a married individual is a joint and survivor annuity of at least 50%. For a single individual the normal form of benefit is typically a life annuity, or in a contributory plan, a modified cash-refund annuity.

Normal Pension Costs—See Funding Standard Account (FSA).

Normal Retirement—A termination of employment involving the payment of a regular formula retirement allowance without reduction because of age or service and with special qualifications such as disability.

Normal Retirement Age—The age, as established by a plan, when retirement normally occurs; usually it is the age when unreduced Social Security benefits are available. The normal Social Security retirement age is rising gradually from age 65 until it reaches age 67 in 2027. See also Social Security Retirement Age.

Normal Retirement Date (NRD)—The earliest date at which a participant qualifies for normal retirement under the plan.

North American Free Trade Act (NAFTA)—Signed in 1994, this agreement between the United States, Canada and Mexico initiated a schedule for the phasing out of tariffs and eliminated a variety of fees and other hindrances to encourage free trade among the three North American countries. NAFTA also encouraged investments among these countries.

Notary—A person authorized by law to witness the statement or act of another.

Note—See Bond.

Notice of Intent to Terminate—The 60-day advance notice to affected parties advising them of a proposed standard termination of a defined benefit plan covered by PBGC.

Nurse Advice Line—A utilization management strategy that employs a registered nurse to answer health care questions for patients or plan members. May include counseling and patient education, guidance in obtaining services, and referrals to network or other physicians.

Nurse Practitioner—A registered nurse who has completed a nurse practitioner program at the master's or certificate level and is trained in providing primary care services. Generally, nurse practitioners provide services at a lower cost than primary care physicians.

Nursing Home—A licensed institution that provides skilled nursing care and related services but does not qualify as a *skilled nursing facility* as defined by Medicare. Nursing homes are usually operated for profit. Medicare and private Medigap insurance plans reimburse only a small portion of the costs; Medicaid covers the entire cost for qualified individuals.

O

Occupational Death Benefit—A benefit payable upon death of an employee resulting from his performance of an act or acts relating to the duties of his position in the employer's service.

Occupational Differentials—Comparably stable differences in wage rates between or among occupations.

Occupational Disability Benefit—A benefit payable on account of disability arising out of and in the course of employment.

Occupational Disease—A disease or condition of health resulting from performance of an occupation. In most states, occupational disease is now covered under workers' compensation.

Occupational Hazards—Occupations that expose the insured to greater-than-normal physical dangers by the very nature of the work in which the insured is engaged, and the varying periods of absence from the occupation, due to disability, that can be expected.

Occupational Health Services—Employer-sponsored services designed to protect the physical health and safety of employees at work.

Occupational Illness—Impairment of health caused by conditions in the work environment.

Occupational Pension Plan—Pension plan sponsored by an employer, labor union or professional organization. Occupational plans can be called private pension plans, company pension plans, registered pension plans or employer-sponsored pension plans.

Occupational Safety and Health Act (OSHA)—Federal statute establishing national standards for health and safety conditions in the workplace. Enforced by the Labor Department, the act also provides for the reporting and compiling of statistics pertaining to occupational illnesses and injuries.

OCONUS (International Benefits)—Outside the Continental United States. Used for assigning values to certain fringe benefits such as travel and meal allowances.

Odd Lot—An amount of stock less than the established 100-share unit or ten-share unit of trading: from one to 99 shares for the great majority of issues; one to nine for so-called inactive stocks. Odd lot prices are geared to the auction market.

Offer—The price at which a person is willing to sell.

Offering Price—With reference to mutual funds, the price an investor will pay per share. The offering price is the net asset value plus a sales charge (for funds that have a sales charge). See also Asked (Asking) or Offering Price.

Office of Management and Budget (OMB)—Arm of the executive branch of the federal government responsible for cost-efficient management.

Office of the Superintendent of Financial Institutions (OSFI) (Canada)—The federal agency that assures that pension plans governed by the Pension Benefits Act comply with its requirements. The agency also oversees all federally regulated financial institutions, such as banks, insurance companies, trust and loan companies, and co-operative credit associations.

Office Visit—A formal face-to-face contact between

the physician and the patient in a health center, office or hospital outpatient department.

Officer—An executive, key employee or highly compensated employee who is in regular and continued service with an employer.

Offset—A tax law provision in which one type of tax is allowed to be used to decrease another area of tax liability.

Offset Approach—Generally, a method of coordinating the amount of one benefit with that due from another source, such as an employer-provided pension with Social Security or other government benefits (benefits from a private plan are decreased by a certain percent from benefits received from the government); or a disability pension where disability insurance benefits are also provided.

Offset Integration (Canada)—Provision in a pension plan for directly reducing a plan benefit by all or a portion of pensions payable to the individual from a government program.

Offset Plan—A plan under which (1) no employee is ineligible to participate because his or her compensation does not exceed a minimum level, (2) no portion of compensation is excluded in computing benefits and (3) all the provisions including the benefit rates apply uniformly to all covered employees regardless of compensation, except that an employee's benefit otherwise computed under the plan formula is reduced or offset by a stated percentage of such employee's old age insurance benefit under the Social Security Act.

Old Age Security (OAS) (Canada)—A monthly pension to qualified Canadian residents regardless of past earnings or current income. This pension is indexed to the Consumer Price Index. This benefit is taxed back wholly or partially for those with incomes over a certain level.

Old-Age, Survivors, and Disability Insurance (OASDI)—A program under Social Security funded through a payroll tax on employers equal to a certain percentage of wages paid to employees.

Older Workers Benefit Protection Act (OWBPA)—Restores the requirement for equal benefits or equal cost in employee benefit plans that provide different treatment based on participants' ages. The law also added some employer requirements and

covers all companies subject to ADEA except the federal government. The law addresses early retirement window plans, severance pay and disability benefits, health benefits, cost determinations and waivers of age discrimination rights.

Omnibus Budget Reconciliation Act (OBRA)—Annual tax and budget reconciliation acts of Congress, which often impact employee benefits, pension plans and Medicare.

Omnibus Budget Reconciliation Act of 1986 (OBRA '86)—Key provisions: Made changes to Medicare reimbursement to physicians and hospitals. Amended COBRA to make the loss of retiree health coverage because of a firm's Chapter 11 bankruptcy filing a qualifying event for continuation of health insurance coverage for retirees and their dependents. Required that employers with pension plans provide pension accruals or allocations for employees working beyond age 64, and for newly hired employees who are within five years of normal retirement age.

Omnibus Budget Reconciliation Act of 1987 (OBRA '87)—Key provisions: Allowed states to extend Medicaid coverage to pregnant women and infants in families with incomes up to 185% of poverty level. Contained provisions affecting the minimum funding standards, including the Pension Protection Act of 1987.

Omnibus Budget Reconciliation Act of 1989 (OBRA '89)—
—Key provisions: Allowed COBRA continuees who become covered under another plan to continue their former employer coverage for a health problem considered to be a preexisting condition under the new plan. Extended the continuation period for individuals who are disabled at termination of employment and raised the premium for the extended period.
—Partially repealed the interest exclusion on ESOP loans. Imposed mandatory Labor Department civil penalties on violations by qualified plan fiduciaries and created a tax penalty for substantial overstatement of pension liabilities in determining deductibility Required that various forms of deferred compensation be included in determination of average compensation and, in turn, the Social Security taxable wage base.

Omnibus Budget Reconciliation Act of 1993 (OBRA '93)—Key provisions: Impacts many direct and indirect components of pay (such as qualified retirement plan limits), increases the Medicare tax base, eliminates the deduction for executive pay in excess of $1 million under most circumstances, and extends the tuition reimbursement exclusion.

1% Owner—An individual owning, directly or indirectly, at least 1% of the employer's stock. If the employer is not a corporation, the individual's capital or profits interest in the employer is considered. See also Key Employee; Top-Heavy Plan.

Open-End Fund/Open-End Investment Company—Open-end funds, or *mutual funds,* are formed when a sponsor creates an investment portfolio with its own money and registers it with the Securities and Exchange Commission. Individual investors then buy shares of the investment company that issued the fund. Since the fund company is always ready to issue or buy back shares of the fund, individual investors are relieved of this concern. This factor also helps to reduce the volatility or changeableness of the fund's share price. The mutual fund invests whatever funds it has. See also Economic Growth and Tax Relief Reconciliation Act of 2001 (EGTRRA); Investment Company or Trust; Mutual Fund.

Open-End Mortgage—A mortgage that permits the borrower to reborrow the money paid on the principal, usually up to the original amount.

Open Enrollment—A period during which subscribers in a health benefit program have an opportunity to select an alternate health plan being offered to them; or a period when uninsured employees and their dependents may obtain coverage without presenting evidence of insurability.

Open Mortgage—A mortgage that can be paid off at any time before maturity without penalty.

Open Panel—A managed care plan (such as an HMO) that contracts with physicians who operate out of their own offices. Permits any willing provider, if qualified, to contract with an HMO.

Opinion Letter—A written statement issued by government agencies to approve an action. For example, the IRS issues such a statement when ruling on the acceptability of a prototype retirement plan.

Option—A standardized contract between a party and one of the exchanges, or a custom contract between two parties, which gives the buyer the right (not the obligation) to exercise an option to buy or sell at a preset price on a specified date. A *call option* gives the holder the right to buy the underlying asset by a certain date at a certain price. A *put option* gives the holder the right to sell the underlying asset by a certain date at a certain price. See also Call Option.

Option Agreement—The agreement a customer must sign within 15 days of his or her approval for options trading. In it the client agrees to abide by the rules of the listed options exchanges and not to exceed the exchanges' position limits.

Optionee—The person who received an option on property; buyer.

Optioner—Person who gives an option on his or her property; seller.

Ordinary Care—The prudent man standard, under the circumstances of a given case.

Ordinary Life Insurance—A form of whole life insurance usually issued in amounts of $2,000 or more with premiums payable on an annual, semiannual, quarterly or monthly basis to the death of the insured or to the end of the mortality table employed, whichever occurs first and at which time (benefits) proceeds are due. The term is also used to mean *straight life insurance.*

Ordinary Life Pension Trust—A trust-funded pension plan that provides death benefits through the purchase of ordinary or whole life insurance contracts for employees covered. The trust pays premiums on the insurance coverage until the employee reaches retirement age. The trust also accumulates, in an auxiliary fund, the additional sums necessary to purchase the retirement benefits of the plan for the employees, using the paid-up cash value of the life insurance policy for each employee as part of the purchase price of the annuity.

Organizational Culture—A company's shared beliefs and values that result in norms of behavior.

Osteopathic Medicine—A system of medicine that emphasizes the theory that the body can make its own remedies, given normal structural relationships, environmental conditions and nutrition. Osteopathic physicians are granted the Doctor of Osteopathy (DO) degree.

Other Diagnosis—All conditions that exist at the time of admission or develop subsequently that affect the treatment received and/or the length of stay in a hospital. Diagnoses that relate to an earlier episode, which have no bearing on the present hospital stay, are to be excluded.

Out-of-Area Benefits (HMO)—Those benefits that the plan supplies to its subscribers when outside the geographical limits of the HMO. These benefits usually include emergency care benefits plus low indemnity payments for nonemergency benefits. Most plans stipulate that area services for emergency care will be provided until the subscriber can be returned to the plan for medical management of the case.

Out-of-Pocket Maximum (OOP Maximum)—See Maximum Out-of-Pocket Payment.

Outcomes Management—The optimization of health outcomes through the continuous development of clinical guidelines and interventions as well as the monitoring and evaluating of data.

Outcomes Measurement—The collection and use of data to show how well a given medical intervention is meeting the health and cost goals of plan sponsors as well as those of patients.

Outliers—Patients displaying atypical characteristics relative to other patients in a DRG, i.e., low and high length of stay, death, leaving against medical advice, admitted and discharged the same day, clinical outliers and low-volume DRGs.

Outpatient—A person who visits a clinic, emergency room or health facility and receives health care without being admitted as an overnight patient. (Antonym: inpatient)

Outpatient Services—Medical and other services provided by a hospital or other qualified facility or supplier, such as a mental health clinic, rural health clinic, mobile X-ray unit or freestanding dialysis unit. Such services include outpatient physical therapy services, diagnostic X-ray and laboratory tests, X-ray and other radiation therapy.

Outpatient Surgery—Same day surgery without anticipation of the overnight stay of patients. Often performed at an ambulatory surgery center. (Synonyms: *ambulatory surgery; day surgery*)

Outplacement Assistance—Employment counseling, employment agency services and other aid for employees who are dismissed when an organization downsizes or modifies its business strategy.

Outsourcing—
—The practice of purchasing parts or finished goods from domestic nonunion shops or from foreign companies.
—Means of eliminating in-house management, administrative and/or clerical duties associated with a particular employee benefit plan by contacting with an external service provider specializing in that particular benefit area.

Over the Counter (OTC)—
—Pharmaceutical products available without a prescription.
—A market for securities made up of securities dealers who may or may not be members of a securities exchange. Over the counter is mainly a market made electronically. Thousands of companies have insufficient shares outstanding, stockholders or earnings to warrant application for listing on the New York Stock Exchange. Securities of these companies are traded in the over-the-counter market between dealers who act as either principals or brokers for customers. The over-the-counter market is the principal market for U.S. government and municipal bonds.

Over-the-Counter Market—The public trading market for securities not traded over the New York Stock Exchange or the American Stock Exchange. Shares are traded by buyers and sellers, rather than brokers, usually electronically or by telephone. Trading is overseen by the National Association of Securities Dealers (NASD).

Overcoding—Reporting a more complex and/or higher cost procedure than was actually performed.

Overfunded Plan—A defined benefit plan in which the company's current contributions exceed both current liabilities and projected future liabilities.

Overinsurance—When persons covered under one or more plans can recover total benefits that exceed their actual medical expenses.

Overtreatment—Providing more services than are consistent with or justified by diagnosis and treatment plan; being neither necessary nor appropriate;

often used with or synonymous to overutilization. See also Undertreatment.

Owner-Employee—Self-employed individual who owns the entire interest in an unincorporated business, or a partner who owns more than 10% of the capital or profit interest of the partnership. If the owner-employee established a plan just for his or her employees but does not cover himself or herself, the rules for qualification and tax treatment of contributions and benefits are the same as those plans established by corporate employers. The requirements and limitations of HR 10 apply when a self-employed individual is included.

Owners' Equity—The owners' financial interest in a company, consisting of the difference between the company's assets and its liabilities; capital invested by stockholders.

P

Paid Claims—The dollar value of all claims paid (e.g., hospital, medical, surgical) during the plan year, regardless of the date that the services were rendered. Measures a plan's performance.

Paired Comparison—A ranking job evaluation method that compares each job being evaluated individually to every other job in pairs to determine which job has a higher value. The final score for a job is the number of times it is considered the most valuable in the comparisons. Ranks are then created from these scores.

Panic—A bear market of severe correction that is compressed into a period of a few weeks.

Paper Profit—A profit still existing in the security on paper, which has not yet been sold and therefore realized. An unrealized profit.

Par Value (Bonds)—The par value of a bond is its principal or face value. It is the amount the issuer promises to repay the lender upon maturity or earlier. Interest income that bonds pay is derived from a bond's par value, and the price of most bonds is quoted as a percentage of par.

Par Value (Stocks)—When applied to common stock, par value is an arbitrary dollar amount assigned to each share by the company's charter, which has little significance to the actual market value of a stock.

Parachute—An arrangement with an employee, particularly an officer or executive of a corporation, which protects the employee financially in the event of change of control of the corporation or loss of employment. The arrangement may be a stipulated severance payment, an employment contract with a substantial notice of severance requirement, insurance or other protection. See also Golden Parachute; Silver Parachute; Tin Parachute.

Parity Rule—A break-in-service rule that says a participant loses pension rights if the break in service exceeds the greater of five years or the length of time worked.

Partial Disability—An illness or injury that prevents an insured person from performing one or more of the functions of his or her regular job.

Partial Termination—Reducing benefits or making participation requirements less liberal although not amounting to a complete termination of the plan, may be considered a partial termination, resulting in the vesting of accrued benefits for at least part of the plan.

Partial Vesting—That form of immediate or deferred vesting under which a specified portion of the accrued benefits of a participant becomes a vested benefit.

Partial Withdrawal—An employer does not completely withdraw from a multiemployer plan, but a specified event occurs that significantly reduces the employer's obligations for contributions under the plan.

Participant—See Plan Participant.

Participant-Directed Plan—A plan under which participants determine the investment of their account balance. Also known as *self-directed investment*. See also 404(c) Plan; Section 404(c) (ERISA); Self-Directed Investment.

Participating Group Annuity Contract—A contract with an insurance company providing income to participants (usually ten or more) in which both the mortality risk and the investment experience are shared in varying degrees between the policyholder and the insurance company.

Participating Preferred Stock—A type of preferred stock that offers the holder a share of the earnings remaining after all senior securities have been paid. This payment is made in addition to the fixed dividend received. Dividends may be cumulative, noncumulative or convertible. See also Convertible Preferred Stock; Cumulative Preferred Stock; Noncumulative Preferred Stock; Preferred Stock.

Participation—Membership is a plan.

Participation Requirements—Most pension and other employee benefit plans provide that a new employee must wait a specified length of time before he or she is eligible to participate in the plan. Under ERISA, in general, the maximum permissible service requirement is one year, although up to two years may be used in pension plans (without CODAs) that provide for full and immediate vesting. The highest minimum age that can be used is 21. See also Minimum Participation Standards.

Partition—The segregation of a portion of the assets and liabilities of a multiemployer plan ordered by the PBGC. The segregated portion of assets and liabilities is held as a separate plan after the partition.

Partnership—Co-ownership of a business by two or more people. Each owner is equally and personally responsible for the debts of the whole business, not just a share.

Part-Time Employees—
—Refers to employees who work less than 1,000 hours for an employer in a year. Such employees may be kept from participating in qualified retirement plans.
—According to the Department of Labor, Bureau of Labor Statistics, employees who usually work between one and 34 hours each week (at all jobs within a company) regardless of the number of hours worked in a given week.

Party in Interest—A party that, because of his, hers or its close relationship with the plan, is prohibited from certain transactions with the plan. Examples of parties in interest include plan fiduciaries, service providers, employees or sponsors; or a relative of these. See also Prohibited Transaction.

Passive Management—A style of investment management that seeks to attain average risk-adjusted performance.

Pass-Through Securities—These represent undivided interests in pools of mortgages. The sponsoring organization, for example, the Government National Mortgage Association (GNMA), passes through interest and principal payments to the certificate holders as these payments are received on a monthly basis. This results in an uneven cash flow because of prepayments caused by foreclosures or delinquent payments. Pass-through securities are offered by private organizations also.

Password—Confidential authentication information composed of a string of characters.

Past Service Benefit—Credit toward a pension, provided by the employer, for all or part of a participant's years of service with the company before the adoption or amendment of a pension plan, or before the employee's entry into the plan.

Patient Days—Accumulated total, for the reporting period, of the number of patients in a hospital each day (excluding newborns). A patient day is one patient in one hospital bed for one day.

Patient Protection Act (PPA)—Refers to various pieces of state legislation introduced since 1995; proposals often include any willing provider provisions or other standards aimed at protecting the provider, broad disclosure requirements, utilization review fairness, fairness for physicians, a point-of-service option and choice of health plans.

Pay As You Go—
—Paying pension benefits as they become due without advance funding. See also General Asset Plan.
—(Canada) Also called a *pay-go plan*. A modified pay-as-you-go plan is partially funded.

Pay for Knowledge—See Knowledge-Based Pay.

Pay or Play—A proposal that would require all employers either to provide health insurance for their workers or to pay a tax that would enable the government to provide insurance. Employers can either "pay" (pay into the public health insurance program) or "play" (provide coverage for their employees in the private market).

Pay-Related Plan—A plan that has a benefit formula that bases benefits or benefit coverage on compensation, such as a final pay plan.

Payer—In health care, generally refers to entities, other than the patient, that finance or reimburse the cost of health services. In most cases, refers to insurance carriers, other third-party payers and/or health plan sponsors (employers or unions).

Pay Plan—A schedule of pay rates or ranges for each job in the classification plan. May include rules of administration and the benefit package.

Pay Range—The range of pay rates, from minimum to maximum, established for a pay grade or class. Typically used to set individual employee pay rates.

Payroll Audit—
—An examination of the insured's payroll records by a representative of the insurer to determine the premium due on a policy. Some insurance, notably workers' compensation, charges its premium on the basis of the policyholder's payroll. The company sends out "payroll auditors" to determine the accuracy of the policyholder's figures.
—In the multiemployer plan context, frequently a part of the collections enforcement procedure, in which the payroll records of a contributing employer are audited by a trust fund representative or fund employee to ensure that contributions are being made in accordance with the provisions of the collective bargaining agreement.

Payroll-Based Stock Option Plan (PAYSOP)—Defined contribution plans established under the Tax Reduction Act of 1975, used to transfer stock to employees to provide equity ownership to workers.

P/E Ratio—See Price/Earnings (P/E) Ratio.

Peer Comparison—In some incentive plans, a company's results in specified financial measures are compared with those of a group of other companies determined to be peer companies. The results can be used in incentive formulas.

Peer Review—A process established to provide for review by unbiased physicians of the effectiveness and efficiency of care provided under a plan's benefits.

Penny Stocks—Low-priced stock selling at less than a dollar, usually highly speculative and volatile in terms of price movements and trading volume, but periodically very rewarding.

Pension—
—A series of periodic payments, usually for life, payable monthly or at other specified intervals. The term is frequently used to describe the part of a retirement allowance financed by employer contributions. Compare with Annuity.
—A regular payment, usually monthly, to a person who has retired from employment because of advanced age or disability.

Pension Adjustment (PA) (Canada)—An adjustment to the amount that individuals who contribute to an occupational pension plan may contribute to an RRSP. The amount contributed by the individual is deducted from the amount allowed by the government.

Pension Adjustment Reversal (Canada)—Introduced by the federal government in 1998, a recalculation of a pension adjustment at time of the individual's termination to allow him or her to belatedly contribute more to his or her RRSP.

Pension Administrator—See Administrator (Employee Benefit Plans).

Pension and Welfare Benefits Administration (PWBA)—See Employee Benefits Security Administration (EBSA).

Pension and Welfare Disclosure Act—A 1958 law requiring companies to file certain pension information with the Department of Labor.

Pension Benefit Formula (Plan's Benefit Formula or Benefit Formula)—The basis for determining payments to which participants may be entitled under a pension plan. Pension benefit formulas usually refer to the employee's service or compensation or both.

Pension Benefit Guaranty Corporation (PBGC)—The federal agency, established as a nonprofit corporation, charged with administering the plan termination provisions of ERISA Title IV and the Multiemployer Pension Plan Amendments Act of 1980. Employers pay premiums to the PBGC, which guarantees benefits up to a specified maximum for participants and beneficiaries when defined benefit plans terminate.

Pension Committee—In general, persons other than the trustees designated by management and/or the union to determine the eligibility of employees to receive a pension, the selection of providers and other plan issues.

Pension Funding Equity Act—Legislation passed in 2004 that changes plan sponsors' minimum required quarterly contributions to defined benefit pension plans. The act updates the interest rate used for determining a plan's current liability for funding purposes. Many companies and multiemployer funds will see lower amounts of additional plan contributions for plans that were underfunded under the former interest rates. The act also includes special rules for multiemployer plans and certain industries, such as the steel and airline industries.

Pension Plan—A plan established and maintained by an employer, which may be a company, labor union, governmental entity or other organization, to provide retirement benefits to employees. The plan can be funded by insurance plans or from general assets. Sections 401 through 419 of the Internal Revenue Code established requirements for qualified pension plans, which offer favorable tax treatment for employers and employees. The amount of the pension benefit is either specified or can be calculated according to a set formula based on various factors, such as age, earnings and service, but not profit. The amount of annual contributions, which can be estimated by actuaries, must cover the specified benefits offered.

Pension Simplification Act—A provision of the Small Business Job Protection Act of 1996. The Pension Simplification Act encourages small businesses to offer retirement plans and establishes simplified small employer pension plans known as savings incentive match plans for employees (SIMPLE). SIMPLE plans may be in the form of an IRA or part of a 401(k) plan.

Pension Trust—A fund consisting of money contributed by the employer and/or the employee plus earnings to provide pension benefits.

Pensionable Salary (International Benefits)—The salary used to calculate a pension. May be the average of a number of years prior to retirement or of the last year's salary.

Per Diem Rate—
—The rate set in advance to cover hospital or other health care facility costs on a daily basis. Sometimes includes only room and board charges and not ancillary service charges.

—Methods of calculation include dividing the total of operating costs, finance charges and depreciation by the number of inpatient days in a hospital or health care facility, as well as applying a uniform overall charge.

Percentage Participation Clause—See Coinsurance.

Percentile—A range of a distribution of provided charges determined by a third-party payer for specific medical/dental services. For example, if the third-party uses a 90th percentile, maximum payment may be made for any charge at or below that level.

Performance-Based Fees—Investment management fees that are related to investment results, not to the size of assets managed. Also known as *incentive fees*.

Performance Sharing (Goal Sharing)—A process in which performance is defined in terms of selected criteria (for example, quality, customer satisfaction, responsiveness, profit, etc.); standards are established; and incentive awards are made contingent upon meeting these standards, usually at the companywide level.

Period Certain—See Annuity Certain.

Permanent Disability—Employee's inability to work at any job, rather than at the specific job held at the time the disability was incurred. Permanent disability is typically covered by insurance for those employees who become disabled before reaching the age of 60.

Permitted Disparity—
—A term for the Social Security integration method of allocating employers' contributions. A qualified pension or profit-sharing plan maintained by a private employer for the benefit of its employees is permitted to be integrated with benefits available to employees under the federal Social Security system. The effect of integration is to reduce the employer's cost of contributing to the plan, due to the credit available for the employer's Social Security contribution for plan participants. Permitted disparity can be an important factor in formulating the plan's participation standards in that the required inclusion of a particular employee may result in no obligation to actually make contributions for such person's benefit.

—The allowable difference between benefit and contribution rates for highly compensated and nonhighly compensated participants in qualified pension plans as permitted by IRS regulations.

Perquisites (Perks)—Special benefits for top executives and other managerial employees. Treated as taxable income to the employee. Examples include legal counseling, special parking and club memberships.

Person—An individual, partnership, joint venture, corporation, mutual company, joint stock company, trust, estate, unincorporated organization, association or employee organization.

Personal Earnings and Benefit Estimate Statement—This statement provides workers with information about their individual Social Security records, showing them the earnings that have been reported for them over the years and estimates of the different types of benefits for which they may qualify.

Personal Financial Planning—Developing and implementing of total, coordinated plans for reaching one's financial goals. See also Financial Planning.

Personal Financial Specialist (PFS)—A certified public accountant that also provides financial planning services. The PFS title is authorized by the American Institute of Certified Public Accountants. Applicants for the designation must complete an exam and have at least three years of financial planning experience, among other requirements.

Personal Information Protection and Electronic Documents Act (PIPEDA) (Canada)—As of January 1, 2004, this act provides that both private sector and federally regulated companies must obtain a person's consent when collecting, using or disclosing personal information, and they can only use that information for the purpose for which the person gave consent.

Personal Pension (United Kingdom)—Individual policy that enables a person to save for retirement if he or she has contracted out of the state earnings-related pension scheme or does not have access to an occupational plan.

Phantom Stock Plan—
—A nonqualified deferred compensation plan under which deferred compensation units are created, assigned a value equivalent to the value of the company's stock and awarded to certain key employees.
—*Full value:* a long-term executive incentive plan in which the participant receives a payment in cash, representing the value of a number of shares of phantom stock, using the company's actual stock price as the value determinant and the valuation date specified in the plan or award.
—*Incremental value:* the same as the full value phantom stock grant except the amount is paid in stock or cash, and is equal to the increase in value of the company's shares from the time of the grant of the phantom stock to the date of payment.

Pharmacy Benefits Manager/Management (PBM)—Refers either to an individual or to a company that manages pharmacy benefits. Company services typically include development of formularies and drug utilization review to help contain costs.

Phased Retirement—Various arrangements helping workers who are at or near retirement to gradually move from full-time work to retirement; for example, working in a reduced capacity on a part-time or temporary basis. Workers can continue to perform and be paid at their highest level and skill, access health benefits and earn and receive pension benefits, while the employer retains valuable, experienced workers. See also Gradual Retirement.

Physical Safeguards—In regard to HIPAA privacy regulation, physical measures, policies and procedures to protect a covered entity's electronic information systems and related buildings and equipment from natural and environmental hazards, and unauthorized intrusion.

Physical Therapy—Treatment of disease and injury by physical means, including exercise, manipulation, electricity, heat, cold and water.

Physician-Hospital Organization (PHO)—Alliances between physicians and hospitals to help providers attain market share, improve bargaining power and reduce administrative costs. These entities sell their services to managed care organizations or directly to employers.

Physician's Assistant (PA)—An allied health professional who is trained to perform certain medical procedures, like physical exams, previously reserved to the physician, and who works under the supervision of a physician.

Piecework—Work compensated according to the number of units produced.

Plan—An arrangement under which employer and employee contributions, if any, are deposited with a trustee who is responsible for the administration and investment of these monies and the income earned on accumulated assets of the fund, and who is normally responsible for the direct payment of benefits to eligible participants under the plan. Benefits are often paid by an insurance company with transfers from the trust fund as required. The trustee may be a corporate trustee (trust company) or an individual.

Plan Administrator—See Administrator (Employee Benefit Plans).

Plan Amendment—See Amendment.

Plan Assets—Stocks, bonds and other investments, including securities of the employer if they are transferable, that have been segregated and restricted (usually in a trust) so they can only be used to provide for postretirement benefits. Plan assets include amounts contributed by the employer (but not amounts accrued and unpaid), amounts contributed by plan participants for a contributory plan and amounts earned from investing the contributions, less benefits, income taxes and other expenses incurred.

Plan Document—For purposes of qualified retirement plans, a definite written program maintained by an employer for the benefit of employees or beneficiaries that is intended to be permanent and is communicated to employees. Sets forth the benefits available under an employee benefit plan and the eligibility requirements. This document is often separate from the trust agreement in order to allow plan modifications without frequent trust agreement amendments.

Plan Liabilities—Include normal costs, accrued liability, past service liabilities and experience losses. Plan liabilities are to be determined under the funding method used generally to determine costs under the plan. Experience gains and any decreases in plan benefits that reduce plan liabilities are also subject to this rule. Plan costs must be determined on the basis of actuarial assumptions that, in the aggregate, are reasonable.

Plan Loan—Loan from a participant's accumulated retirement assets, such as a 401(k) plan, that must not exceed 50% of the balance or $50,000, whichever is less. The loan feature is optional. See also 401(k) plan.

Plan Participant—Any employee or former employee of an employer, member or former member of an employee organization, sole proprietor, or partner in a partnership who is or may become eligible to receive a benefit of any type from an employee benefit plan, or whose beneficiaries may be eligible to receive any such benefit. See also Active Participant; Participation Requirements.

Plan Sponsor—The party that establishes and maintains the plan, which is (1) the employer, in the case of an employee benefit plan maintained by a single employer; (2) the employee organization, in the case of a plan maintained by an employee organization; or (3) the association, committee, joint board of trustees or other similar group of representatives of the parties involved, in the case of a plan maintained by one or more employers and one or more employee organizations.

Plan Suspension—An event in which the pension plan is frozen and no further benefits accrue. Future service may continue to be the basis for vesting of nonvested benefits existing at the date of suspension. The plan may still hold assets, pay benefits already accrued and receive additional employer contributions for any unfunded benefits. Employees may or may not continue working for the employer.

Plan Termination—
—When the plan ceases to exist and benefits are settled. Replacement with another plan is not a termination. ERISA requires that all accrued benefits (to the extent funded) must be fully vested upon the termination or partial termination of a plan. (A partial termination might result from a large reduction of the workforce or a sizable reduction of benefits under the plan.) See also Termination.
—(Canada) Voluntary or involuntary discontinuance of a plan. The Pension Benefits Act regulates the wind-up procedure.

Plan Termination Date—If the plan is terminated by the plan administrator, the termination date is the date established by the administrator and agreed to by the Pension Benefit Guaranty Corporation. If the plan is terminated by the PBGC, it is the date established by the PBGC and agreed to by the administrator. In either case, if the administrator and PBGC cannot agree, the date will be set by the court.

Plan Termination Insurance—Insurance protecting pension plan participants from loss of pension benefits due to plan termination. The federal program set forth under Title IV of ERISA insures defined benefit pension plans against the failure of the employer to properly fund. It is administered by the Pension Benefit Guaranty Corporation. All defined benefit pension plans are subject to these regulations. The Multiemployer Pension Plan Amendments Act of 1980 extended mandatory Title IV coverage to multiemployer plans (such coverage was discretionary under ERISA as originally enacted) and adjusted the multiemployer per participant premium.

Plan Year—The calendar, policy or fiscal year on which the records of the plan are kept.

Plant Closing Bill of 1988—Requires employers that anticipate a major layoff to notify the affected workers 60 days in advance.

Play or Pay—See Pay or Play.

PM/PM—Per member per month; the revenue or cost of a risk payment that is typically made to providers by HMOs for providing a defined amount of care for each enrolled patient each month.

Point—
—In the case of shares of stock, a point means $1. If ABC shares rise three points, each share has risen $3.
—In the case of bonds, a point means $10, since a bond is quoted as a percentage of $1,000. A bond that rises three points gains 3% of $1,000, or $30 in value. An advance from 87 to 90 would mean an advance in dollar value from $870 to $900 for each $1,000 bond.
—In the case of market averages, the word *point* means merely that and no more; its value is relative and is assigned arbitrarily. If, for example, the Dow Jones Industrial Average rises from 870.25 to 871.25, it has risen a point. A point in this average, however, is not equivalent to $1.
—The term is frequently used when referring to

mortgage premiums and is 1% of the principal amount. It is a method used by lenders to obtain additional revenue over the legal interest rate.

Point-of-Service Plan (POS)—A type of managed care plan that allows members to choose, at the point where care begins, to receive services from a participating or nonparticipating network provider, usually with a financial disincentive for going outside the network. More of a product than an organization, POS plans can be offered by HMOs, PPOs or self-insured employers.

Poison Pill—An attempt by a company's management to insulate the firm from either a two-tier bid or a low-ball bid by creating additional equity at very low prices, thereby substantially increasing the acquiring company's acquisitions cost. It is an anti-takeover ploy.

Policy—The contract between the insurance company and the policy owner under which the insurance company agrees to pay the policy benefit when specific losses occur, provided the insurer receives the required premiums.

Policy Dividend—See Dividend.

Policyholder—The owner of the policy. Under a group purchase plan, the policyholder is the employer, labor union or trustee to whom a group contract is issued. In a plan contracting directly with the individual or family, the policyholder is the individual to whom the contract is issued.

Pool—In some cases refers to a large number of small groups that are analyzed and rated as a single large group. Risk pools may be any account that attempts to find the claims liability for a group with a common denominator.

Pooled Trust—A common trust fund generally sponsored by one employer and used to accumulate the assets of different plans of the employer and its subsidiaries.

Pop-Up Option—A variation of the usual joint and survivor option in which, if the participant survives the contingent annuitant, the amount of benefit payable reverts back (or "pops up") to the original life-only amount of benefit. More frequently seen in multiemployer plans.

Portability—
—Any provision for retaining pension rights and credits when changing from one employer to another. Vested rights are nonforfeitable. The retention of nonvested (contingent) rights depends upon remaining within the scope of a multi-employer plan, or its reciprocating plan under a reciprocal agreement.
—The ability of the consumer to take health insurance from job to job. See also Job Lock.
—The right of an employee to take with him or her, upon separation from the employer, the total accumulation of monies carried in his or her account.
See also Reciprocal Agreement; Reciprocity.

Portfolio—
—The mix and composition of an investor's holdings among different classes of securities such as bonds, mortgages and common stocks.
—All of the products an insurance company offers.

Portfolio Mix—A combination or selection of investments, including stocks, bonds, real estate and selected limited partnership interests.

Portfolio Optimization—Starting with a universe of securities that has been valued in terms of (1) expected return, (2) variances of expected return and (3) covariance of return with every other security under consideration, the process of portfolio optimization involves selecting the portfolio that minimizes risk for a given level of risk. In practice, the computerized optimization programs can impose manifold constraints on the characteristics of the resultant portfolio. Typical constraints would be that the resultant portfolio have no more than 5% of the portfolio's value in a single stock or that the average current yield be at least 4% per annum.

Postretirement Adjustment—A change (usually an increase) in the amount of a retirement allowance after its commencement to reflect changes or anticipated changes in cost-of-living or living standards. See also Cost-of-Living Adjustment (COLA).

Postretirement Benefits—All forms of benefits, other than retirement income, provided by an employer to its retirees.

Power of Attorney (P/A)—An instrument authorizing another to act as one's agent or attorney in fact.

Practice Guideline—A statement concerning the known cost, benefits and risks of using a certain medical intervention to bring about a given medical income. Practice guidelines are intended to assist in health care decision making by practitioners, patients and others about appropriate health care in a particular situation. See also Protocols.

Practitioner—One who practices medicine; may include physicians, chiropractors, dentists, podiatrists and physicians' assistants.

Pre-Authorization—See Prior Authorization.

Preadmission Certification—See Precertification.

Preadmission Testing (PAT)—A plan benefit designed to encourage patients to obtain needed diagnostic services on an ambulatory basis before a nonemergency hospital admission in order to reduce hospital length of stay.

Precedent—A previously decided court case that can serve as an authority in deciding a present controversy. In law, the term *stare decisis* refers to the practice of adhering to decided cases and settled principles, providing for the development of a consistent body of law.

Precertification—The process of obtaining certification or authorization from the health plan for hospital admissions (inpatient or outpatient) or for surgery, based on the judgment of medically appropriate care by a qualified peer. Failure to obtain precertification often results in a financial penalty to either the provider or the subscriber. Also known as *preadmission certification* or *preadmission review.*

Preemption of State Law (ERISA)—The regulatory portion of ERISA supersedes all state law that otherwise would be applicable to plans covered by the reporting, disclosure, fiduciary responsibility, participation and vesting, funding and plan termination insurance provisions of ERISA. However, the preemptive effect of the act does not relieve any person from state law regulating insurance, banking or securities. Nor does the act preempt any generally applicable state criminal law.

Preexisting Condition—A physical and/or mental condition of an insured person that existed prior to the issuance of his or her policy. Some plans may cover these conditions after a waiting period of six months to a year, while others may permanently exclude a person with a preexisting condition from coverage. See also HIPAA.

Preferred Provider Organization (PPO)—A managed care plan that contracts with employers, insurance companies or other third-party administrators to provide comprehensive medical service. Providers exchange discounted services for increased volume and prompt payment. Participants' out-of-pocket costs are usually lower than under a fee-for-service plan.

Preferred Risk—A person classified as an above-average risk because the person's physical condition, health history, occupation and/or lifestyle indicate the probability of a lower-than-usual mortality rate.

Preferred Stock—Securities or shares representing an ownership interest in the business, but which have "preference" over other shares (i.e., common stock) as regards dividends, or in distribution of assets up to a certain fixed amount in the event of liquidation, or both. Preferred dividends are normally fixed, whereas common stock dividends may fluctuate depending upon company earnings. See also Convertible Preferred Stock; Cumulative Preferred Stock; Noncumulative Preferred Stock; Participating Preferred Stock.

Pregnancy Disability—Disability that is caused, or contributed to, by pregnancy, childbirth or related medical conditions. Under Title VII of the Civil Rights Act of 1964, employers must treat such disabilities on a parity with other, non-pregnancy-related conditions.

Pregnancy Discrimination Act of 1978 (PDA)—An amendment to Title VII of the Civil Rights Act of 1964 that requires covered employers to treat pregnancy the same as any other disability in providing employee benefits and in granting leaves of absence.

Premature Distributions—Unless a participant is disabled, any distribution from an individual retirement account or annuity to an individual for whose benefit the account or annuity was established is subject to a 10% premature distribution tax if he or she has not reached age 59½. This includes a constructive distribution resulting from the disqualification of the account or annuity. Whether the individual is disabled is determined under the annuity rules.

The Tax Reform Act of 1984 imposes a 10% tax on amounts that an individual receives from a qualified plan where he or she is, or has been, a 5% owner of the business under which the plan is established, and where he or she receives the distribution before reaching the age of 59½. The premature distribution tax would not be applied if the reason for the distribution was that the individual became disabled. The tax would apply only to the extent that the amounts distributed are attributable to contributions paid on behalf of the individual (other than contributions made by him or her as a 5% owner) while he or she was a 5% owner. The 10% tax is in addition to other income taxes imposed on the distribution.

Thus, Keogh plan participants who are not 5% owners do not have to pay the 10% premature distribution tax for amounts distributed to them before they reach the age of 59½.

Premium—

—The amount of money a policyholder agrees to pay an insurance company for an insurance policy or an annuity, in consideration of which the insurance company guarantees the payment of specified benefits. May be a single sum or a series of periodic payments. Synonymous with *purchase payment* or *contribution*.

—An insurance concept: premium rate is based on sex, amount and issue age, and is usually level to retirement age. Generally based on the same mortality, interest and expense assumptions used in the calculation for regular insurance contracts. Some insurance companies offer special pension series of contracts with a different set of actuarial assumptions that can be justified on the basis of special tax credit for investment income earned on pension reserves and differences in experience in pension underwriting.

—(1) The difference between the original offering price of a security and the price to which it may rise in the "after-offering" market. (2) The amount by which a security sells over its *face (par value)*. A $1,000 par value bond selling at 105 (worth $1,050) would be selling at a $50 or 5% *premium*. The opposite of a *discount*. The premium is also that part of an investment paid at the time of purchase that will not be returned at maturity.

—The price paid by the purchaser of an option and the amount received by the seller (writer).

—(International Benefits) An incentive paid to ex-

111

patriates for undertaking a foreign assignment, usually 10-20% of base pay.

Premium Tax—
—A state tax levied on gross premiums, usually adjusted for dividends or retroactive rate adjustments.
—(Canada) A provincial tax levied on net premiums.

Prepaid Care Plan—See Prepaid Group Practice.

Prepaid Group Practice—A term used before the term *health maintenance organization* was coined to refer to multispecialty physician groups paid on a salaried or capitated basis.

Prepaid Pension Cost—Cumulative employer contributions in excess of accrued net pension cost.

Prepaid Program—A program that finances the cost of care in advance of receipt of service through a third party.

Prepayment—A method providing in advance for the cost of predetermined benefits for a population group, through regular periodic payments in the form of premiums, dues or contributions.

Prepayment Clause—A clause in a mortgage instrument spelling out the details under which the mortgagor is permitted to pay all or part of the unpaid loan balance before it becomes due, thereby saving the interest or clearing the way for a new mortgage.

Prepayment Penalty—A fee imposed on a mortgagor for paying the mortgage off before it becomes due, where there is no prepayment clause.

Preretirement Counseling—Program to help employees prepare financially and, sometimes, emotionally for retirement. See also Financial Planning Education.

Preretirement Death Benefits—These are the payments payable on the death of a participant prior to attaining retirement age. If the program is based upon investments only, then customarily the full value of the investment accounts. If the plan uses life insurance, then usually this would constitute the payment. A combination of both investments and life insurance is permissible; however, in no event may the total sum delivered to the beneficiary exceed 100 times the projected monthly pen-

sion benefit, unless the former participant was in the last years of his or her service period. In such an instance, the death benefit may equal the cash value of a retirement income contract, issued under similar circumstances.

Preretirement Surviving Spouse Benefit—A benefit providing that, if the participant dies while actively employed, the spouse will receive 50% of the pension calculated as though the employee had retired the day death occurred. This benefit is required under REA at time of vesting.

Prescription Benefits Management—See Pharmacy Benefits Manager/Management (PBM).

Prescription Drug Formulary—A listings of prescription medications that will be covered by a plan or insurance contract that often fosters substitution of generic or therapeutic equivalents on a cost-effective basis.

Prescription Drug Plan—Usually a provision under medical coverage plans whereby the beneficiary can obtain prescription drugs without incurring potentially large out-of-pocket expense. Different types of prescription drug plans are available. Examples are discount plan, closed panel drug plan, service-delivered plan, mail-order plan and maintenance drug option with major medical plan.

Prescription Drug Reimportation—The practice of importing prescription drugs from Canada or another foreign country as a cost-savings measure, especially for seniors and those who do not have prescription drug coverage. The practice is currently supported by some pharmacy chains, state governors and attorneys general, and insurance companies. Drug companies, as well as the federal Food and Drug Administration (FDA), contend they cannot be sure the imported drugs are safe. Legislation approving prescription drug reimportation was pending at press time.

Present Value—See Actuarial Present Value (APV).

Preservice Review—See Prospective Review.

Presumptive Method—A method of calculating and allocating withdrawal liability that generally requires an employer entering or continuing in a multiemployer plan after September 25, 1980, who subsequently withdraws, to fund a share of the increase in the plan's unfunded vested benefits during the period of the employer's required contributions to the plan.

Pretreatment Estimate—See Prior Authorization.

Prevailing Fee—A fee that falls within the range of fees most frequently charged by providers in a given locality for a particular medical service or procedure.

Prevailing Wage Rate—The amount paid by other employers in the labor market for similar work.

Preventive Care—Comprehensive care emphasizing priorities for prevention, early detection and early treatment of conditions, generally including routine physical examinations, immunization and well-person care. See also Wellness (Health Promotion) Programs.

Price/Earnings (P/E) Ratio—A stock's market price divided by its current or estimated future earnings. A measure of the attractiveness of a particular security versus all other securities as determined by the investing public. P/E ratios indicate the value of a company, based in part upon its price.

Price Index—A relative measure of the general price level over time. It is obtained by computing the ratio of the prices of a collection of goods and services during one period with the prices of the same goods and services during a selected base period. See also Consumer Price Index (CPI).

Price-to-Book Ratio—The current market price of a stock divided by the book value per share, or net worth.

$$P/B = \frac{\text{Market Price of a Common Stock}}{\text{Book Value per Share}}$$

Primary Care—Basic or general health care as opposed to specialist or subspecialist care. Primary care providers often oversee the total care of patients, referring the patient to other professionals as appropriate. Physicians whose practices are predominantly primary care include general or family practitioners, internists and pediatricians. Primary care also may be provided by nurse practitioners, physicians' assistants or other midlevel practitioners.

Primary Care Case Management—See Gatekeeper.

Primary Care Network (PCN)—A group of primary care physicians who have formed a network to share the risk of providing services to enrollees in a prepaid plan.

Primary Care Physician (PCP)—The physician in a managed care plan who is responsible for coordinating all care for an individual patient, from providing direct care services to referring the patient to specialists and hospital care. Can be a physician specializing in family practice, general practice, obstetrics/gynecology or pediatrics.

Primary Insurance Amount (PIA)—A figure used to compute how much Social Security a person is to receive upon reaching Social Security retirement age. It is based on the individual's wages, compensation, self-employment income and deemed military wage credits for years after 1950.

Primary Offering—A corporation's offering of stock to the public. Proceeds of the offering go directly to the corporation. See also Initial Public Offering (IPO).

Primary Payer—The insurance carrier that has first responsibility under coordination of benefits.

Prime Rate—The minimum rate on bank loans set by commercial banks and granted only to top business borrowers. It is affected by overall business conditions, the availability of reserves and the general level of money rates; it may vary geographically. Lending rates are also greatly influenced by the size of the loan; the largest loans naturally command the lowest rates.

Principal—
—One of the main parties in a real estate transaction; the purchaser or the seller.
—In agency law, the party to a contract who authorizes an agent to act on its behalf.
—In finances, an amount loaned, the sum that earns interest.
—The basic amount of money as distinguished from interest. The capital sum; the amount upon which interest is paid.

Principal Sum—
—A lump-sum payment made upon the insured person's accidental death.
—The value payable to the participant upon maturity of an endowment contract.

Prior Authorization—A cost-control procedure that requires the service or medication to be approved in advance by the doctor and/or the insurer. Without prior authorization, the health plan or insurer will not pay for the test, drug or services.

Prior Service Benefit—See Past Service Benefit.

Prior Service Cost—The cost of retroactive benefits granted in a plan amendment or under a new plan.

Priorities (Plan Termination) (Canada)—A set of rules, in an employment pension plan or legislation, under which the assets of a plan that is discontinued are allocated among members and beneficiaries to provide as far as possible for all accrued benefits.

Private Letter Ruling—See Letter Ruling.

Private Pension Plans—Pension plans established by private agencies, including commercial, industrial, labor and service organizations; nonprofit organizations; and nonprofit religious, educational and charitable institutions. Includes both single employer and multiemployer plans. Basically, all nongovernmental plans.

Private Placement—Usually associated with debt instruments where marketability is not required, but not always the case. The private placement of a loan with an institutional investor, such as a pension fund or insurance company, precludes the borrower from any SEC registration requirements, eliminates problems connected with changing market interest rates, and provides the investor with a higher interest rate and often a tailor-made maturity that might be difficult for the investor to obtain in a public offering.

Privatization—Occurs when services formerly performed by public employees are contracted to private sector firms.

Pro Rata Agreement—See Reciprocal Agreement; Reciprocity.

Probate—The entire process of reviewing or testing a will before a court of law to ensure that the will is authentic, and managing and distributing the decedent's assets by an executor (if there is a will) or a court-appointed administrator (if there is not a will).

Probationary Period—A specified number of days after the date of the issuance of the policy during which coverage is not afforded for sickness. The purpose of the period is to eliminate sickness actually contracted before the policy went into force.

Productivity—The relationship between output, or the quantity of goods and services produced, and inputs, or the amounts of labor, material and capital needed to produce the goods and services. Usually measured in terms of output per worker, per hour. It is affected by technology level, changes in plant and equipment and quality of the labor force.

Professional Employer Organization (PEO)—A firm that leases downsized employees back to the client company to alleviate staffing problems. The PEO offers comparable benefits to those earned by full-time permanent employees. The client contracts with the PEO and functions as a co-employer; but the PEO is considered the employer. See also Leased Employee.

Profit—Money remaining after all costs of operating a business are paid.

Profit and Loss Statement—A detailed summary of the income and expenses of a business over a period of time (usually quarterly, semiannually or annually) showing the net income or loss incurred. Also known as *income account* or *income statement.*

Profit-Sharing Plan—Plan established and maintained by an employer to provide for the participation in its profits by its employees or their beneficiaries. The plan must provide a definite predetermined formula for allocating the contributions made to the plan among the participants and for distributing the funds accumulated under the plan after a fixed number of years, the attainment of a stated age, or upon the prior occurrence of some event such as layoff, illness, disability, retirement, death or severance of employment. Deferred profit-sharing plans are subject to the participation, vesting, reporting and disclosure, and fiduciary rules of ERISA. They are excluded from the funding and plan termination provisions of the act.
  —Current profit-sharing plan (cash). Profits paid directly to employees in cash, check or stock as soon as profits are determined.
  —Deferred profit-sharing plan. A defined contribution plan; a qualified program of retirement benefits wherein the employer provides

retirement benefits subject to a written agreement and based on the limitations described in the IRC. The employees' benefits at retirement are based strictly upon the sum total of the contributions made and the investment result thereon.

Profit Taking—The act of selling stock, convertible securities and/or bonds that have appreciated in value to translate a paper profit into a realized gain. Often used to explain the reason for a market decline after a noticeable runup in prices.

Prohibited Group—Employees who are officers, shareholders or highly compensated. A qualified pension plan may not discriminate in favor of this group of employees.

Prohibited Transaction—
—With certain exceptions, a trustee or other plan fiduciary may not engage in any financial transaction with the employer or individuals in control of the employer (referred to as *parties in interest* under the regulatory provisions and as *disqualified persons* under the tax provisions) if he or she knows or should have known that such transaction is prohibited by ERISA. This includes the selling or leasing of property, the lending of money, the furnishing of goods, services or facilities, or the transfer of any assets to or for the use of a party in interest (or disqualified person). In addition, plans other than eligible individual account plans may not invest more than 10% of plan assets in the employer's securities and/or real property. A plan may not hold or acquire an employer security or employer real property that is not a "qualifying employer security" or "qualifying employer real property." See also Disqualified Person; Party in Interest; Self-Dealing.
—In regard to an IRA, any action that results in a constructive distribution from an IRA. According to the IRS, such actions are borrowing money from an IRA, selling property to an IRA or receiving unreasonable compensation for managing an IRA. The effect is a loss of favorable tax treatment.

Prohibited Transaction Exemption (PTE)—A statutory or administrative exemption that permits transactions between plans and parties in interest to occur that would otherwise be prohibited. In granting exemptions from the prohibited transaction rules, the DOL requires the exemption to be administratively feasible; in the interests of the plan, its participants and beneficiaries; and protective of the rights of the plan's participants and beneficiaries.

Projected Benefit Obligation (PBO)—The present value of accrued benefits for a defined benefit plan, assuming no future service but anticipating salary increases; a required disclosure under FAS 87. See also Accumulated Benefit Obligation (ABO).

Projected Benefits—Those pension plan benefit amounts that are expected to be paid at various times under a particular set of actuarial assumptions, taking into account such items as the effect of advancement in age and past and anticipated future compensation and service credits. That portion of an individual's projected benefit allocated to service to date, determined in accordance with the terms of a pension plan and based on future compensation as projected to retirement, is called the *credited projected benefit*.

Proprietorship—A form of business organization in which a single owner has total control over his or her own business and makes all the management decisions.

Proration—The adjustment of benefits paid because of a mistake in the amount of the premiums paid or the existence of other insurance covering the same accident or disability.

Prospective Future Service Benefit—That portion of a participant's retirement benefit that relates to his or her period of credited service to be rendered after a specified current date.

Prospective Pricing—Setting a specific, total all-inclusive price for a service prior to the delivery of the service, often on a DRG basis (usually established by the plan or payer and not by the provider, but may be the result of negotiation).

Prospective Review—Requires the granting of authorization for payment *before* medical care is provided.

Prospectus—A legal document setting forth the complete history and current status of a security issue, which must be made available to all interested purchasers in advance of a public offering under the Securities Act of 1933.

Protected Health Information—See Electronic Protected Health Information (ePHI).

Protocols—Step-by-step guidelines for treatment of a specific condition after a diagnosis has been made. The purpose of protocols is to establish minimum standards for services to obtain the best overall outcome in the majority of cases. See also Practice Guideline.

Prototype Plan—A standardized plan, approved and qualified as to its concept by Internal Revenue Service, that is made available by insurance companies, banks and mutual funds for the use of employers. See also Master Plan.

Provident Fund (International Benefits)—A saving plan in which accumulations of employee and employer contributions are generally paid out in a lump sum when a vested employee ceases active employment.

Provider—Individual or organization whose primary source of income is derived from the provision, administration or financing of health services, or from research or teaching in the health field.

Provider Sponsored Organization (PSO)—Health care delivery network owned and operated by physicians and hospitals that provides services under contract to employers and insurers.

Provincial Government Plan—See Medicare (Canada).

Proxy—A written authorization given by a shareholder to someone else to vote his or her shares at a stockholders annual or special meeting called to elect directors or for some other corporate purpose.

Proxy Statement—Required SEC filing for a publicly traded company that notifies shareholders of the company's annual (or any special) meeting, transmits information about matters that will be voted upon by shareholders at the meeting (including election of directors), and encloses a ballot for voting.

Prudent Expert Act—A revision to the *prudent man rule* required by ERISA to guide managers of pension and profit-sharing portfolios: The manager must act as someone familiar with matters relating to the management of money, not just prudence. See also Prudent Man Rule.

Prudent Investor Rule—Part of developing fiduciary prudence evaluation, this term differs from the traditional *prudent man rule*. It indicates no asset is automatically imprudent but must meet the needs of the trustees; the entire portfolio is viewed when evaluating fiduciary prudence; and certain action can be delegated to other agents or fiduciaries. ERISA Section 404(a)(1)(C) generally follows the prudent investor rule. See also Prudent Man Rule.

Prudent Layperson Standard—Determines when an emergency medical condition exists and services for the condition qualify for emergency insurance coverage. An *emergency medical condition* is characterized by acute symptoms such as severe pain, such that a prudent layperson with average knowledge of health and medicine would expect the lack of medical attention to result in placing the health of the victim in serious jeopardy. See also Emergency Medical Condition.

Prudent Man Rule/Prudent Person Rule—
—A common law standard applicable to the investment of trust funds. Briefly stated:

All that can be required of a trustee in the investment of trust funds is that he conduct himself faithfully and exercise sound discretion. He is to observe how men of prudence, discretion and intelligence manage their own affairs, not in regard to speculation, but in regard to the permanent disposition of their funds, considering the probable income as well as the probable safety of the capital to be invested. (International Foundation *Trustees Handbook*)

—According to ERISA, a fiduciary must act "with the care, skill, prudence, and diligence under the circumstances then prevailing that a prudent man acting in a like capacity and familiar with such matters would use in the conduct of an enterprise of a like character and with like aims." (Section 404(a)(1).)

—An investment standard adapted by the majority of states that allows a fiduciary to invest in only those securities which would be acquired by prudent men of discretion and intelligence who are seeking a reasonable return and preservation of their capital. Some states have a legal list published by the superintendent of banking to which savings banks, trust funds and similar institutions must adhere. See also Fiduciary.

PS 58 Costs—Refers to the law that determines annual cost of current life insurance protection provided by a retirement plan that is includable in the participant's taxable income.

Public Employee Retirement System (PERS)— An organization providing a formal program of retirement benefits for employees of states, provinces or their political subdivisions. See also CalPERS.

Public Offering—The sale of stocks and bonds, which have been registered with government agencies, to the public.

Public Sector Plan (Canada)—An employment pension plan offered by an employer in the public sector, covering civil servants, teachers, municipal employees, etc.

Punitive Damages; Exemplary Damages—Damages awarded by a court over and above compensatory damages because of the wanton, reckless, malicious or oppressive character of the acts committed by the wrongful party. Intended to punish or "make an example of" the wrongdoer.

Purchaser—Program sponsor, often an employer or union, that contracts with a benefits organization to provide benefits to an enrolled population.

Purchasing Power—The goods and services that can be purchased with a given amount of money. Inflation is reflected in loss of purchasing power of currency. For example, if it takes $2 to pay for goods and services that formerly cost $1, the purchasing power of the dollar has been cut in half.

Purchasing Power Risk—The risk that an investment will lose its buying power due to high levels of inflation.

Pyramiding—
—In stock and commodity market terminology, the practice of using unrealized paper profits to make additional purchases on margin.
—As related to financial statements, the practice of creating a highly leveraged capital structure by which only a relatively small amount of stock in the parent company controls a large number of subsidiary or related companies. Sometimes associated with conglomerates.
—An illegal form of selling in which franchise agreement are sold to operators, along with stocks of the goods to be sold. The goods are then sold on down a distribution and sales

chain. The distributors make the most money, but the commissions earned by the salespeople are unlikely to pay back their investments made in the stock.

Q

Qualification Period (Canada)—The period of time between the beginning of a disability and the start of a policy's benefits. Called a *waiting period* in the United States.

Qualification Requirement—The rules and regulations, issued in order to determine whether a proposed pension or profit-sharing plan will be fully deductible for tax purposes.

Qualified Beneficiary—
—An active employee, former employee and his or her spouse and dependents who are eligible for continuation coverage under COBRA because of their status on the day before a qualifying event.
—An individual covered by a group health plan, or a dependent of such an individual, as of the day before a qualifying event takes place.

Qualified Benefits—Employer-provided benefits that are nontaxable; that is, the employee may exclude the cost from federal income tax calculation. Nontaxable benefits that can be included in a cafeteria plan: group term life insurance, accident and health insurance, dependent care assistance and cash or deferred arrangements.

Qualified Cash or Deferred Arrangement—See Section 401(k).

Qualified Cost—The limit on an employer's tax deduction for contribution to a welfare benefit fund. It equals the fund's qualified direct cost and permitted additions to a qualified asset account, minus the fund's after-tax income for the taxable year.

Qualified Deferred Compensation Plan—A deferred compensation plan is qualified, or tax exempt, if it provides contributions or benefits for nonexecutive employees that are proportionate to those provided for executives.

Qualified Disability Benefit—A disability benefit provided by a plan that does not exceed the benefit that would be provided if the participant separated from service at normal retirement age.

Qualified Domestic Relations Order (QDRO)—A domestic relations order is a judgment, decree or order (including an approval of property settlement agreement) that (1) relates to the provision of child support, alimony payments or marital property rights to a spouse, former spouse, child or other dependent of a participant and (2) is made pursuant to a state domestic relations law (including a community property law). A domestic relations order is a qualified domestic relations order if it creates or recognizes the existence of an alternate payee's right, or assigns to an alternate payee the right, to receive all or a portion of the benefits payable to a participant under a plan, specifies required information and does not alter the amount or form of plan benefits. An alternate payee is a spouse, former spouse, child or other dependent of a participant who is recognized by a domestic relations order as having a right to receive all, or a portion of, the benefits under a plan with respect to the participant. See also Assignment of Benefits.

Qualified Employee—An employee who works more than 30 hours per week or 120 hours per month. Qualified employees usually receive benefits, including health insurance, while temporary, seasonal or part-time employees do not.

Qualified Impairment Insurance—A form of substandard or special class insurance, which restricts benefits for the insured person's particular condition.

Qualified Joint and Survivor Annuity (QJSA)—An annuity from a pension plan that runs for the life of the participant, with a survivor annuity for the life of the spouse not less than 50% nor more than 100% of the annuity payable for their joint lives, and that is the actuarial equivalent of a single annuity for the life of the participant. See also Joint and Survivor Annuity.

Qualified Matching Contributions (QMACs)—Matching contributions that are 100% vested at all times and that are subject to the same restrictions on distributability as elective contributions. QMACs may be treated as elective contributions for ADP testing if they are from plans with the same plan year and meet certain requirements.

Qualified Medical Child Support Order (QMCSO)—A judgment, decree or order that (1) is issued by a court of competent jurisdiction pursuant to a state domestic relations law or community property law; (2) creates or recognizes the right of an alternate recipient to receive benefits under his or her parent's employer's group health plan; and (3) includes certain information relating to the participant and alternate recipient.

Qualified Medicare Beneficiary (QMB)—A person whose income falls below 100% of federal poverty guidelines, for whom the state must pay the Medicare Part B premiums, deductibles and copayments.

Qualified Nonelective Contributions (QNECs)—Nonelective contributions that are 100% vested at all times and that are subject to the same restrictions on distributability as elective contributions. QNECs may be treated as elective contributions for ADP testing or as matching contributions for ACP testing if they are from plans with the same plan year and meet certain requirements.

Qualified Plan—Commonly refers to plans established under Sections 401(k), 401(a) or 403(b) or any retirement plan that meets IRS criteria that allow employers to deduct pension costs as a business expense and defer current income tax on its earnings, and allow employees to defer income tax on the employer's contributions and savings.

Qualified Preretirement Survivor Annuity (QPSA)—If a pension plan participant dies before starting pension benefits, the surviving spouse receives this type of annuity. Amount of QPSA depends on type of plan and age of participant at death. See also Automatic Survivor Coverage.

Qualified Professional Asset Manager (QPAM)—A bank, savings and loan, insurance company or registered investment adviser satisfying certain equity capital, net worth or total assets of managed funds requirements.

Qualified Retirement Annuity—A tax-deductible investment product typically purchased through insurance companies using employer contributions; used in lieu of a company pension plan.

Qualified Total Distribution—One or more distributions that (1) constitute lump-sum distributions; (2) are made within one taxable year to the employee because of termination of the plan or, in

118

the case of a profit-sharing or stock bonus plan, complete discontinuance of plan contributions; or (3) constitute a distribution of accumulated deductible contributions.

Qualifying Event—An occurrence entitling a person to elect continuation coverage under COBRA, such as termination of employment (or a reduction in hours), death of a covered employee, divorce or legal separation, a covered employee's eligibility for Medicare, a dependent child's loss of dependent status, or loss of coverage due to the employer's filing of a bankruptcy proceeding.

Quality Assurance—A specific process within health plans that examines the services the patient has received to see that they were of high standard, and reviews and fixes problems in patient care or other parts of the health care system.

Quality of Care—Refers to the degree of success by which a medical provider increases the probability of desired patient outcomes and reduces the likelihood of undesired patient outcomes, given the state of medical knowledge. Quality of care is dependent on the training, credentialing and experience of medical providers. Measurements for quality of care can include preventive services, death rates, surgery rates, inpatient stays, outpatient utilization, use of drug therapies and survival rates for catastrophic illness.

Quality Review Committee—A committee established by a professional organization or institution to assess and/or assure quality. Unlike peer review committees, it can function on its own initiative on a broad range of topics.

Quarters of Coverage (QC)—The basic unit of measurement for determining Social Security coverage. A QC is one-fourth of a year, or three months. The number of QCs during which an individual must earn enough money to receive credit toward Social Security eligibility depends on the individual's age; 40 is the maximum number required.

Quebec Pension Plan—See Canada Pension Plan/ Quebec Pension Plan (CPP/QPP) (Canada).

Quick Assets—Those assets consisting of cash or the equivalent and receivables due within one year (i.e., current assets) minus inventories.

Quick Assets Ratio—See Acid Test Ratio.

Quitclaim Deed—Used to release any present interest the grantors might have in the property. Quitclaim deeds are used extensively to clear from the title any clouds or defects when the County Recorder's office indicates that some person other than the record owner might be able to prove some claim to or interest in the property.

Quotation—Often shortened to "quote." The highest bid to buy and the lowest offer to sell a security in a given market at a given time.

R

Rabbi Trust—So named because one of the first was created for a rabbi. Under this nonqualified arrangement, the employer sets aside money specifically for payment of excess pensions or deferred pay. Employer takes no tax deduction, and the beneficiaries pay no tax on contributions to the trusts until they start receiving their money. Although funds are subject to employer's creditors, they are unaccessible to present and future management. Rabbi trusts are often used for executives and key employees.

Radiation Therapy—Use of ionizing radiation in the treatment of cancer patients, such service being provided by a radiation therapist or a physician qualified in therapeutic radiology.

Range—
—(Compensation) In reference to a pay grade, the amount by which the maximum pay exceeds the minimum pay.
—(Investments) The difference between the highest and lowest prices recorded during a given trading season, week, month, etc.

Range Penetration—The level of an individual's pay compared to the total pay range (rather than compared with midpoint, as in compa-ratio). See also Compa-Ratio.

Rate—
—(Insurance) The cost of one unit of a specific type of insurance.
—(Investments) The ratio of interest earned to the principal during a period of time. It is gener-

ally expressed as a percentage and is one of the factors used in computing interest.

—(Compensation) Money paid to an employee per hour.

Rate of Interest—The charge made by a borrower to a lender for use of the latter's money, expressed as a percentage upon the principal and usually in terms of one year's charges—unless otherwise stated. Thus, if the interest rate is 5%, $5 is paid for the annual use of $100.

Rate of Return—The yield obtainable on a security based on its purchase price (yield to maturity) or its current market price (current income return).

Rated Policy—A policy issued to cover a person classified as a substandard risk. The policy's premium rate is higher than the rate for a standard policy or the policy is issued with special limitations or exclusions or both. Sometimes called an *extra risk policy.*

Rating—The process that determines how much a particular package of benefits will cost and what will be charged (premium) to cover those expected costs for a specific group of people. See also Community Rating; Experience Rating.

Ratio Test—The requirement that the percentage of nonhighly compensated employees covered by a plan be at least 70% of highly compensated employees covered. One of the IRS minimum coverage tests.

Real Estate—Equity ownership in land, buildings and improvements. Ownership by employee benefit funds can be directly held or indirectly held through participation in commingled accounts, mutual funds, investment trusts or limited partnerships.

Real Estate Investment Trusts (REITs)—Companies that invest in income-producing real estate such as apartments, shipping centers and office buildings. Investors can own a fractional interest in these companies by purchasing REIT shares on the major stock exchanges. REITs are required to distribute (or pass through) 90% of their income in the form of dividends.

Real Income—
—Money income measured in terms of purchasing power; inflation-adjusted income.
—Commodities and services a person receives in kind, plus what can be purchased with his or her monetary income.

Real Interest Rate—The nominal interest rate minus the rate of inflation.

Real Rate of Return—The return achieved by the fund after adjusting for the change in general prices of goods and services in the economy. Greater purchasing power for a fund results from a positive real rate of return; less purchasing power results from a negative real rate of return. The production of a real rate of return, over the longer term, can assist in providing retirement benefits at levels that are competitive to the increase in the cost of living. See also Nominal Return.

Real Terms—How purchasing power is affected by inflation.

Real Wages—See Real Income.

Reasonable Accommodation—Under the ADA, this may include: (a) making existing facilities used by employees readily accessible to and usable by individuals with disabilities; and (b) job restructuring, part-time or modified work schedules, reassignment to a vacant position, acquisition or modification of equipment or devices, appropriate adjustment or modifications of examinations, training materials or policies, the provision of qualified readers or interpreters, and other similar accommodations for individuals with disabilities.

Reasonable and Customary (R&C) Charge—The prevailing charge made by physicians of similar expertise for a similar procedure in a particular geographic area. See also Usual, Customary and Reasonable (UCR) Fees.

Reasonable Care—The care that prudent persons would exercise under the same circumstances.

Reasonableness of Compensation—Compensation and fringe benefits paid to an employee (or former employee) are deductible as ordinary and necessary business expenses to the extent that such payments and the cost of such benefits represent overall compensation for services rendered.

Rebalancing—The process of adjusting an asset allocation whenever market activity has caused it to deviate from its target policy. The decision to rebalance a portfolio can be made on a calendar basis or a contingency basis.

Receivership—A situation where the bankruptcy laws apply; usually arises from the inability of the company to meet its obligations as they are due. A U.S. district court appoints a receiver who operates the company under the court's direction until a more permanent disposition of the matter is agreed to by all parties at interest. See also Bankruptcy.

Recertification—See Continued Stay Review (CSR).

Recession—The downward phase of a normal business cycle that follows prosperity and precedes a depression. Usually, unemployment rises, business slows and the standard of living falls. It is the opposite of recovery, which follows a depression and precedes prosperity. See also Business Cycle.

Recharacterization—A mechanism that treats excess contributions as employee contributions in order to correct an ADP test that does not meet the requirements of the law. When the contribution ratios of highly compensated employees need to be reduced, the excess elective contributions are treated as after-tax employee contributions and the excess is included in the employees' gross income or distributed to them.

Recidivism (Health Care)—A relapse requiring readmission to a facility or program.

Reciprocal Agreement; Reciprocity—An agreement between multiemployer plans, under which service with any signatory to the agreement will be recognized for purposes such as (1) satisfying minimum service requirements for plan participation; (2) fulfilling minimum service requirements for benefit entitlement; (3) preventing a break in continuous service; or (4) accumulating benefit credits. Two principal types are the *pro rata agreement,* under which each plan pays its proportionate share of pension benefits, and the *money-follows-the-man agreement,* under which employer contributions are remitted to the participant's home or terminal fund, which then pays the full retirement benefit.

Reciprocity (Medical)—The right of a member of a group health plan, temporarily away from home, to receive necessary medical care from a group health plan in the area the member is visiting.

Recognition Program—A program of acknowledging employee contributions after the fact, usually without predetermined goals or performance expectations. Examples include giving employees gifts on milestone anniversaries, granting an extra personal day for perfect attendance or paying a one-time cash bonus for making a cost-saving suggestion. Also known as *service awards.*

Recordkeeping—The tracking of employer and employee contributions, investment gains and losses, and dividend distributions. Includes the accompanying technology systems that support delivery of plan information to both participants and sponsors.

Recurring Clause—
—A provision in some health insurance policies that specifies a period of time during which the recurrence of a condition is considered a continuation of a prior period of disability or hospital confinement.
—(Canada) Also known as a *recurrence clause.*

Red Circle Rate—An individual pay rate above the established range maximum assigned to the job grade. Usually the employee is not eligible for further base pay increases until the range maximum surpasses the individual pay rate.

Redeemable Bonds—Also known as *callable bonds.* May be paid at the option of the issuer during a specified period prior to maturity.

Redemption Fee—A charge levied when investors sell their mutual fund shares before a specified time, ranging from 30 days to two years; from 0.25% to the legal limit of 2%. Unlike contingent deferred sales charges, redemption fees go to the fund to compensate long-term investors for transaction costs incurred by short-term traders.

Redemption Price—
—The price at which a bond may be redeemed before maturity, at the option of the issuing company. Redemption value also applies to the price the company must pay to call in certain types of preferred stock.
—The price at which a mutual fund's shares are bought back (redeemed) by the firm.

Referee—A person to whom a cause pending in a court is referred by the court. Takes testimony, hears the parties and reports thereon to the court.

Referral—A formal request within managed care plans by the primary care doctor, to specialists, hospitals or other services, for additional care. Also an informal suggestion from one provider for the patient to see another provider. When used in a formal environment, having a qualified referral has a direct impact on who pays for the service and how much.

Referral Agency—An agency or institution to which a person is referred for continuing treatment by a primary health source, an employee assistance program, an employee benefit plan or another health institution. For employee assistance programs, this procedure may involve referring a person with a known condition to an agency or organization that may offer counseling and other treatment.

Refinancing—A situation arising in the event a company decides to retire existing securities by the issuance of new securities to save interest costs, consolidate debt or lengthen maturities, or some combination of these three goals.

Reflation—Restoration of deflated prices to a desirable level.

Refund Annuity—A form of annuity under which any excess contributions and interest over the total of annuities actually paid are refunded after the annuitant's death to a designated beneficiary of his or her estate. Two types are *cash refund annuity* (unliquidated purchase price is refunded in a lump sum at the time of the annuitant's death) and *installment refund annuity* (monthly payments are continued to the beneficiary until the full cost has been received).

Refunding—The redemption of an obligation on or before its maturity in order to reduce the fixed interest charge, reduce the amount of fixed payment or postpone payment, due to inability to conveniently liquidate an indebtedness when it matures.

Regional Fund—A mutual fund that invests in the securities of just one country, such as Japan or Germany, or of just one geographical region, such as Southeast Asia, the Pacific Rim, Latin America or Europe.

Regionalization—The concept of shared facilities and resources for maximizing health care services.

Registered Bond—A bond that is registered on the

books of the issuing corporation in the owner's name and negotiable only when endorsed by the registered owner. Most bonds held by pension funds are in the nominee name of a bank or in a street name held by a broker to make them readily negotiable and to simplify the collection of interest. The opposite of bearer bond.

Registered Education Savings Plan (RESP) (Canada)—A plan that allows a contributor, on a tax-deferral basis, to accumulate assets on behalf of a beneficiary for the purpose of obtaining a post-secondary education.

Registered Home Ownership Savings Plan (RHOSP) (Canada)—A trusteed arrangement registered under Section 146.2 of the Income Tax Act whereby, subject to prescribed maximums, a resident Canadian taxpayer makes tax deductible contributions to the trust for the purpose of providing an amount that is to be used by the beneficiary for the purpose of purchasing an owner-occupied home for the beneficiary or his or her spouse, neither of whom, whether separately or jointly in the year (in which application is made for the plan) or the immediately preceding year, owns or has owned any interest in an owner-occupied home.

Registered Investment Adviser—An individual or organization that has filed with the Securities and Exchange Commission in order to provide investment advice or financial planning, or both, to clients for a fee.

Registered Pension Plan (RPP) (Canada)—An employer-sponsored pension plan that meets certain criteria and is registered for purposes of the federal Income Tax Act. Usually funded through contributions by both employees and employers. Contributions to RPPs are tax-deductible and distributions from the plans are taxable. Defined benefit pension plans provide a pension that is generally calculated on the basis of earnings and years of service. Money purchase (defined contribution) plans provide whatever pension income that accumulated from the contributions and income earned from those invested funds.

Registered Retirement Income Funds (RRIFs) (Canada)—Funds established at financial institutions and registered under the Income Tax Act that provide retirement income to individuals. Monies are directly transferred from RRSPs or lump-sum payments from RPPs. Amounts withdrawn from

RRIFs are taxable. A minimum amount must be withdrawn annually, beginning in the year after the RRIF is established.

Registered Retirement Savings Plan (RRSP) (Canada)—A voluntary individual retirement plan funded with an individual's own earnings. Contributions to an RRSP are tax-deductible and investment income is tax free until withdrawn. (Similar to an IRA in the United States.)

Registration (Securities)—Before a public offering may be made of new securities by a company or of outstanding securities by controlling stockholders—through the mails or in interstate commerce—the securities must be registered under the Securities Act of 1933. The registration statement is filed with the SEC by the issuer. It must disclose pertinent information relating to the company's operations, securities, management and purpose of the public offering. Securities of railroads under jurisdiction of the Interstate Commerce Commission, and certain other types of securities, are exempted. On security offerings involving less than $300,000, less information is required. Before a security may be admitted to dealings on a national securities exchange, it must be registered under the Securities Exchange Act of 1934. The application for registration must be filed with the exchange and the SEC by the company issuing the securities. It must disclose pertinent information relating to the company's operation, securities and management.

Registration of Plans—
—All plans subject to the vesting requirements of ERISA must register with the IRS annually. Thus, plans that are not qualified for tax purposes, as well as those that are qualified, must register. The registration statement that the administrator of the plan is required to file is intended to inform the IRS of plan participants with vested deferred benefits who were separated from service during the plan year. The registration statement must contain the nature, amount and form of vested deferred benefits to which the separated employees were entitled. Each separated employee is entitled to a statement of his or her vested deferred benefits, and evidence that he or she has been provided with such statement must accompany the registration statement.
—A plan administrator who is required to file a registration statement is also required to inform the IRS of any changes in the status of the plan at such times as the regulations specify. Changes that must be reported are (1) change in plan name, (2) change in name or address of the administrator, (3) termination of the plan and (4) merger or consolidation of the plan with another plan or division of it into two or more plans.

Rehabilitation—
—Services and facilities patients use as part of recovering from an accident or illness.
—Restoration of a totally disabled person to a meaningful occupation.
—A provision in some long-term disability policies that provides for continuation of benefits or other financial assistance while a totally disabled insured is retraining or attempting to resume productive employment.

Reimbursement Account—See Flexible Spending Accounts (FSAs).

Reinstatement—The resumption of coverage under a policy that has lapsed.

Reinsurance—An added level of coverage purchased by a self-funded employer, at-risk managed care plan or another insurance company to protect against a payout of claims in excess of a designated limit, to protect themselves from major losses or catastrophic claims. See also Stop-Loss Insurance.

Reinvestment Risk—The risk that investors will not be able to earn the same interest on an investment that they earn today. Applies primarily to bonds.

Reliance—Assurance from the IRS that an employer's plan is qualified under the IRC. Standardized plans receive automatic reliance; nonstandardized plans must apply for a Determination Letter.

Relief—The thing sought by a plaintiff in a lawsuit; usually whatever it is that would make the plaintiff whole or at least compensate for the injury.

Relocation Services—Benefits offered by an employer to a current employee accepting an assignment in a new location. Examples include reimbursement for house-hunting expenses, household moving costs or interim travel expenses; or help in orienting to a new culture or learning a new language.

Remedy—The judicial means or court procedures by which legal and equitable rights are enforced.

Remembrance Fund—A fund, often organized by unions, that provides flowers or small gifts for employees or family members in the event of illness, termination, hospitalization or death. The fund is exempt from reporting for ERISA purposes.

Renegotiable Rate Mortgage (RRM)—Sometimes called a rollover mortgage. Features an interest rate that is renegotiated every three to five years. The rate can rise or fall by a maximum of half a percentage point a year. The total increase or decrease during the life of the mortgage is limited to five percentage points. Increases and decreases are based on an index linked to average mortgage rates.

Renewal—Continuance of coverage under a policy beyond its original term by the insurer's acceptance of a premium for a new policy term.

Repatriation—The process of making the transition from an overseas assignment to the home country.

Repetitive Motion Injury—A work-related disorder that develops over time as a result of worker exposure to ergonomic hazards. Includes hand, wrist and back discomfort and eyestrain. Also referred to as *cumulative trauma disorder.*

Replacement Ratio—The portion of preretirement earnings under any retirement plan that is replaced by benefits following retirement.

Reportable Event—An event that must be reported to the PBGC (usually within 30 days after its occurrence) unless expressly waived by the PBGC. Notice is required to allow the PBGC adequate time to protect the benefits of participants and beneficiaries. A reportable event includes (1) disqualification for tax purposes; (2) benefit decrease by amendment; (3) a decrease in participation to less than 80% of that at the start of the plan year; (4) an IRS Determination Letter indicating partial or complete plan termination; (5) failure to meet minimum funding standards; (6) inability to pay benefits when due; (7) a distribution to "a substantial owner"; (8) filing an actuarial statement with the IRS before a plan merger, consolidation, or the transfer of assets or the granting of an alternative method of ERISA compliance by the Department of Labor; or (9) any other event determined by the PBGC, including bankruptcy, insolvency, liquidation, dissolution or a change in the plan sponsor of a single employer plan with un-

funded, nonforfeitable benefits and 100 or more participants.

Reporting—Refers to government filing requirements by plan administrators. Reporting requirements include filing annual reports with IRS, filing annual premium reports with the PBGC, and making certain documents available for inspection by the DOL.

Repurchase Agreement—The sale of a money instrument such as a bond or CD, usually in large amounts (by a dealer or a bank to an investor), and the simultaneous repurchase of the same security at the same price. Although the trades occur simultaneously, the settlement dates (when money changes hands and interest begins) are different. The period between gives the investor a very short-term (usually one to ten days or two weeks) investment at an attractive rate of return. Repurchase agreements that allow banks to buy temporarily idle funds isolate the investor from market fluctuation because both the purchase and the results are done at a guaranteed rate that is mutually acceptable.

Request for Proposal/Request for Information (RFP/RFI)—Two types of instruments used to solicit information from vendors interested in supplying a service. Includes services for employee benefit plans such as accounting, auditing, administration, investment consulting, computer systems, health care and legal counsel. Plan trustees prepare a list of specifications based on their goals, identify appropriate guidelines, solicit bids and proposals from candidates, conduct interviews regarding candidates' qualifications, check references, discuss fees and choose the provider accordingly.

Required Distributions—
—Payments that must be made once a participant reaches age 70½ or retires (whichever is later); they are calculated to span his or her life expectancy.
—When a participant dies, the payments that must be made to the beneficiary.

Reserve—A sum set aside by an insurance company or self-funded plan to assure the fulfillment of commitments for future claims.

Reserve Requirements—The ratio of funds to deposits that banks and other institutions have to keep in their vaults. This ratio varies with the size of the bank's deposits. The Federal Reserve stipulates what these ratios must be. Changes in reserve requirements are used by the Federal Reserve to influence monetary conditions. If the Federal Reserve wants to make money and credit easier to obtain, it lowers reserve requirements; if a tightening of monetary conditions is desired, the reserve requirements are raised.

Reserves—Represent claims against, or deductions from, assets in the balance sheet and are established to reduce or revalue assets to identify the existence of liabilities and to earmark a part of surplus for some future use.

Residential Care Facility—A facility that provides custodial care to persons who—because of their physical, mental or emotional condition—are not able to live independently.

Residential Treatment Center (RTC)—A term generally used for residential centers used to provide mental health treatment.

Residual Disability Benefits—A provision in an insurance policy that provides benefits in proportion to a reduction of earnings as a result of disability, as opposed to the inability to work full time.

Resource-Based Relative Value Scale (RBRVS)—A classification system to pay providers for Medicare services based on the time, training, skill and other factors required to deliver various services. Used initially by Medicare, but has influenced other sectors to more properly assess the skill and resource relationships to specific CPT codes, thereby dictating reimbursement levels.

Respite Care—Services provided to the primary caregiver to allow him or her to take temporary periods of relief or rest from caring for a sick or elderly person. Can be provided by a home health agency or another state-licensed facility and may be reimbursable under a long-term care policy.

Respondeat Superior—Literally, "Let the master respond." Refers to the legal doctrine of vicarious liability, which holds an employer liable for employees' negligent actions while on the job.

Restricted Stock Plan—An executive is given stock or allowed to buy it at a discount. He or she may not sell or transfer it until a certain period of time has elapsed, usually four or five years. The executive receives the dividends, but if he or she leaves the organization before the end of the restriction period, the stock usually is forfeited.

Restructuring—Describes a variety of activities, including writeoffs, debt-for-equity swaps and reorganizations. The common denominator is dramatic change within the corporation. Although there may be long-term benefits, the objective is usually short term. In many situations, the goal has been to ward off would-be suitors.

Retained Earnings—Profits added to a company's capital after dividends and taxes are paid.

Retention—
—The portion of the premium retained by an insurer to cover the cost of risk, expense charges, profit or a contribution to surplus.
—Net retention plus any amounts of other reinsurance permitted under the reinsurance contract.

Retired Life Fund—See Annuity Purchase Fund.

Retired Lives Reserve Insurance (RLR)—Tax-favored application of group term life insurance by which an employer may provide employees with substantial postretirement insurance through several funding mechanisms.

Retiree Medical Account—A separate account that is contained in a pension or annuity plan, providing health benefits subordinate to the plan's retirement benefits.

Retiree Medical Plans—Generally, group-sponsored medical plans that are integrated with Medicare and are not scheduled or Medicare supplement policies.

Retirees—The group of plan participants that includes retired employees, their beneficiaries and covered dependents.

Retirement Allowance—A series of payments, usually for life, payable monthly or at other specified intervals. The term is used to describe the entire benefit payable, including both the annuity derived from the participant's accumulated contributions and the pension financed by the employer's contributions.

Retirement Allowance (Canada)—An amount paid

by an employer to an employee (or former employee) upon retirement from office or service in recognition of long service or in respect of loss of office or employment.

Retirement Annuity—An insurance term describing a contract where there is no element of pure insurance. The death benefit would be the larger of the reserve or the premium paid, without interest.

Retirement Benefits—See Pension.

Retirement Bonus Plan—See Life Cycle Pension Plan.

Retirement Compensation Arrangement (Canada)—A funded supplementary pension arrangement that provides retirement benefits, but is not a registered pension plan.

Retirement, Compulsory—See Compulsory Retirement.

Retirement, Deferred—See Deferred Retirement.

Retirement, Early—See Early Retirement.

Retirement Equity Act of 1984 (REA)—
—A federal law that amended ERISA with the purpose of providing greater pension equity for women workers and surviving spouses. Established qualified domestic relations orders (QDROs).
—REA liberalizes ERISA participation, vesting and break-in-service requirements. The law requires these and other changes to be clearly communicated to employees.

Retirement Income—Income from pensions and other sources to which a retired person is entitled. May include both private and public pension payments, income from personal savings, government income supplements and imputed income.

Retirement, Normal Age—See Normal Retirement Age.

Retirement Plan—
—An overall plan intended to provide for all aspects of one's retirement, including medical care, travel, residence and budgeting.
—Any financial plan specifically designed to provide funds to cover expenses in one's retirement years.

—(Legal) A plan maintained by an employer or employee organization (such as a union) or both that is designed to provide employees with retirement income and that allows employees to defer receipt of income until the end of their employment or even later. See also Pension Plan.

Retirement Protection Act of 1994 (RPA)—Primary purpose was to strengthen PBGC. Key provisions include: raised minimum funding and liquidity requirements and PBGC variable premiums for underfunded plans; increased disclosures to participants and the PBGC; modified interest assumption limitation for lump-sum calculations; and rounded down cost-of-living adjustments. The law was passed as part of GATT to offset loss in tariff income. See also General Agreement on Tariffs and Trade (GATT); Uruguay Round Agreements Act of 1994.

Retroactive Benefits—Benefits granted in a plan amendment (or initiation) that are attributed by the pension benefit formula to employee services rendered in periods prior to the amendment. The cost of the retroactive benefits is referred to as *prior service cost*. See also Past Service Benefit.

Retroactive Rate Reduction—See Experience Refund.

Retrogressive Tax—See Locked In.

Retrospective Premium—Arrangement by which a policyholder agrees to pay an additional premium at the end of the contract year if claims and retention exceed paid premium.

Retrospective Rating—An insurance plan for which the premium is not determined until the completion of the coverage period, and is then based upon the plan's actual experience for that period, subject to a stated minimum and maximum, and providing for recovery of expense and administrative factors. See also Experience Rating.

Retrospective Reimbursement—The most common method of payment to health facilities, when payment is made after the services are rendered on the basis of costs incurred by the facility.

Return—The amount of money received annually from an investment, usually expressed as a percentage.

Return on Equity (ROE)—Return to stockholders measured by relating profits to equity of stockholders.

$$ROE = \frac{Net\ Profit\ After\ Tax}{Stockholder's\ Equity}$$

Return on Shareholders' Equity—See Return on Equity.

Return-to-Work Program—An employer-sponsored program of rehabilitation, job modification and monitoring to get disabled employees back to work as soon as possible.

Revalued Earnings (International Benefits)—Earnings that are adjusted, up or down, based on an index. Such indexes are provided by the government and use is mandated.

Revenue Anticipation Note—An obligation issued by a state or political subdivision to be redeemed by anticipated revenue when received.

Revenue Bonds—Bonds payable out of revenue from the operation of public facilities, or a special source of revenue, and not out of general tax collections. See also Municipal Bonds; Special Assessment Bonds; Tax-Exempt Securities.

Revenue Procedure—Issued by the IRS, it is somewhat similar to a Revenue Ruling but deals with procedural matters or details the requirements to be followed in connection with various dealings with the IRS. Revenue procedures also set forth (at times) guidelines that the IRS follows in handling certain tax matters.

Revenue Ruling—Issued by the IRS, these rulings express the views of the IRS about the tax results that apply to a specific problem.

Reverse Mortgage—A federally sponsored program enabling elderly home owners to meet living expenses by tapping the equity in their property. Mortgages offered by lenders are authorized to make FHA insured loans. Lender disburses money to home owner (borrower) in monthly checks or lump sums, and the borrower keeps the home. When borrower dies or vacates the home, he or she, or the heirs, pay off the debt by selling the property. Also known as *home equity conversion mortgage*.

Reverse Stock Split—Reducing the number of outstanding shares of corporate stock by exchanging one new share of stock for two or more old shares.

Reversion of Employer Contributions—A qualified plan (or trust) is prohibited from diverting corpus or income for purposes other than the exclusive benefit of employees. However, this prohibition does not preclude the return of a contribution made by an employer if the contribution was made, for example, by reason of a mistake of fact or conditioned on the qualification of the plan or the deductibility of the contribution.

Reversionary Annuity—A deferred annuity payable during the lifetime of a beneficiary only if the beneficiary survives a specified retiree.

Rewards System—A company's plan for cash and noncash motivational elements and the combination of its total compensation program used to support its business strategy.

Rider—A document that amends the policy or certificate. It may increase or decrease benefits, waive the condition of coverage, or in any other way amend the original contract. See also Endorsement.

Right of Direct Payment—A type of mandated benefit that requires a plan to pay for services not prescribed by a licensed physician (such as the services of a midwife).

Right-to-Work Laws—State laws that ban any form of compulsory union membership.

Rights of Participants—A participant or beneficiary cannot be discharged, fined, suspended, expelled or disciplined, or discriminated against for exercising any right under the regulatory provisions of ERISA or for giving information or testimony in an inquiry or proceeding relating to ERISA. Likewise, the interference with a participant's attaining of any right under the regulatory provisions of ERISA is prohibited. This provision is enforceable by investigation and civil suit.

Risk—
—(Investments) The chance that investments will not achieve the targeted return and result in financial loss. The level of risk an investor is willing to assume should be determined with the understanding that the higher the expected return,

the higher the risk. Types of risk include inflation, interest rate, exchange and political.

—(Insurance) A possible and real hazard that can result in a financial loss to the insured party. Insurance companies protect against various risks.

Risk Appraisal—See Underwriting.

Risk Aversion—The attitude of an investor who is not willing to accept increasing amounts of uncertainty about future investment returns without commensurate increases in the level of return anticipated. Another manifestation of this attitude is the investor who prefers less risk for the same rate of return expectation.

Risk Benefits (International Benefits)—Those benefits relating to the life and health of an employee, i.e., life insurance and so on. In many countries, a pension plan may also encompass the risk benefits—lump-sum benefit, widow's or orphan's income and so forth.

Risk Classification—The process by which a company decides how its premium rates for life insurance should differ according to the risk characteristics of individuals insured (e.g., age, occupation, sex, state of health) and then applies the resulting rules to individual applications. See also Underwriting.

Risk Factors—Conditions that influence a person's health and are capable of provoking ill health, including inherited or biological, environmental and behavioral risk factors.

Risk-Free Asset—Typically a noncallable, default-free bond such as a short-term government security. Although such an asset is not risk free in an inflation sense, it is (under the rationale that the government can always print money) risk free in a dollar sense.

Risk-Free Return—A theoretical return that is earned with perfect certainty; it is without risk. We approximate the risk-free return with 91-day Treasury bill yields.

Risk Load—A factor that is multiplied into the premium rate to offset some adverse parameter in the group.

Risk Management—The use of insurance and other techniques that minimize an organization's exposure to loss or injury.

Risk Pool—The population of individuals (or groups) across which costs for insured expenses are spread through premiums or other mechanisms.

Risk-Reward Spectrum—A construct used to illustrate that (in a rational marketplace) higher and higher anticipated rewards are always accompanied by incremental increases in risk (measured as the deviations between expected and actual results). The left end of the spectrum represents the lowest risk investment—typically short-term government obligations. Moving to the right on the spectrum—through a continuum of common stock investments—Each incremental increase in expected return is accompanied by an incremental increase in risk.

Risk Sharing—A method by which premiums and costs of medical protection are shared by plan sponsors and participants.

Rollover—The reinvestment in a qualified plan, IRA or Keogh plan of money or property received in a distribution from another qualified plan that meets certain requirements. If the reinvestment is made within 60 days of the distribution, federal income tax on the distribution is deferred until the benefits involved are finally distributed from the recipient plan. See also Unemployment Compensation Amendments of 1992.

Rollover Mortgage—See Renegotiable Rate Mortgage (RRM).

Roth IRA—A type of IRA created by the Taxpayer Relief Act of 1997. It is funded with aftertax dollars, and qualifying distributions are not taxed. Eligible individuals can contribute $3,000 a year ($3,500 if over the age of 50), and earnings can be withdrawn tax-free after five years, provided the individual is at least age 59½, is disabled or is using the money for a first-time home purchase.

Round Lot—A unit of trading or multiple thereof usually thought of as 100 shares of stock listed on the NYSE and 100,000 par value of bonds, particularly where institutions are concerned.

Rule of 72—A convenient technique for either mental or pencil and paper estimation of compound interest rates, derived from the fact that a 7.2% return per year is the interest rate that will double the value of an investment in ten years. Hence, "years to double" an investment with a given annual rate of return can be estimated by dividing the rate of return into 72.

S

Safe Harbor 401(k) Plan—A 401(k) plan exempt from nondiscrimination testing of elective and/or matching contributions in exchange for providing certain minimum levels of matching or nonelective contributions. Effective for plan years beginning after December 31, 1998.

Safe Harbor Rules—A series of guidelines set forth by the Department of Labor that, when fully complied with, may limit a fiduciary's liabilities. Safe harbor rules require:
1. The use of prudent experts
2. A due diligence process for selecting managers
3. Investment discretion be given to selected managers
4. Managers' acknowledgment of cofiduciary status in writing
5. Monitoring of the activities of selected managers.

Salaried Administrator—Person employed full time by the trustees of a multiemployer fund to provide administrative services.

Salary—Remuneration received by an employee and paid weekly, monthly or yearly as opposed to hourly pay. Usually applies to employees of higher levels with nonrepetitive jobs that may or may not be supervisory in nature. These positions are exempt from the Fair Labor Standards Act provisions, including overtime.

Salary Continuation Plan—A benefit option designed to provide some form of protection during disability. Also refers to a retirement plan for key employees where there is no qualified plan. See also Sick Leave; Supplemental Executive Retirement Plan (SERP); Workers' Compensation.

Salary Progression—Relates to the estimated rates at which compensation levels will increase in future periods. This assumption generally includes factors of inflation, the participant's share of productivity gains and merit and seniority increases.

Salary Reduction Plan—A qualified retirement plan that lets participants have a portion of their compensation (otherwise payable in cash) contributed pretax to a retirement account on their behalf. Also known as *cash or deferred arrangement (CODA),* examples include 401(k) plans (private sector employers), 403(b) plans (nonprofits and state and local government employers) and 457 plans (public sector). These plans are named for the section of the Tax Code that establishes the rules for them. See also Cash or Deferred Arrangement (CODA), 401(k) Plan, 403(b) Plan and 457 Plan.

Salary Reduction Simplified Employee Pension Plan (SARSEP)—An employee saving plan similar to a 401(k) plan that was available only to companies with 25 or fewer employees. Terminated by the SBJPA of 1996; existing SARSEPs can continue. See also Savings Incentive Match Plan for Employees (SIMPLE).

Salary Structure—The hierarchy of job grades and pay ranges established within a company. Salary structure may be expressed as job grades, job-evaluation points or policy lines.

Sallie Mae (SLMA)—Securities issued by the Student Loan Marketing Association.

Sarbanes-Oxley Act of 2002—The act first aims to redress accounting and financial reporting abuses, calling for major changes in corporate governance, internal financial controls and record managing rules for public traded and companies and public accounting firms. Another significant provision applies to *blackout periods,* when plan participants or corporation insiders cannot access their accounts because of insufficient information. Administrators of individual account plans must now notify participants 30 days in advance of any such blackout periods; and directors and executive officers (insiders) may not trade in any company stocks during a blackout if they acquired such stocks in connection with their employment. The act also contains changes to rules pertaining to executive compensation. This legislation was named for Senator Paul Sarbanes of Maryland and Congressman Mike Oxley of Ohio. See also Blackout Period.

Savings and Loan Association—A financial institution that is state or federally chartered and privately owned by the depositors or stockholders. Its prime functions are to furnish first mortgage loans on improved real estate and to provide government-insured, interest-bearing savings accounts.

Savings Bond—A U.S. security sold by the government that offers a fixed income with minimum risk and return. Interest accumulates over a designated period. See also Series EE Bond; Series HH Bond.

Savings Incentive Match Plan for Employees (SIMPLE)—A simplified retirement plan for small businesses (100 or fewer employees) created by the Small Business Job Protection Act of 1996. Employers avoid the administrative fees and paperwork required by plans such as 401(k)s. A SIMPLE plan can be structured like an IRA or a 401(k). See also Pension Simplification Act.

Savings Plan—See Thrift Plan.

SBJPA—See Small Business Job Protection Act of 1996 (SBJPA).

Schedule—A list of coverages or amounts concerning things or persons insured.

Scheme (International Benefits)—Frequently used interchangeably with *plan.*

S Corporation—A small business corporation in which the shareholders elect to be taxed like a partnership with profits and losses passing directly through to the shareholders. Income is not taxed at the corporate level. To be eligible, a corporation must meet certain requirements as to kind and number of shareholders, classes of stock and sources of income.

Second Country National—An employee from another country working in the country in which the company is based.

Second Injury Funds—Funds that reimburse employers for the difference between the total compensation benefits and the partial compensation benefits that would have been paid to a disabled employee, had he or she not been disabled previously while working for another employer.

Second Surgical Opinion Program (SSOP)—This cost-management strategy encourages or requires participants to obtain the opinion of another doctor after a physician has recommended that a nonemergency or elective surgery be performed. Programs may be voluntary or mandatory in that reimbursement is reduced or denied if the participant does not obtain the second opinion. Plans usually require that such opinions be obtained from board-certified specialists with no personal or financial interest in the outcome.

Secondary Care—Medical services provided by medical specialists that do not have first contact with patients. Usually secondary care involves inpatient hospitalization that does not require complex medical services or equipment. May also include ambulatory surgery services.

Secondary Payer—The insurance carrier that is second in responsibility under coordination of benefits. Often mentioned in the context of Medicare's efforts to recoup payments made as primary payer when other primary, duplicate coverage exists.

Secretary—The term *secretary* when used in connection with an employee welfare benefit plan or an employee pension plan refers to the secretary of labor.

Section 125 Plan—A plan in compliance with Section 125 of the IRC, which protects an employee from *constructive receipt* of the cash he or she has as a choice of benefits under a cafeteria plan. This means that employee contributions to a Section 125 plan may be made with pretax dollars. Also called *Flexible Benefit Plan.* See also Cafeteria Plan; Constructive Receipt; Flexible Benefit Plan.

Section 218 Agreements—Voluntary agreements between the state and the commissioner of Social Security that allow the states, if they so desire, to provide Social Security coverage for the services of state and local government employees.

Section 401(k)—Section of the IRC that allows profit-sharing and stock bonus plans to offer cash or deferred arrangements (CODAs) to participants. State and local governments are not eligible to maintain CODAs under 401(k) unless such a plan was adopted before May 6, 1986.

Section 403(b)—Extends tax-deferred defined contribution plans to public school employees, charities and other tax-exempt organizations. 403(b) plans, also called *tax-sheltered annuities* or *tax-deferred annuities,* are available to these employees. Contributions to the plans may be made by employers or employees. See also 403(b) Plan; Tax-Sheltered Annuity.

Section 404(c) (ERISA)—Section 404(c) of ERISA protects employers that offer defined contribution plans, such as 401(k) plans and other participant-directed plans, against liability for losses incurred by employees who make bad investment decisions, provided the employers meet certain requirements. Employers must provide at least three investment vehicles with different risk/return characteristics; allow transfers among investments at least quarterly; provide basic investment information to help participants make investment decisions; and provide information on the various investment options, including prospectuses, lists of plan assets in each investment fund, transaction fees charged to participant accounts and the identity of the fund manager. See also 404(c) Plan; Participant-Directed Plan; Self-Directed Investment.

Section 415 Limits—IRC Section 415 limits the contribution and/or benefit amount that retirement plans can provide to individual participants on a tax-deductible basis.

Section 423 Plan—See Stock Purchase Plan.

Section 457—Section of the IRC that allows employees of state and local governments to defer a portion of their income in a deferred compensation plan that is not taxable until a distribution is made. See also 457 Plans.

Section 501(c)(9)—See Voluntary Employees' Beneficiary Association (VEBA).

Section 529 Plan—See 529 Plan.

Sector Funds—Mutual funds that confine their investments to one economic or industrial sector (e.g., utilities or technology).

Secular Trust—So named to distinguish it from a rabbi trust. An irrevocable trust established for the exclusive purpose of holding assets to pay employees' nonqualified retirement and/or deferred compensation benefits. It has a design similar to that of a rabbi trust, but the assets contained within the trust are not subject to the claims of the company's general creditors in bankruptcy.

Securities Acts—Federal laws enforced by the Securities and Exchange Commission to protect investors; they include the Investment Advisers Act, Investment Company Act, Securities Act of 1933, Securities Exchange Act of 1934, Trust Indenture Act and Public Utilities Holding Company Act.

Securities and Exchange Commission (SEC)—
—An organization created by the Securities Exchange Act of 1934. The SEC is an independent bipartisan, quasi-judicial agency of the United States government. The laws administered by the commission relate in general to the field of securities and finance and seek to provide protection for investors and the public in their securities transactions.
—The SEC is charged with enforcing the Securities Acts.

Securities Lending—A practice whereby owners of securities either directly or indirectly lend their securities to primarily brokerage firms for a fee, and against which either cash, securities or a letter of credit is pledged to protect the tender.

Security—Any note, stock, Treasury stock, bond, debenture, evidence of indebtedness, certificate of interest or participation in any profit-sharing agreement, collateral trust certificate, preorganization certificate or subscription, transferable share, investment contract, voting trust certificate, certificate of deposit for security, fractional undivided interest in oil, gas or other mineral rights or, in general, any interest or instrument commonly known as a security, or any certificate of interest or participation in, temporary or interim certificate for, receipt for, guarantee of, or warrant or right to subscribe to or purchase any of the foregoing.

Security Incident—In HIPAA privacy rules, the attempted or successful unauthorized access, use, disclosure, modification or destruction of information or interference with system operations in an information system.

Security Measures—In the context of HIPAA privacy rules, all of the administrative, physical and technical safeguards in an information system.

Segregated Fund Contract (Canada)—Assets of a pension plan held by an insurance company for investment management only. Funds are segregated from the assets of the insurance company. The employer assumes responsibility for the adequacy of the fund, but also retains more control over the asset mix.

Self-Administered Plan—
—(Directly Invested or Trusteed) A plan funded through a fiduciary, generally a bank, but sometimes a group of individuals, that directly invests the funds accumulated. Retirement payments are made from the fund as they fall due. This term is used to designate a plan that is not funded through an insurance company.
—(Health Care) A plan administered by the em-

ployer or welfare fund without recourse to an intermediate insurance carrier. Some benefits may be insured or subcontracted while others are self-funded.

Self-Care—An approach or philosophy that sees the patient as the primary health care provider. Includes a variety of health education strategies that allow the patient to become skilled in self-diagnosis and treatment for 70-90% of symptoms. See also Demand Management.

Self-Correction Program (SCP)—One of the three IRS-sponsored programs making up the Employee Plans Compliance Resolution System (EPCRS), which allows sponsors to correct operational and plan document errors affecting their tax-qualified plans. SCP allows a plan sponsor that has established compliance practices and procedures to, at any time without paying any fee or sanction, correct insignificant operational failures under a qualified plan, provided the plan is established and maintained by an approved document. In certain cases, the plan sponsor may correct even significant errors without penalty. See also Correction on Audit Program (Audit CAP); Employee Plans Compliance Resolution System (EPCRS); Voluntary Correction Program (VCP).

Self-Dealing—Under ERISA, certain activities are prohibited for fiduciaries, including using plan assets for personal profit, taking bribes or kickbacks from someone who deals with the plan, or acting on behalf of a party whose interests are adverse to those of the plan.

Self-Directed Brokerage Account (SDBA)—An option under a 401(k) plan that allows contributors to invest in various additional mutual funds or stocks to provide greater investment flexibility. The administrator is usually a large financial institution, which charges a commission for transactions just as a broker would.

Self-Directed Investment—Any plan in which plan participants control the investment of their accounts. Also known as *participant-directed plans*. See also 404(c) Plan; Participant-Directed Plans.

Self-Employed Retirement Plan—See Keogh Plan.

Self-Funding—See Self-Insurance (Self-Funding).

Self-Insurance (Self-Funding)—A fully noninsured or

self-insured plan is one in which no insurance company or service plan collects premiums and assumes risk. In a sense, the employer is acting as an insurance company—paying claims with the money ordinarily earmarked for premiums. Regardless of the specific self-funding technique a firm chooses, it will need to either buy its administrative services (ASO) outside the company or develop them in-house. Hence, self-funded arrangements are referenced as ASO or self-administered.

There are two standard self-funding techniques that companies interested in this approach usually evaluate for appropriateness to their own situation: 501(c)(9) trust and disbursed self-funded plan. See also Disbursed Self-Funded Plan; 501(c)(9) Trust.

Self-Pay Option—Under some multiemployer health care plans, the opportunity offered to laid-off workers, or those with insufficient hours worked, to maintain eligibility for health benefits through the individual's payment of a premium, thus avoiding lapses in coverage. The self-pay premium frequently does not cover the costs of carrying such individuals, but represents a partial subsidy by the plan.

Self-Referral—
—The process whereby a patient seeks care directly from a specialist without seeking advice or authorization from the primary care physician.
—The practice of referring patients to clinics, laboratories or other medical facilities in which the physician is an investor.

Sensitivity—The degree to which a portfolio's fluctuations are more or less volatile than market fluctuations. See also Beta; Systematic Risk.

Separate Account—A fund established by a life insurance company. The fund is maintained separately from the insurance company's general assets and is generally used for investing pension assets. Allows greater choice of investment options.

Separate Line of Business (SLOB)—The separate line of business exception permits electing businesses that are part of a controlled group to ignore affiliates when testing retirement and dependent care plans for nondiscrimination, thereby treating each business as a stand-alone company for these purposes.

Serial Bonds—Bonds that mature in relatively small amounts at periodic stated intervals.

Serial Maturity—See Balloon Maturity.

Series EE Bond—A nonmarketable U.S. government savings bond that is issued at a discount from par. See also Savings Bond.

Series HH Bond—A nonmarketable interest-bearing U.S. government savings bond that is issued at par. See also Savings Bond.

Serious Mental Illness—As defined by the National Advisory Mental Health Council, includes disorders with psychotic symptoms such as schizophrenia, manic depressive disorder and autism, as well as severe forms of other disorders such as major depression, panic disorder and obsessive-compulsive disorder.

Service—Employment taken into consideration under a pension plan. Years of employment before the inception of a plan constitute an employee's past service; years thereafter are classified in relation to the particular actuarial valuation being made or discussed. Years of employment (including past service) prior to the date of a particular valuation constitute prior service; years of employment following the date of the valuation constitute future service; a year of employment adjacent to the date of the valuation, or in which such date falls, constitutes current service (included in future service).

Service Area—
—An approved area of operation for a managed care organization under either federal or state regulations.
—The geographic area from which a particular health care program draws the majority of its users. See also Catchment Area.
—The territory within certain boundaries that an HMO designates for providing services to members. It is generally believed that a member should not have to drive longer than 30 minutes in order to gain access to the system.

Service Awards—See Recognition Program.

Service Credits—See Credited Service.

Service Plan—A prepayment plan that guarantees to provide covered health care services to subscribers, as opposed to indemnifying expenses.

Service Provider—Any of the following who provide service to a benefit plan: persons, such as accoun-

tants, attorneys, enrolled actuaries, investment managers, trustees or other plan fiduciaries; entities, such as third-party administrators or insurance carriers.

Settlement—
—(Investment) An arrangement between brokerage houses for the payment or receipt of cash or securities. It represents the final consummation of a securities transaction and is handled through the stock clearing corporation.
—(Pension) An irrevocable action that relieves the employer (or the plan) of primary responsibility for a pension benefit obligation and eliminates significant risks related to the obligation and the assets used to effect the settlement. Examples of transactions that constitute a settlement include (1) making lump-sum cash payments to plan participants in exchange for their rights to receive specified pension benefits and (2) purchasing nonparticipating annuity contracts to cover vested benefits.

Severance Pay—A lump-sum benefit payable on termination of employment either in lieu of or in addition to a pension.

Sex Discrimination—Under the Civil Rights Act, gender may not be used, by and of itself, in any decision regarding employees. Under the Equal Pay Act, men may not be paid more than women for substantially similar jobs. Title XIX forbids gender discrimination in educational institutions.

Sexual Harassment—Unwelcomed sexual advances, requests for sexual favors or other verbal or physical conduct of a sexual nature, when (1) submission to such conduct is made either explicitly or implicitly a term or condition of an individual's employment or (2) submission to or rejection of such conduct by an individual is used as the basis for employment decisions affecting such individual. Violates the Civil Rights Act of 1964.

Share—One of the equal parts into which the capital stock of a corporation is divided. It represents the owner's proportion of interest in the company and is issued to the shareholder in the form of a stock certificate.

Shared Employee—When the services of an employee are shared by several professionals, corporations or partnerships, he or she may be considered a full-time employee of each employer, whereby contributions to each employer's pension plan must be based on the portion of compensation paid by each professional or corporation.

Shared Funding—See High Self-Insured Deductible (HSID).

Shareholder—An individual who owns shares of stock in a company or shares of a mutual fund. Also called *stockholder*. See also Stockholder.

Shareholder-Employee—In regard to a subchapter S corporation, a more-than-5% shareholder.

Shareholders' Equity—See Net Worth (NW).

Shoe Box Effect—When an indemnity plan has a deductible, there may be beneficiaries who save up their prescription drug or other receipts to file for reimbursement at a later time, but never actually file claims.

Short-Term Assignment (International Benefits)—An assignment that lasts over three months, but less than a year. Also known as *expatriate assignment*.

Short-Term Bond—A debt security with a holding period usually less than one year to maturity.

Short-Term Disability (STD)—Often considered to be a disability lasting usually not longer than two years.

Short-Term Disability Income Insurance—A provision to pay benefits to a covered disabled person as long as he or she remains disabled up to a specified period.

Short-Term Income Protection—See Unemployment Compensation.

Short-Term Investment Fund (STIF)—A collective investment fund consisting of highly liquid and readily marketable interest-bearing securities.

Short-Time Compensation—Prorated unemployment insurance for workers whose hours are reduced through a work-sharing plan.

Sick Leave—Plans that provide employees protection against short-term disability and typically specify a maximum number of benefit days per year or per disability that an employee may take at full pay

before insured short-term or long-term disability benefits are initiated.

Sidecar IRA—See Deemed IRA.

Side Fund—See Conversion Fund.

Significant Break in Coverage—Under HIPAA, a period of 63 consecutive days during which an individual does not have any creditable health care.

Significant Other—An individual who has an important impact on one's welfare, happiness or emotional security, such as spouse, lover, partner, parent, child, grandparent, daughter/son-in-law, friend or companion.

Silver Handshake—An early retirement incentive consisting of increased pension benefits for several years or a cash bonus.

Silver Parachute—A severance and benefit plan to protect nonexecutives if their firms are acquired by another firm.

SIMPLE Plans—See Savings Incentive Match Plan for Employees (SIMPLE).

Simplified Employee Pension Plan (SEP)—A SEP is a simplified alternative to a profit-sharing or 401(k) plan. A SEP is a pension plan to which contributions are made by the employer to an individual retirement account or annuity (IRA) established by an employee (subject to special rules on contributions and eligibility). As of January 1997, no new SEPs may be formed.

Single Employer Plan—A pension plan maintained by one employer. Also, the term may be used to describe a plan maintained by related parties such as a parent and its subsidiaries.

Single Life Annuity Plan—An employee's accrued benefit from mandatory contributions to a defined benefit plan that provides a benefit in the form of a single life annuity (without ancillary benefits) beginning at normal retirement age is the employee's accumulated contributions multiplied by a conversion factor. (Since the accrued benefit from voluntary contributions must be separately accounted for, it does not come into consideration.) Initially, the conversion factor is to be set at 10% for a normal retirement age of 65. The conversion factor for other normal retirement ages will be fixed by regulation.

An employee's accumulated contribution consists of (1) mandatory contributions; (2) interest, if any, on mandatory contributions to the end of the last year before the vesting rules are applicable; and (3) 5% compound interest on (1) and (2) after the vesting rules are applicable.

The interest rate and conversion factor mentioned above can be adjusted by the regulations.

Single Payer System—A centralized method of financing health care delivery through public funds, with the government acting as the only payer for health care services.

Single Premium Deferred Annuity (SPDA)—A deferred annuity purchased with one investment or premium.

Single Premium Funding Method—A method of funding whereby the cost of providing an insurance or pension benefit is paid in one lump sum. When the single premium is paid at retirement age for a life annuity, it is frequently referred to as terminal funding. See also Actuarial Cost Method.

Sinking Fund—Money set aside to pay for losses. This form of self-insurance is used by some businesses and individuals to cover a portion of certain losses.

Skill-Based Pay—A system for individual wage differentiation, based on the number of specified skills or tasks mastered by the job incumbent. Pay level is not dependent on whether any of the skills are utilized. See also Knowledge-Based Pay.

Skilled Nursing Care—Around-the-clock nursing and rehabilitative care that can only be provided by, or under the supervision of, skilled medical personnel.

Skilled Nursing Facility (SNF)—A care setting for patients who have chronic diseases or no longer require hospital care, but need 24-hour nursing care and other defined health care services.

Sliding Fee Scale—A fee schedule under which the fee charged the patient for services varies with the patient's ability to pay.

Small Business Job Protection Act of 1996 (SBJPA)—Federal legislation that raises the minimum wage 90 cents by September 1, 1997; contains significant changes to encourage small businesses to offer retirement plans; and offers ways for all employers to reduce nondiscrimination burdens and ease the ad-

ministration of qualified plans. The law allows tax-exempt organizations to offer 401(k) plans, requires multiemployer plans to use the same vesting standards as single employer plans, and simplifies the general definition of *highly compensated employees* for contribution limits. See also Pension Simplification Act.

Small Cap Funds—*Capitalization,* or *cap,* describes the value of a company in terms of its size. The figure is calculated by multiplying the current stock price of a company by the number of shares available for trading. For example, a company that currently trades its stock at $52 per share and has five million shares to sell has a market capitalization of $260 million. A small cap fund is one valued at less than $3 million. See also Large Cap Funds; Mid Cap Funds.

Small Welfare Plan—An employee welfare plan that covers fewer than 100 participants at the beginning of the plan year.

Social Insurance—A compulsory insurance program legislated to provide certain minimum economic protections or security for large groups of people, particularly those of low income.

Social Security—
—A federal program of old age and related benefits covering most workers and their dependents. Social Security benefits are provided by OAS-DHI. Programs are provided under the U.S. Social Security Act of 1935, plus amendments and additions thereto. Funded through a payroll tax paid by employers and employees.
—(Canada) Benefits arising from the Old Age Security Plan (which provides benefits for essentially all old age persons), the Canada and Quebec Pension Plans (which cover workers and their families), and other income support programs.
—(International Benefits) Used generally in reference to any government program providing economic security for portions of the public.

Social Security Benefits or Wage Base Increase Effects—ERISA prohibits reductions in private pension benefit payments to a retiree because of an increase in Social Security benefits or the wage base. In addition, ERISA prohibits a reduction of private plan benefits because of an increase in Social Security benefits or wage base where the employee was separated from the employer's service prior to retirement and has vested deferred rights to benefits under the plan.

Social Security Disability Insurance (SSDI)—Provides for subsidized payments to eligible workers who are unable to continue working.

Social Security Freeze—A long-term disability policy provision which establishes that the offset from benefits paid by Social Security will not be changed regardless of subsequent changes in the Social Security law.

Social Security Integration—See Integration With Social Security.

Social Security Retirement Age—The age at which unreduced Social Security benefits are payable. The Social Security retirement age for individuals born before 1938 is age 65; for those born 1938 through 1942, age $65\frac{2}{12}$ through $65\frac{10}{12}$; for those born 1943 through 1954, age 66; for those born 1955 through 1959, age $66\frac{2}{12}$ through $66\frac{10}{12}$; and for those born 1960 and after, age 67. See also Normal Retirement Age.

Socially Responsible Investments—Generally considered to include those investments that (1) carry a lesser rate of return and/or, (2) have a lower credit rating and quality and/or (3) have less liquidity or marketability than other forms of investment or specific investments readily available in the marketplace, but that will (1) create employment opportunities for plan participants and/or (2) have a greater social or moral quality.

Also includes "socially sensitive" investments that otherwise are equal to other investments when compared by traditional financial analysis, but have favorable noneconomic characteristics. Socially responsible investments are known as *divergent, target* and *political investments*.

See also Economically Targeted Investments (ETIs).

Soft Dollars—The portion of a plan's commissions expense incurred in the buying and selling of securities that is allocated through a directed brokerage arrangement for the purpose of acquiring goods or services for the benefit of the plan. In many soft dollar arrangements, the payment scheme is effected through a brokerage affiliate of the consultant.

Software—Computer programs and systems necessary to direct the hardware of a computer system and used to extend the capabilities of computers. *Hardware* refers to the physical (hard) components of the computer and its accessories.

Sole Proprietor—The owner of 100% of an unincorporated business. See also Proprietorship.

Solvency—In a pension plan, the ability of the plan to meet its present and future obligations; the adequacy of provisions for funding.

Special Assessment Bonds—Bonds made to cover the cost of improving facilities. Property owners who directly benefit from the improvements are assessed for the improvement with the assessment spread over a series of years. See also Municipal Bonds; Revenue Bonds; Tax-Exempt Securities.

Special Class Insurance—Insurance for applicants of health insurance who cannot qualify for a standard policy by reason of health.

Special Risk Insurance—Coverage for risks or hazards of a special or unusual nature.

Spend Down—Depleting income and assets to meet eligibility requirements for Medicaid. However, HIPAA imposed restrictions on this practice.

Spinoff—
—Division of an employee benefit plan into two or more separate plans.
—A divestiture in which the stock of a subsidiary is given to the parent company's stockholders.

Split Dollar Life Insurance—The employer and employee share in the expenses, equity and death benefits of the policy. See also Corporate Owned Life Insurance.

Split Funding—The use of two or more funding agencies for the same pension plan. In some cases, part of the contributions to the plan is paid to a life insurance company and the remainder is invested through a corporate trustee, generally in equities.

Sponsor—See Plan Sponsor.

Spousal Consent—Elections to waive QPSA and QJSA benefits and to elect some other form of benefit or to designate some other beneficiary are not valid unless the spouse of the participant consents in writing in the election.

Spousal Individual Retirement Account (Spousal IRA)—A trust or custodial account or subaccounts created for the exclusive benefit of an individual and his or her nonworking spouse. Such account or subaccounts also may be established by purchasing individual retirement annuities from an insurance company. Maximum contributions vary.

Stabilization Fund (International Benefits)—A fund established under a multinational pool with a loss-carry forward feature, which is to protect the carrier against excess losses. Also called a *contingency fund*.

Stable Value Funds—Usually the least risky investment options offered by 401(k) plans and other defined contribution plans. These funds allow participants to withdraw or transfer their funds without any market value risk or other penalty for early withdrawal.

Staff-Model HMO—A type of closed-panel HMO in which the physicians are employees of the HMO. The providers see members in the HMO's own facilities.

Stagflation—Stagnation in the economy accompanied by a rise in prices.

Stand-Alone Plan—A separate plan that provides benefits such as mental health or prescription drugs. See also Carve-Out.

Standard & Poor's 400—An index of the 400 industrial stocks that comprise the S&P 500.

Standard & Poor's 500 Stock Price Index (S&P 500)—A well-known gauge of stock market movements computed by Standard & Poor's Corporation and determined by the price action of a carefully selected list of 500 largest industrial issues, plus 20 transportation issues, 40 utilities and 40 finance issues.

Standard Deviation—Measures the total risk of an asset or a portfolio. This risk is defined as the normal variation of returns from an expected return. Standard deviation is a measure of the dispersion of a set of numbers around a central point. If the standard deviation is small, the frequency distribution is concentrated within a narrow range of values. For many distributions, about two-thirds of the observations will fall within one standard deviation of the mean.

Standard Rate—The pay rate for a job, based on job evaluations and/or job pricing.

Standard Risk—Average risk; a person who has an average or less-than-average likelihood of loss.

Standard Termination—A voluntary pension plan termination in which plan assets are sufficient to pay all vested and nonvested employee benefits.

Standardized Plan—A qualified prototype plan written to satisfy various tax qualification requirements under the Internal Revenue Code.

State Disability Plan—A plan for accident and sickness, or disability insurance required by state legislation of those employers doing business in that particular state. See also Temporary Disability Insurance (TDI).

State Earnings Related Pension Scheme (SERPS) (United Kingdom)—The second tier of the state pension scheme that provides an additional pension linked to one's earnings and paid at state pension age out of national insurance contributions.

Statutory Benefits—See Legally Required Benefits.

Statutory Reserve—In the context of insurance, especially life insurance, money held in reserve for payment of claims. May be specific or general, as required by law.

Step Rate—A method of calculating benefits by assigning a different value to income below and above a certain breakpoint, such as the Social Security level.

Step Rates—Standard progression pay rates established within a pay range. Step rates generally are a function of time in grade and are often called "automatic." They also can be variable or used with merit programs.

Step Therapy—In the context of pharmacy benefits, the practice of utilizing the most cost-efficient method to treat a patient according to protocol that calls for using one drug therapy before proceeding to another drug therapy that is more expensive or difficult to use.

STIF Account—See Short-Term Investment Fund (STIF).

Stock—A certificate of ownership; a contract between the issuing corporation and the owner that gives the latter an interest in the management of the corporation, the right to participate in profits and, if the corporation is dissolved, a claim upon assets remaining from all debts that have been paid. Also known as *equity securities* or *equities*. See also Common Stock; Preferred Stock.

Stock Appreciation Right (SAR)—An executive can receive the difference between the stock option price and current market price of the company's stock without buying any; often used in conjunction with an incentive stock option.

Stock Bonus Plan—A qualified defined contribution plan established and maintained by an employer to provide benefits similar to those of a profit-sharing plan, except that the contributions by the employer are not necessarily dependent upon profits and the benefits are distributable in stock of the employer company. For the purpose of allocating and distributing the stock of the employer that is to be shared among employees or their beneficiaries, such a plan is subject to the same requirements as a profit-sharing plan. See also Employee Stock Ownership Plan; Profit-Sharing Plan.

Stock Certificate—An engraved piece of paper representing legal evidence of ownership of a stipulated number of shares of stock in a corporation.

Stock Dividend—A dividend payable in shares of stock and generally disbursed in lieu of cash by corporations wanting to conserve capital for expansion or other purposes.

Stock Fund—A mutual fund comprised mostly of stocks.

Stock Option—The right to buy company stock at a certain price within a particular period of time.

Stock Purchase Plan—
—(Nonqualified) A plan that allows senior management or other key personnel to purchase employer stock. Certain restrictions apply: (1) the stockholder must be employed for a particular length of time, (2) the employer has the right to buy back the stock and (3) stockholders cannot sell the stock for a specific time period.
—(Qualified) A program under which employees buy shares in the employer's stock. The employer contributes a certain amount for each unit of employee contribution. Also, stock may be offered at a fixed price (usually below market) and paid for in full by the employees.

Stock Purchase Warrant—See Warrant.

Stock Split—A division made of the capital stock of a corporation to create more shares, primarily to improve marketability and heighten investor interest. Stock splits are generally on a two-for-one basis (two shares of new stock are made exchangeable for one share of old).

Stock Swap—Allowing an executive to deliver already-owned stock, instead of paying cash, to exercise a stock option.

Stock Yield—The rate of return on a stock based upon its market value as of a particular date and the dividend currently being paid by the company.

Stockholder—The owner of one or more shares of corporate stock who is entitled to (1) a proportionate share of the issuing company's undivided assets; (2) dividends when declared by the directors; (3) the right of proportionate voting power; and, frequently, (4) the opportunity to subscribe to additional stock before public offerings are made.

Stockholder of Record—A stockholder whose name is registered on the books of the issuing corporation.

Stockholders' Equity—The residual claims that stockholders have against a company's assets. Calculated by subtracting total liabilities from total assets.

Stop-Loss Insurance—Contract established between a self-insured group and an insurance carrier providing carrier coverage if claims exceed a specified dollar amount over a set period of time. May apply to an entire plan or a single component. Also called *excess loss insurance*. See also Reinsurance.

Stop-Loss Provision—A health insurance policy provision. A stop-loss provision is determined in two ways: either after a certain amount of benefits are paid from the plan or after a certain amount of out-of-pocket expenses are paid by the individual or family unit. When the dollar amount specified is reached, the coinsurance factor is raised to 100%.

When there is a stop-loss provision in the plan (besides the separate maximums and coinsurance levels on outpatient mental and nervous disorders), outpatient mental and nervous charges usually do not apply toward the dollar figure used to calculate when the stop-loss begins; after the stop-loss does begin, it does not apply to these charges.

Straight Bonds—As opposed to income or convertible bonds. Bonds conforming to the standard description (i.e., unquestioned right to repayment of principal at a specified future date; unquestioned right to fixed interest payments on stated dates; and no right to additional interest, interest in assets or profits, or voice in management).

Straight Life Insurance—Whole life insurance on which premiums are payable for life.

Subpoena—A process issued by a court requiring the attendance of a witness at a trial or the production of documents.. Term is derived from the first words of the document, "Under penalty of . . ." or "Subpoena . . ."

Subrogation—The right of the employer or insurance company to recoup benefits paid to participants through legal suit, if the action causing the disability and subsequent medical expenses was the fault of another individual. Used as a cost-containment measure. Generally, the substitution of one person or entity for another in regard to a legal right, interest or obligation.

Subscriber—The employee or member who elects coverage under the plan.

Subsidiary Company—A firm that has a majority of its voting stock owned by a parent company.

Substantive Plan—According to Financial Accounting Statement 106, it is a welfare plan not just as it is written, but as it is understood by employee and employer. It includes historical practices and employer practices.

Successor Plan—A plan established after the termination of a group health plan. If an employer terminates a group health plan and does not establish a new plan, it is not required to provide COBRA continuation coverage; however, if a new group health plan is established shortly after the old plan is terminated, the employer may have to provide continuation coverage.

Term also applies to 401(k) plans in merger situations.

Sullivan Principles—A code of conduct advocated by the Rev. Leon H. Sullivan for corporations doing business in South Africa. The code dictates non-segregation in work facilities; equal pay for equal work; fair employment practices; training programs for blacks, those of mixed race and Asians; and improved facilities in housing, schooling and other quality-of-life areas.

Summary Annual Report (SAR)—A summary report on the financial status of an employee benefit plan; must be given to participants. See also Annual Report (Employee Benefit Plans).

Summary of Material Modifications (SMM)—A description of important changes to a benefits plan or its summary plan description (SPD), such as plan administrators, claims procedures and eligibility. ERISA requires the SMM to be provided to each participant and beneficiary.

Summary Plan Description (SPD)—A written, easy-to-read summary statement describing the provisions and features of a benefit plan, including eligibility, coverage, employee rights and appeals procedures. The SPD must be provided to participants, beneficiaries and, upon request, to the Department of Labor.

Superannuation—Plan or scheme that provides benefits in the event of retirement, death or disability. Can refer to private company plans as well as industry or union funds. Frequently used in British Commonwealth countries.

Superimposed Major Medical—See Supplemental Major Medical Coverage.

Supplemental Benefits—Benefits provided by a pension plan in addition to regular retirement benefits. Supplemental benefits vary according to the terms of a plan and include such items as the payment of benefits in the event of terminations, death, disability or early retirement. See also Supplemental Unemployment Benefits (SUB); Voluntary Benefits.

Supplemental Executive Retirement Plan (SERP)—A nonqualified pension plan that allows an employer to offer greater benefits to its highly paid employees to bring the total compensation package to a predetermined level. See also Top-Hat Plan.

Supplemental Major Medical Coverage—This coverage is designed to insure expenses not covered by a basic medical plan. Covered persons are first reimbursed for their medical expenses under the employer's basic plan, usually with no deductible or copayment applied, to the extent that the basic plan covers the expenses. Expenses not covered by the basic plan can be reimbursed under the supplemental major medical plan, usually after the satisfaction of a corridor type deductible. After the covered expenses exceed the deductible, the major medical plan takes over and typically pays a percentage, such as 80%, of the covered expenses in excess of the deductible amount. There frequently is a limit on the amount of covered expenses that are subject to a coinsurance provision, after which the covered expenses are reimbursed in full.

Supplemental Security Income (SSI)—A federal income support program for those over the age of 65, the blind and disabled who fall below specified income and resource thresholds.

Supplemental Unemployment Benefits (SUB)—Amounts provided under a labor contract as additions or supplements to the unemployment compensation provided by law. See also Unemployment Compensation.

Supplementary Medical Insurance (SMI)—Also known as Medicare Part B, it is a voluntary insurance program that provides insurance benefits for physician and other medical services in accordance with the provisions of Title XVIII of the Social Security Act for aged and disabled individuals who elect to enroll under the program. See also Medicare.

Surplus—
—That part of the accumulated profits of a corporation that has not been capitalized.
—The balance of income in a trust that, at the end of the fiscal year, may be paid to the beneficiary.

Surrender Charge—A charge for the cancellation of an insurance or annuity policy.

Surrender Value—Generally, the net proceeds, after applicable charges, available from the termination or cancellation of an insurance or deferred annuity contract.

Surviving Spouse Benefit—Payments to the spouse of a deceased participant. See also Automatic Survivor Coverage.

Survivor Annuity—See Joint and Survivor Annuity; Qualified Joint and Survivor Annuity (QJSA); Reversionary Annuity.

Suspension—Some contributory plans that do not permit employees to withdraw from the plan while continuing in employment do permit them, on application, to suspend contributions temporarily. The term also refers to a temporary interruption of employer contributions that may sometimes be permitted by an insurance company and/or the secretary of the treasury without terminating the plan.

Syndicate—A group of investment banking firms that bands together to underwrite (i.e., distribute to the public) a new security issue or that engages in a secondary distribution of an already outstanding security.

Systematic Risk—Tendency of the asset price to move along with the market index. The measure of systematic risk is widely known as beta. If *beta* is 1.0, the asset price tends to fall in the same proportion that the market falls, other things being equal, and to rise by the same proportion that the market rises. If beta is 1.5, the asset price tends to fall (or rise) proportionally by 1.5 times as much as the market falls (or rises).

T

Table of Allowances—A list of covered health care services that assigns to each service a sum that represents the total obligation of the plan with respect to payment for such service, but that does not necessarily represent the provider's full fee for that service. Sometimes called a *fee schedule*. See also Covered Expenses.

Taft-Hartley Act (Labor-Management Relations Act of 1947)—An amendment to the National Labor Relations Act of 1935 based on the theory of equalizing the bargaining power of management with that of labor. Principal provisions: (1) specification of unfair labor practices by labor, (2) granting individual workers the right to prosecute for unfair labor practices by union or company officials, (3) anti-Communist provisions, (4) restriction of the closed shop, (5) prohibition of secondary boycott. See also Multiemployer Plan.

Taft-Hartley Plans—Benefit plans that have an equal number of trustees who are employer representatives and trustees who are union representatives. The plans are governed by federal law.

Tangible Assets—Physical property, including land, buildings, machinery and equipment, timber and other growing products, mineral resources, merchandise and others.

Target Benefit Plan—A defined contribution pension plan that has many features of a defined benefit plan. Contributions are based upon an actuarial valuation designed to provide a target benefit to each participant upon retirement. The plan does not guarantee that such benefit will be paid; its only obligation is to pay whatever benefit can be provided by the amount in the participant's account. A hybrid of a *money purchase plan* and a *defined benefit plan*. See also Cash Balance Plan.

Target Compensation—The expected pay for a job or position, including base pay, incentives and bonuses.

Tax Anticipation Bills (TABs)—See Treasury Bills.

Tax Deferral—Tax treatment granted to qualified retirement plans where taxes are not imposed when benefits are accrued (under a defined benefit plan) or contributions are made (under a defined contribution plan), but instead are imposed when benefits are paid to participants in cash.

Tax-Deferred Annuity—Offered by savings and loans, brokers and others, it offers high interest rates when the account is opened, but future interest rates are not guaranteed. Tax is deferred on the account until money is withdrawn. See also 403(b) Plan.

Tax Equity and Fiscal Responsibility Act of 1982 (TEFRA)—Lowered limits on contributions and benefits for corporate plans; allowed certain loans from plans to be treated as distributions; reduced estate tax exclusion for retirement plan death benefits to maximum of $100,000; repealed special Keogh plan and subchapter S restrictions; added "top-heavy" plan requirements; stopped employers and health plans from forcing employees ages 65 to 69 to use Medicare rather than group health plan.

Tax-Exempt Securities—Certain obligations issued by state and local governments, the interest of which is exempt from federal income tax. See also Municipal Bonds; Revenue Bonds; Special Assessment Bonds.

Tax-Qualified Plan—See Qualified Plan.

Tax Reduction (International Benefits)—The corporate taxation policy that, depending upon the foreign country involved, (1) permits expatriates to gain from the differences in income taxes in their home countries and the foreign country to which they are assigned or (2) adjusts the compensation of expatriates so they experience no loss in income as a result of the net effect of income taxes, both foreign and their home country.

Tax Reform Act of 1984—Among major changes made: delayed until 1988 cost-of-living increases in contributions and benefits; repealed the estate tax exclusion for death benefits from a pension plan or an IRA; allowed partial distributions from a pension plan to be rolled over to an IRA; applied restrictive distribution rules to 5% owners only. It attempted to redefine net earned income from self-employment. Top-heavy plan rules were modified. Deductions were extended to stock held under an ESOP. Welfare benefit rules were modified.

Tax Reform Act of 1986—Dictated extensive changes in the law governing the qualifications of pension and profit-sharing plans and the tax treatment of employers and employees. Imposed the comprehensive nondiscrimination rules of IRC Section 89.

Tax Shelter—
—An investment that provides tax savings by creating losses to offset taxable income.
—An investment upon which taxes are deferred.

Tax-Sheltered Annuity (TSA)—A special type of tax-qualified deferred compensation arrangement for employees of nonprofit organizations or public educational systems. Such plans must meet the requirements of IRC Section 403(b). See also 403(b) Plan; Section 403(b).

Taxable Wage Base (TWB)—With respect to any year, the maximum amount of earnings that may be considered wages for such year under Code Section 3121(a)(1); i.e., Social Security wage base.

Taxable Year—The 12-month period used by an employer to report income for income tax purposes.

The employer's taxable year does not have to co-incide with the year used by the plan to keep its records.

Taxpayer Relief Act of 1997—Contains a number of retirement plan provisions simplifying plan administration and creating new retirement planning options, such as the Roth IRA. Key tax relief provisions for individuals include: reduced tax rate on capital gains, new rules on gains exclusion upon sale of principal residence, new IRA provisions that permit withdrawals for education and home purchases prior to age 70½ without penalty, as well as contributions of up to $500 per year for children under age 18 for education, and extension of employer-provided education assistance. See also Roth IRA.

Teacher's Annuity—See 403(b) Plan.

Technical Analysis—An approach to analysis of futures markets and future trends of commodity prices that examines the technical factors of market activity. Technical analysts normally examine patterns of price change, rates of change and changes in volume of trading and open interest, often by charting, in hopes of being able to predict and profit from future trends.

Technical and Miscellaneous Revenue Act of 1988 (TAMRA)—Revised Section 89 nondiscrimination rules and amended the penalties for noncompliance with COBRA. Provided technical definitions and rules concerning required distributions, excess distributions, IRA rollovers, and vesting schedules for all pension and profit-sharing plans. Increased excise tax on excess pension assets upon termination of qualified plans.

Technical Safeguards—In the HIPAA privacy context, the technology and the policy and procedures for its use that protect electronic-protected health information and control access to it.

Telecommuting—An arrangement whereby an employee performs full- or part-time work at home, usually with a computer, while maintaining communication with the office via a modem.

Telemedicine—A technology that allows medical services to be conducted over a geographic distance. It involves application of interactive audio-visual technology in actual patient care, as well as education of physicians and other health care personnel. Can be especially useful in home monitoring of patients.

Temporary Disability Insurance (TDI)—Insurance that covers off-the-job injury or sickness and is paid for by deductions from an individual's paycheck; administered by state agency. Mandated in certain states. Also called *unemployment compensation disability* or *state disability insurance.*

Tender Offer—An offer to buy securities for cash, other securities or both.

Term Certain—See Annuity Certain.

Term Insurance—Life insurance payable to a beneficiary only when an insured dies within a specified period. There are no permanent policy benefits such as cash or loan value. Premiums are age based.

Terminal Illness (TI) Benefit—See Living Benefits.

Termination—Describes the final phase of an interrupted pension program. If the plan has enough assets to meet all its obligations, it is called a *standard termination.* In the case of a *distress termination,* the PBGC acts as trustee and uses its insurance funds as necessary to guarantee pension payments. Strict regulations govern all payout periods. Essentially all participants must vest 100%. However, the assets will have to be distributed according to the present formula. No money may return to the employer, except in the case of an actuarial error. It is also possible to discontinue contributions, but keep the trust in force, in order to preserve the tax-sheltered status of future payouts. See also Distress Termination; Plan Termination; Standard Termination.

Termination Benefits—See Severance Pay.

Termination Indemnities (International Benefits)—Obligation by law for payments on separation based on age, service or reason for termination.

Termination Insurance—See Plan Termination Insurance.

Termination Rate (Canada)—Rate of termination of employment for reasons other than death or retirement.

Tertiary Care—Specialized health care, needed by relatively few people, such as select rehabilitation services, highly technical medical procedures, burn centers and so on. The highest level of care.

Therapeutic Substitution—The practice of substituting one drug for another when both are thought to produce the same therapeutic effects.

Third-Country Nationals (TCNs) (International Benefits)—Citizens of one country who are employed by a company headquartered in a second country to work in a third country.

Third-Party Administrator (TPA)—The party to an employee benefit plan that may collect premiums, pay claims and/or provide administrative services. Usually an out-of-house professional firm providing administrative services for employee benefit plans. (Synonyms: *administrative agent, contract administrator*)

Third-Party Payer—The party that pays for the services provided to a patient. Can be an insurance company, the government, a self-insured employer or a managed care organization.

Thirteenth Check—An annual supplemental retirement allowance arising from earnings on the investments of a system in excess of those determined as needed for other purposes.

30 and Out—A retirement option that permits retirement after 30 years' credited service, regardless of age.

Three-Legged Stool—Theory that a combination of an individual's savings, Social Security and a private pension will provide secure retirement income.

3% Rule—The employee's accrued benefit must be at least equal to 3% of the projected normal retirement benefit for each year of participation, to a maximum of 100% after 33⅓ years of participation. See also Accrued Benefit.

Thrift Plan—A defined contribution plan to which employees make contributions on an aftertax basis, usually as a percentage of salary. Incentive matching or partially matching contributions may be made on behalf of the participating employees by the employer. Also known as *savings plan*.

Tin Parachute—A play on the term *golden parachute*, it assures that rank and file workers receive cash payment, if the company changes hands against the will of the board of directors. Helps discourage hostile takeovers. See also Golden Parachute.

Title XVIII—The section of the Social Security Act that describes the Medicare program's coverage for eligible persons (i.e., the aged, the blind and the disabled).

Title Insurance—A policy of insurance that indemnifies the owner of real estate for any loss sustained by reason of defects in the title.

Title XIX—The section of the Social Security Act that describes the Medicaid program's coverage for eligible persons who may be medically indigent.

Title VII of the Civil Rights Act of 1964—A federal law, covering employers with 15 or more employees who are engaged in interstate commerce, that prohibits discrimination on the basis of national origin, race, color, religion and sex; also covered are employment agencies and unions.

Top-Down Investment Manager—Common stock manager who develops the portfolio with a primary emphasis on the economy and industries, as opposed to one who places his or her selection emphasis on recognizing favorable characteristics of individual companies.

Top-Hat Plan—An unfunded deferred compensation plan or welfare plan that is maintained to provide deferred compensation for a select group of management or highly compensated employees.

Top-Heavy Plan—A qualified plan in which the share of benefits allocable to key employees is more than 60%. The plan may be subject to special accelerated vesting provisions and minimum contribution rates. See also 5% Owner; Key Employee.

Tort—Any wrongful act or omission that causes damage to the person, property or reputation of another. Commonly spoken of as a private wrong, as opposed to a public wrong, which is called a *crime*.

Total Compensation—The sum of all financial and nonfinancial elements in the employment package, including base salary, incentives, benefits, perquisites, bonuses, commissions, job satisfaction, status and any other reward of employment that the employee values.

Total Compensation Statement—See Annual Benefits Statement.

Total Disability—An illness or injury that prevents an insured person from continuously performing every duty pertaining to his or her occupation or from engaging in any other type of work for remuneration. (This definition varies among insurance policies and benefit plans.) See also Disability.

Total Quality Management (TQM)—A comprehensive management process designed to control quality and improve all aspects of an organization's activities using statistical techniques, employee teamwork, joint problem solving and open communication on a continuous basis.

Total Return—The aggregate increase in the value of the portfolio resulting from the net appreciation (or depreciation) of the principal of the fund, plus or minus the net income (or loss) experienced by the fund during the period.

Totalization Agreements (International Benefits)—Social security arrangements between countries intended to protect the social security benefits of employees who move between countries and ensure single country social security coverages for employees on assignment.

Trader—A person who actively buys and sells securities for his or her own account using very short time horizons for the most part.

Trading Post—One of 23 trading locations on the floor of the New York Stock Exchange at which stocks assigned to that location are bought and sold. About 75 stocks are traded at each post.

Traditional Pension Plan—See Defined Benefit Plan.

Tranche—
—A class of maturity. For example, a collateralized mortgage obligation (CMO) is a debt security backed by a pool of mortgages divided into separate issues of differing maturities with each issue called a *tranche*. See also Collateralized Mortgage Obligation (CMO)
—(International Benefits). In France the term refers to a pay bracket.

Transactions—All the activity of a portfolio: purchases and sales of securities, contributions to the fund and disbursements out of the fund, transfers, income re-

ceipts from dividends or bond interest, and payment of any administrative expenses.

Transfer Payment (International Benefits)—A payment from one pension scheme to another when a member/employee has changed jobs. The individual thus receives some credit in the new scheme for rights accrued in the old.

Transportation Benefits—Some companies sponsor public transportation subsidies, van pools, employer-sponsored vans or buses that transport workers to the workplace. Aims to increase employee attendance and retention.

Trauma—A severe, life-threatening injury that requires emergency care and possibly extensive life-saving measures.

Treasury Bills—Short-term U.S. government-backed bonds maturing in three months to one year. Treasury bills are purchased at a discount and then grow to their full par value by maturity. The yield is exempt from state and local taxes; they are the safest and most liquid investment next to cash. Also known as *T-bills,* investors can purchase them directly from the Treasury (commission-free) at the government's DirecTreasury Web site, www.treasurydirect.gov.

Treasury Bonds—Long-term U.S. government-backed bonds maturing in more than ten years. They sell at face value and pay a fixed rate of interest twice a year, and are exempt from state and local taxes. Investors can purchase them directly from the Treasury (commission-free) at the government's DirecTreasury Web site, www.treasurydirect.gov.

Treasury Inflation-Protected Securities (TIPS)—U.S. Treasury securities that adjust in value based upon changes in the inflation rate as measured by the consumer price index (CPI). They mature in two to 30 years and pay a fixed rate semiannually. Taxes must be paid yearly on the increased value of the bonds.

Treasury Notes—Intermediate term U.S. government-backed bonds maturing in one to ten years. They pay a fixed rate of interest twice a year, and the yield is exempt from state and local taxes. Also known as *T-notes,* investors can purchase them directly from the Treasury (commission-free) at the government's DirecTreasury Web site, www.treasurydirect.gov.

Treasury Regulations—Regulations promulgated by the U.S. Department of the Treasury. IRS is a part of the Treasury Department, and regulations interpreting the Internal Revenue Code are technically Treasury regulations.

Treasury Stock—Common stock that has been issued and reacquired (purchased) by the corporation from the public at the current market price.

Trend Rate—See Health Care Cost Trend Rate.

TRICARE—A regionally managed health care program for active duty and retired members of the uniformed services, their families and survivors. TRICARE brings together Army, Navy and Air Force health care resources and supplements them with networks of civilian health care professionals to provide better access to high-quality service. Replaces CHAMPUS. See also Civilian Health and Medical Program of the Uniformed Services (CHAMPUS).

Trust—A legal entity that is created when a person or organization transfers assets to a trustee for the benefit of designated persons.

Trust Agreement—
—An agreement that spells out the methods of receipt, investment and disbursement of funds under a benefit plan. It contains provisions for investment powers of trustees; irrevocability and nondiversion of trust assets; payment of legal, trustee and other fees relative to the plan; exculpatory clauses pertaining to the liability of trustees; periodic reports to the employer or union by the trustees; records and accounts to be maintained by the trustees; conditions for removal, resignation or replacement of trustees; benefit payments under the plan; and the rights and duties of the trustees in case of amendment or termination of the plan. The plan agreement is often separate from the trust. See also Plan; Plan Document.
—(Canada) Also called a *trust deed*.

Trust Fund—A fund whose assets are managed by a trustee or a board of trustees for the benefit of another party or parties. Restrictions as to what the trustee may invest the assets of the trust fund in are usually found in the trust instrument and in applicable state and federal laws. In the case of ERISA-controlled employee benefit plan trust funds, there are specific requirements that should be referred to.

Trustee—
—A person, bank or trust company that has responsibility over financial aspects (receipt, disbursement and investment) of funds. Where this responsibility is not exercised by a bank or trust company, it is usually exercised by a board of trustees in which the individual trustee has but one vote.
—One who acts in a capacity of trust as a fiduciary and to whom property has been conveyed for the benefit of another party. Under the terms of ERISA, a *fiduciary* is "one who occupies a position of confidence or trust and who exercises any power of control, management or disposition with respect to monies or other property of an employee benefit fund or who has authority or responsibility to do so."

Trusteed Pension Plan—
—A pension plan in which the corporation's contributions to the plan are placed in a trust for investment and reinvestment, as distinguished from a plan in which the benefits are secured by life insurance.
—A negotiated employee benefit plan established under the Taft-Hartley Act and governed by a board of trustees composed of equal numbers selected by the employers, or management, and individuals selected by the union. All trustees of a trusteed plan are charged with the fiduciary responsibility of discharging their duties with respect to the plan "solely in the interests of participants and beneficiaries." See also Trust Fund.

Tuition Reimbursement Plan—See Educational Assistance Program.

Turnover, Turnover Rate—
—The rate at which securities within a portfolio are exchanged for other securities.
—Termination of employment for a reason other than death or retirement.
—In general labor terms, the number of persons hired to replace those leaving or dropped, within a stated period of time; also, the ratio of this number to the average workforce maintained. In pension plans, the ratio of those

145

leaving or dropped to the total number of plan participants at any age or length of service.

12(b)-1 Fees—Named for the SEC rule that permits them, these fees are advertising and marketing fees charged by an investment company to sell its mutual funds. They are an ongoing charge included in the fund's annual expense ratio, which is provided in the company's prospectus for the fund. See also Management Fees (Investments).

24-Hour Coverage—A combination of workers' compensation benefits and regular medical insurance coverage. A single plan would cover both medical and disability benefits for any injury, job related or not. See also Integrated Disability Management.

Two-Tier Pay Plan—A dual pay structure that attempts to control labor costs by grandfathering the current structure for existing employees, but starting new employees under a second, lower level pay structure.

U

Ultrasound—A technique that uses high-frequency sound waves to provide structural information on many parts of the human anatomy that cannot be obtained by traditional X-ray and radioisotopic methods. It permits visualization of both surface and internal structures of many body organs. Often used for fetal monitoring.

Unbundled Services—A 401(k) plan sponsor using separate service providers for investment and administration. Compare with Bundled Services.

Unbundling—
—Charging separately for procedures normally covered as one billing unit so the total exceeds what should be charged.
—Under Part B of Medicare, billing for nonphysician services provided to hospital inpatients by a source other than the hospital.

Unconditional Vesting—That form of vesting in a contributory plan under which entitlement to a vested benefit is not conditional upon the nonwithdrawal of the participant's contributions.

Underdistribution—See Excess Accumulation.

Underfunded Benefit Plan—An employee benefit plan in which the company's past contributions are insufficient to cover current and future liabilities.

Underinsured—People who do not have enough insurance coverage to meet their current or anticipated needs.

Undertreatment—Failure to recommend at the proper time one or more of those services that, consistent with diagnosis and treatment planning, are necessary and appropriate. See also Overtreatment.

Underwriter—
—(Insurance) Can mean (1) the company that receives the premiums and accepts responsibility for fulfilling the policy contract, (2) the company employee who decides whether or not the company should assume a particular risk or (3) the agent who sells the policy.
—(Investments) With respect to a mutual fund, the entity responsible for marketing the shares of the fund. See also Investment Banker.

Underwriting—
—(Insurance) The process of identifying and classifying the potential degree of risk represented by a proposed insured.
—(Investments) The procedure by which investment bankers channel investment capital from investors to corporations and municipalities.

Unemployed Person—Described by the government as a civilian who, during a given week, had no employment but was available for work and sought a job during the prior four weeks or was waiting to be called back to work or to a new position within 30 days.

Unemployment Compensation—Payments made under state-administered programs to workers who are unemployed and meet the requirements of the law involved to qualify for such payments. The requirements usually are (1) that the worker not be unemployed voluntarily; (2) that the worker has worked in employment that is "covered" by the law; (3) that the worker be willing and able to take employment offered him or her; and (4) that an initial period (the waiting period) of unemployment elapse before compensation is due. Programs are entirely employer financed except in four states that require small employee contributions. See also Supplemental Unemployment Benefits.

Unemployment Compensation Amendments of 1992—The law contains three directives for plan administrators of qualified plans and payers of Section 403(b) annuities: (1) provide a direct roll-over option from qualified plans or Section 403(b) annuities, (2) withhold 20% federal income tax on eligible rollover distributions (ERDs) not directly rolled over into an eligible retirement plan and (3) give written notice to recipients before ERDs are made.

Unfunded—Means the plan is not insured or trusteed. The benefits are paid solely from the employer's general assets.

Unfunded Accrued Pension Cost—Cumulative net pension cost accrued in excess of the employer's contributions.

Unfunded Accumulated Benefit Obligation—The excess of the accumulated benefit obligation over plan assets.

Unfunded Actuarial Accrued Liability—The excess of the actuarial accrued liability over the actuarial value of assets. This value may be negative, in which case it may be expressed as a negative unfunded actuarial accrued liability; the excess of the actuarial value of assets over the actuarial accrued liability; or the funding excess.

Unfunded Deferred Compensation Agreement—A contract between employer and employee to pay certain sums of money at any later date, usually upon retirement, without payment by the employer into any funding agency.

Unfunded Past Service Cost—See Unfunded Actuarial Accrued Liability.

Unfunded Plan—A plan funded by the employer out of current income. See also Pay As You Go.

Unfunded Projected Benefit Obligation—The excess of the projected benefit obligation over plan assets.

Uniform Gifts to Minors Act (UGMA) Account—An account established by UGMA to provide parents a vehicle for making gifts of money or securities to minors without having to set up complicated trust accounts.

UGMA accounts allow minors to experience the benefits of investing by having their own investment account, and the first $750 of investment income produced is tax-free if the child is under the age of 14. However, these accounts may affect later eligibility for financial aid for education. See also Kiddie Tax; Uniform Transfers to Minors Act (UTMA).

Uniform Resource Locator (URL)—The address for a Web site.

Uniform Transfers to Minors Act (UTMA)—This act was developed to supersede the Uniform Gifts to Minors Act by providing greater flexibility in terms of what can be transferred. See also Kiddie Tax; Uniform Gifts to Minors (UGMA) Account.

Uniformed Services Employment and Reemployment Rights Act (USERRA)—The federal law that provides protection of jobs and benefits for employees who take a leave of absence to serve in the military, National Guard or other uniformed services.

Unilateral Plan—A pension plan that does not result from collective bargaining. See, in contrast, Collectively Bargained Plans.

Union-Sponsored Plan—A program of health benefits developed by a union. The union may operate the program directly, or may contract for the benefits. Funds to finance the benefits are usually paid out of a welfare fund, which receives its income from (1) employer contributions, (2) employer and union member contributions or (3) union members alone.

Unique User Identification—The assignment of a name and number/password that identifies and tracks user identity.

Universal Life Insurance—A type of life insurance that pays a death benefit and accumulates cash value, which is used to buy term insurance. The policyholder may vary the amount of the policy, the premium payment and the protection periods to suit changing family needs.

Unlisted Securities—Securities not listed on a stock exchange, such as those traded over the counter.

Unrealized Profits—Paper profits that have not yet been made actual.

Unsecured Bond—A bond that is not backed by any pledge of assets that the debt will be paid. The debtor pledges its credit standing, secured by full faith. Government bonds and most corporate debentures are in this category.

Upcoding—A deceptive practice of health care providers in which service codes are reported at their highest service value for payment, although the procedures actually performed were less complex.

Urgent Care Center—An ambulatory care facility that provides extended or 24-hour service to treat minor conditions such as cuts, bruises and suture removal; less costly than emergency room treatment. Also called *emergicenter* or *urgicenter.*

Uruguay Round Agreements Act of 1994—Approved the trade agreements that resulted from the Uruguay Round of multilateral trade negotiations under the auspices of the General Agreement on Tariffs and Trade (GATT). See also General Agreement on Tariffs and Trade (GATT); Retirement Protection Act of 1994 (RPA).

Use-It-or-Lose-It Rule—A rule forbidding cafeteria plans to let participants defer receipt and taxation of compensation from year to year by carrying over unused pretax contributions or plan benefits.

User—In HIPAA privacy concerns, a person or entity with authorized access.

User ID—A unique identifier given to authorized members of the workforce to establish a user account and provide access to the covered entity's information system. Usually a combination of an assigned name and number.

USERRA—See Uniformed Services Employment and Reemployment Rights Act (USERRA).

Usual, Customary and Reasonable (UCR) Fees—*Usual* is the fee usually charged for a given service by a health care provider; *customary* is a fee in the range of usual fees charged by similar providers in area; *reasonable* is a fee that, according to the review committee, meets the lesser of the two criteria or is justified in the circumstances. Reimbursement is limited to the lowest of the three charges. Usual and customary charges are also being applied to workers' compensation. See also Reasonable and Customary (R&C) Charge.

Usury—An illegal rate of interest.

Utilization—
—Proper and efficient use of hospital facilities, labor force, services and equipment.
—The extent to which a given group uses specified services in a specific period. Usually expressed as the number of services used per year per 100 or per 1,000 persons eligible for the services, but utilization rates may be expressed in other types of ratios, e.g., per eligible person covered. Utilization rates are established to help in comprehensive health planning, budget review and cost containment.

Utilization Management (UM)—A wide range of techniques such as second surgical opinion, preadmission certification, concurrent review, case management, discharge planning and retrospective chart review used to evaluate the necessity, appropriateness and efficiency of health care services. The term *utilization management* also refers to management of patient care processes and is preferred by managed care organizations. See also Utilization Review (UR).

Utilization Review (UR)—The evaluation of medical necessity, efficiency or quality of health care services, either prospectively, concurrently or retrospectively. The term *utilization review* is more limited to the physician's diagnosis, treatment and billing amount. See also Utilization Management (UM).

Utilization Review Organization (URO)—Independent review organizations, insurance companies or in-house programs providing utilization review services.

V

Vacation Benefit—A benefit provided through an employer's current assets.

Vacation Pay Plan—A benefit plan, typically established through collective bargaining, to which the employer generally makes a contribution to the trust that pays the benefits. Vacation pay plans are covered by ERISA.

Valdez Principles—See CERES Principles.

Valuation—A determination of the value, as of a given

date, of an investment or investment portfolio (asset valuation). See also Actuarial Valuation.

Valuation Assets—See Actuarial Value of Assets.

Valuation Reserves—Reserves established to anticipate a decreased value of an asset (i.e., depreciation or depletion reserves).

Value Managers—A common stock manager whose style of management results in focusing on price/earnings ratios, book value and *current* relative to *historical* levels. Value managers focus on current year earnings and buy stocks at low prices, relative to their earnings, but have relatively high-dividend yields. Value managers are seen to take a more conservative approach to investing. See also Growth Managers.

Variability—Measures the fluctuations in rates of return. These measurements are used frequently as proxies for risk management.

Variable Annuity—
—Annuity expressed in terms of benefit units instead of fixed dollar amounts.
—Annuity in which the amount of each periodic payment fluctuates according to some variable factor. Under an equity annuity plan, payments vary according to the value of a specific portfolio of common stocks and similar investments. Under a cost-of-living plan, benefits are adjusted to reflect variations in a specific index, such as the consumer price index of the Bureau of Labor Statistics. An insured variable annuity is one under which the benefit varies according to the investment results of an insurance company's separate account (usually invested primarily in common stocks) in which funds have been set aside to provide the annuity.

Variable Benefit Plan—
—A pension plan in which the retirement benefits otherwise specified are varied from time to time to provide a measure of protection to the purchasing power of the benefits. In a *cost-of-living plan,* the benefits are adjusted to reflect variations in a specific index, such as the Consumer Price Index of the United States Bureau of Labor Statistics. In an *equity annuity plan,* the periodic benefit (or, more frequently, one-half of the benefit) is dependent on the investment experience of a specific portfolio containing equity securities.

—A pension plan that describes the monthly pension to be received in units, rather than in dollars. The value of each unit is being determined, based upon the investment portfolio of the plan, at the time of either retirement or payment of actual benefits.

Variable Life Insurance—Life insurance under which the premiums are level but the benefits are not. Above a guaranteed minimum, benefits relate to the value of assets behind the contract at the time benefits are paid.

Variable Pay—Compensation that ties pay to productivity or some other factor that varies with the company's profitability. Variable pay can be based on individual or organizational performance and may include cash awards, profit sharing, team incentives or gainsharing.

Variable Rate Mortgage—The interest rate and the buyer's monthly payment fluctuate, depending on interest rates in the economy. When rates decline, homeowners benefit. When rates go up, however, the monthly payment will go up or the amount or length of the mortgage might be increased. See also Fixed Rate Mortgage.

Variable Universal Life—A form of life insurance (also called *Universal Life II* or *flexible life*) offering a guaranteed death benefit that combines the flexible premium features of universal life with the investment component of variable life.

Variance—A measure of variability based on squared deviations of individual observations from the mean value of the distribution. Its square root is the standard deviation. See also Standard Deviation.

Venture Capital—Capital subject to more than a normal degree of risk, usually associated with a new business or venture. Also called *risk capital.*

Vertical Integration—Connection of dissimilar entities such as an HMO, hospitals, physician practices or PPOs into one local or regional health care delivery network to enhance coordination and value to patient care and support. An *integrated delivery system* can achieve economies of scale and operate more cost-effectively. Can also refer to coordination of all programs related to illness and injury, from prevention to return to work. Vertical integration is also called *full-service integration*. See also Horizontal Integration; Integrated Delivery System.

Vest; Vesting—A term used by employers to indicate the time it takes for employer contributions to a retirement or other account to become property of the employee. An employee's right to receive a present or future pension benefit vests when it is no longer contingent upon remaining in the service of the employer. Employee contributions are always fully vested; however, interest upon such contributions may not be vested or may be paid at a specified rate, depending upon plan provisions. A vested benefit may be paid as a lump sum or, frequently, is paid as a deferred annuity upon retirement. See also Cliff Vesting; Graded Vesting.

Vested Benefit Obligation—The actuarial present value of vested benefits.

Vested Benefits—Accrued benefits of a participant that have become nonforfeitable under the vesting schedule adopted by the plan.

Vested Liabilities—The plan's liability for the nonforfeitable immediate and deferred benefits due at retirement age for participants and their beneficiaries; the present value of vested benefits ultimately owed to separated and current plan participants.

Viatical Settlement—A provision of the Health Insurance Portability and Accountability Act of 1996, this form of living benefit allows severely ill patients tax-free access to the face value of their life insurance policies to help them meet medical and other necessary expenses. A qualified individual can sell his or her policy to a viatical settlement company or other such investor that pays out a percentage of the policy's face value to the policyholder, assumes responsibility for future premium payments and becomes the policy's beneficiary.

Vision Care Coverage or Plan—A separate plan covering medical treatment relating to eye conditions. Ophthalmologists, optometrists or opticians can render care.

Vocational Provisions—The specific stipulations written into a workers' compensation law regarding the employer's duties specific to providing vocational rehabilitation.

Voice Response Technology—A form of communication using a touch-tone phone, in which recorded voice messages lead users through a list of options and prompt a response made by pressing a button on the telephone keypad. Responses are then fed into a computer. Voice response technology, also called *interactive voice response (IVR)*, is used by financial institutions, health care plans, etc. See also Interactive Benefits Communication.

Volatility—That part of total variability due to sensitivity to changes in the market. It is systematic and unavoidable risk. It is measured by the beta coefficient. Efficient portfolios have no additional risk, and volatility is the only source of variability in rates of return.

Volume—The aggregate number of shares of stock traded during a given period.

Voluntary Benefits—Employer-sponsored benefits often available at group rates or discounts that create a value employees could not duplicate on their own. Examples include dental coverage, vision benefits, prescription drug coverage, life insurance, long-term care insurance, financial planning, legal services and college savings plans. Benefits are administered by the employer, but paid for by the employees. Also known as *ancillary benefits* or *supplemental benefits*.

Voluntary Compliance Resolution Program—The IRS allows plan sponsors to identify and correct operational defects in their plans and to obtain a compliance statement indicating how the defects will be fixed. The program allows defects to be corrected without negative tax consequences to workers and without significant financial penalties being imposed on employers. Failure to remedy defects results in plan disqualification. See also Employee Plans Compliance Resolution System (EPCRS); Self-Correction Program (SCP).

Voluntary Contribution—The amount of money the employee pays into the plan. Not required for employee participation; voluntary contributions do not affect the level of employer contributions. See also Contributory Plan.

Voluntary Correction Program (VCP)—One of the three IRS-sponsored programs making up the Employee Plans Compliance Resolution System (EPCRS), which allows sponsors to correct operational and plan document errors affecting their tax-qualified plans. VCP allows a plan sponsor, at any time before audit, to pay a limited fee and receive approval for the correction of a qualified plan. There are special procedures for anonymous submissions. See also Correction on Audit Program

(Audit CAP); Employee Plans Compliance Resolution System (EPCRS); Self-Correction Program (SCP).

Voluntary Employees' Beneficiary Association (VEBA)—Usually covered by IRC Section 501(c)(9), it serves as the base of an employer-sponsored employee benefit plan. It is a tax-exempt fund that pays death, health, accident or other benefits to members, their dependents and/or beneficiaries.

Voting Right—A right enjoyed by a stockholder to participate in the affairs of the company to the extent he or she deems necessary or desirable. In the case of the passing of a preferred dividend, preferred holders may, if the default exceeds a specified time period, have the right to vote their shares to protect their interests. This right may be delegated to another party.

Voucher Program—Refers to an employer-sponsored and -financed dependent care option in which the employee submits monthly vouchers for dependent care expenses to the provider and the employer covers all or a part of the cost of the services.

Vulnerability—In computer terminology, a context of a weakness or flaw in security procedures, practices or controls that could be exploited (accidentally or intentionally) by a threat source.

W

Wage—Pay given to employees covered by the Fair Labor Standards Act, typically at an hourly, rather than monthly or annual, rate.

Wage Loss Insurance—See Disability Income Insurance.

Wagner Act—See National Labor Relations Act of 1935 (NLRA) (Wagner Act).

Waiting Period—
—The duration of time between the beginning of an insured person's disability and the start of the policy's benefits. Called a *qualified period* in Canada.
—The period between employment or enrollment in a program and the date when an insured person becomes eligible for benefits.
—See also Participation Requirements.

Waive—To intentionally give up a known right. It may be done expressly through words, or through conduct involving acts that are inconsistent with the claiming of a known right.

Waived Funding Deficiency—If an employer is not able to satisfy the minimum funding standard without substantial business hardship and if the application of the standard would be adverse to the interests of plan participants in the aggregate, the IRS may waive part or all of the minimum funding standard for the plan year. The amount waived must be amortized in no more than 15 equal annual payments. The term *waived funding deficiency* means the part of the minimum funding standard determined without regard to previously waived amounts and not satisfied by employer contributions.

Waiver—
—Relinquishing the right to a benefit, especially in regard to health benefits, flexible benefits or early retirement window plans.
—An agreement attached to a policy that exempts from coverage certain disabilities or injuries normally covered by the policy. Also known as *exclusion endorsement*.
—A supplementary life insurance policy benefit under which the insurer gives up its right to collect renewal premiums if the policy owner dies or becomes disabled. Also known as *waiver of premium*.
—In health care, a common usage is exemption of a state from participating in the Medicare program under the prospective payment system (PPS) when the state has presented an alternate method of payment that the government has accepted.

Warehousing—The process of borrowing funds on a short-term basis and using mortgage loans as collateral.

Web Site—A collection of "pages" of related topics that are linked together and organized under a home page on the Internet.

Weekly Indemnity Insurance—See Disability Income Insurance.

Weighted Mean—An average of means, found by weighting each individual mean according to the number of data points that made up that individual mean. For example, the weighted mean is an answer to the question, "On average, what are current employees in a particular job paid?"

Weighting—The specification of the relative importance of each of a group of items that is combined. For example, stocks included in indexes may be equally weighted or weighted according to value.

Welfare Fund—When employer and/or employee contributions for health are placed in a fund that is administered by a board, usually with equal representation from labor and management. (Synonym: health and welfare fund)

Welfare Plan—See Employee Welfare Benefit Plan.

Wellness (Health Promotion) Programs—A broad range of employer- or union-sponsored facilities and activities designed to promote safety and good health among employees. The purpose is to increase worker morale and reduce the costs of accidents and ill health such as absenteeism, lower productivity and health care costs. May include physical fitness programs, smoking cessation, health risk appraisals, diet information and weight loss, stress management and high blood pressure screening. See also Preventive Care.

Whistleblower Protection—Prevents an employer from taking any retaliatory action against employees that disclose, or threaten to disclose, any employer activity, practice or policy the employees reasonably believe is illegal.

White Knight—A company, friendly to management, that rescues another firm that is faced with a hostile bid.

Whole Life Insurance—Insurance payable to a beneficiary at the death of the insured, whenever that occurs. Premiums may be payable for a specified number of years (limited payment life) or for life (straight life). The premiums may remain level or decrease (by accumulating cash in the initial years of the policy).

Window Plan—An early retirement program providing an employee with an incentive to terminate employment within a specified time.

Wind-Up (Canada)—The termination or discontinuance of a pension plan. The wind-up of a pension plan stops the accrual of benefits and requires disposal of all plan assets and liabilities.

Withdrawal Liability (Multiemployer Plans)—
—The liability of a contributing employer to a qualified multiemployer defined benefit plan to make contributions necessary to fund benefits of employees before it can cease contributions to the plan.
—The Multiemployer Pension Plan Amendments Act of 1980 (MPPAA) imposes liabilities on contributing employers upon a complete or partial withdrawal of the employer from the plan, rather than on plan termination as is the case for multiple and single employer plans.
—MPPAA removed multiemployer plans from the termination insurance system that governs single and multiple employer plans and substituted a system that imposes liability for certain unfunded vested benefits when an employer partially or totally withdraws from a multiemployer plan.

Withdrawal of Employee Contributions—Whenever a participant whose benefit attributable to employer contributions is less than 50% vested withdraws all or any part of his mandatory contributions, ERISA permits a forfeiture of the benefit attributable to employer contributions. If the benefit attributable to employer contributions is 50% or more vested, no forfeiture is permitted.

If an employee withdraws his or her mandatory contributions, the employee must be permitted to repay the amount he or she received with interest at 5% initially. (The interest rate may be adjusted.)

Withdrawal of Vested Benefits—The right of an employee to withdraw monies credited to him or her in the employer's program. Not permissible under pension plans but often available in profit-sharing plans. Special regulations apply. Typically, the IRS does not allow accumulations to be distributed in less than two years. Thus, after a contribution has been credited to an employee's account for three years, he or she can withdraw an amount equal to the first year's contributions and the investment income credited that year only. The withdrawn amount is taxable as ordinary income in the year received.

Women's Health and Cancer Rights Act of 1998—Requires that health plans covering mastectomies must also cover breast reconstruction.

Work/Life Benefits—A broad range of programs and services designed to improve the balance between work and personal life. Includes work reorganization initiatives such as job sharing, flextime and telecommuting; as well as on-site child care and/or elder care, emergency/sick child care, tuition assistance, concierge services, financial or career counseling, etc. Work/life benefits tend to result in healthier, more productive employees and are seen as a retention tool for employers.

Work Sharing—The practice of spreading a firm's available work hours among its employees during a cutback; used as an alternative to layoffs.

Work Teams—Groups of multiskilled employees responsible for a business product or service.

Workers' Compensation—Every state has a system of providing for the cost of medical care and weekly payments to employees who suffer job-related illnesses or injuries and to dependents of those killed in industry. Absolute liability is imposed on the employer, which is required to pay benefits prescribed by law. See also 24-Hour Coverage.

Workforce—Employees, volunteers, trainees and others who work for a covered entity, whether or not they are paid by the covered entity.

Working Capital—Found by subtracting current liabilities from current assets.

Working Families Tax Relief Act of 2004—Provides various tax reform measures, notably a new definition of *dependent* as "qualifying child" or "qualifying relative." The new definition may affect hardship withdrawals for medical and tuition plans, QDRO rules and deemed IRAs; it directly impacts personal income tax filings, health plans, flexible spending accounts and cafeteria plans. Changes are effective for tax and plan years beginning in 2005.

Works Councils (International Benefits)—Elected representatives of employers and employees of a plant or business that discuss topics such as working conditions, wages or grievances in the workplace. Also a committee elected to negotiate any of these. Most common in Western Europe.

Workstation—An electronic computing device, for example, a laptop or desktop computer, or any other device that performs similar functions and has electronic media stored in its immediate environment.

World Trade Organization (WTO) (International Benefits)—An international organization that supervises all agreements and arrangements concluded under the auspices of the Uruguay Round of multilateral trade negotiations. The WTO agree-

ment was signed by nearly 100 nations in 1995 and is the successor to GATT. See also General Agreement on Tariffs and Trade (GATT) and Uruguay Round Agreements Act of 1994.

World Wide Web (WWW)—A full-color, multimedia database of information on the Internet. The World Wide Web is a universal mass of Web pages connected through links. Users access the Web by means of Web *browsers*.

Wraparound Mortgage—Buyers who do not have enough cash to assume a loan and compensate the seller sufficiently for the equity can sometimes get a lender to combine the seller's old mortgage with additional new financing needed to satisfy the seller. Often the wraparound carries a lower rate than conventional mortgages.

Wraparound Plan—
—A major medical plan and a basic surgical/regular medical plan are wrapped around a basic hospital plan and cover all charges other than those provided for by the basic hospital plan. Commonly used for Medicare.
—A deferred compensation plan for highly compensated employees that augments existing 401(k) investments to enable the employees to save more for their retirement. See also 401(k) Wraparound Plan.

Y

Yankee Bond—A dollar-denominated bond sold in the United States by a foreign entity.

Yankee Certificate of Deposit—A certificate evidencing a time deposit issued by the U.S. branch of a foreign bank.

Year of Service—ERISA defines a *year of service* in terms of 1,000 compensable hours during a consecutive 12-month period.

For the purpose of the participation rules, an individual has one year of service if he or she works for 1,000 hours during the initial 12-month period after he or she is employed. Assuming that he or she has reached age 21 (and that the plan is not one that requires a three-year waiting period), the employee who has met the above requirement must be permitted to participate in the plan on the earlier of (a) the beginning of the first plan year after the anniversary date of his or her employment or (b) six months from the anniversary date of his or her employment. If an employee fails to work 1,000 hours during the initial 12 months of his or her employment, he or she must begin meeting the 1,000-hour requirement in the next 12-month period.

For purposes of determining where an individual stands on the vesting schedule, a year of service is a calendar year, plan year or other consecutive 12-month period designated in the plan during which the employee worked 1,000 hours.

Special rules govern the maritime industry and certain seasonal industries.

Years Certain Annuity—See Annuity Certain.

Year's Maximum Pensionable Earnings (YMPE) (Canada)—The maximum amount of annual earnings, prior to reduction of the amount of the year's basic exemption, upon which benefits and contributions for purposes of the Canada Pension Plan and the Quebec Pension Plan are based. The YMPE has been subject to yearly adjustments and since 1989, it has increased according to the average wage of industrial workers in Canada.

Yield—The return of an investment expressed as a percentage of cost or market. There are various ways to calculate *yield* depending upon whether you are dealing with a bond or stock. *Straight yield* on either a bond or stock is found by dividing the price into the expected dollar amount to be received from interest or dividends. A stock selling at $40 and paying a $2 dividend yields 5% ($2 divided by $40), and a bond with an 8% coupon selling at $1,000 yields 8% (i.e., $80 divided by $1,000). Where a bond is purchased at a premium or discount, the yield will vary depending upon whether the bond is held to its first call date or to maturity. *Amortized yield* allows for an actual gain or loss of principal to be realized at maturity.

Yield to Call—The rate of return on an investment that accounts for the cash difference between a bond's acquisition cost and its proceeds calculated to the earliest date that the bonds can be called in by the issuing corporation.

Yield to Maturity—The yield, or return, provided by a bond to its maturity date; determined by a mathematical process, usually requiring the use of a "basis book." For example, a 5% bond pays $5 a year interest on each $100 par value. To figure its current yield, divide $5 by $95—the market price of the bond—and you get 5.26%. Assume that the same bond is due to mature in five years. On the maturity date, the issuer is pledged to pay $100 for the bond that can be bought now for $95. In other words, the bond is selling at a discount of 5% below par value. To figure *yield to maturity,* a simple and approximate method is to divide 5% by the five years to maturity, which equals 1% pro rata yearly. Add that 1% to the 5.26% current yield, and the yield to maturity is roughly 6.26%.

Z

Zero Balance Reimbursement Account (ZEBRA)—A pre-January 1985 type of flexible spending arrangement under which amounts were allocated to the account only when an expense was incurred. The employee was then reimbursed by the employer by subtracting the amount of the covered expenses from his or her taxable income at the end of the year. Such arrangements are specifically forbidden in cafeteria plans.

Zero-Base Budget—A financial plan in which all expenditures must be justified.

Zero-Based Forecasting—A company uses the current level of employment as a starting point for determining future employment needs.

Zero-Coupon Bond—A bond that is unique in that no interest payments are made to the holder by the issuer. The difference between the purchase price and the redemption value represents the imputed interest paid. A zero-coupon bond is a fixed income security sold at a deep discount from the value at maturity. An attractive feature is that reinvestment rate risk is avoided by the holder. The holder locks in a certain internal rate of return, provided the issuer is financially able to repay the face value of the bond when it matures.

Zero Premium—The practice, in some Medicare marketplaces, of not charging any added monthly premium to what is already paid for Part B coverage, as opposed to the practice of an HMO getting a monthly premium in addition to what is paid to the federal government by the patient.

Zones—In compensation, pay ranges used as guidelines within pay bands, such as maximums, midpoints and minimums.

BENEFITS AND COMPENSATION
ACRONYMS AND ABBREVIATIONS

The employee benefits and compensation field encompasses many subjects: accounting, business, government regulations, health care, human resources, insurance, investments, law, real estate and so forth. Each has a wealth of acronyms (words formed from the initial letters of the major words in compound terms) and other abbreviations. Therefore, the International Foundation of Employee Benefit Plans has published this new edition of its acronyms and abbreviations dictionary. Use this dictionary as a guide rather than as an authority since no such list can ever be complete. Send suggested additions to the glossary editor at the Foundation. An updated version of this dictionary will appear periodically.

Notes on Arrangement

Entries are alphabetized as if they were single words. Ampersands, commas, slashes and spaces are ignored in alphabetization. Letters combined with numbers appear *before* letters combined with letters.

If an entry has more than one definition, those definitions appear in alphabetical order within the entry.

AAA	(1) American Academy of Actuaries
	(2) American Accounting Association
	(3) American Arbitration Association
	(4) Area Agency on Aging
AABD	Aid to the Aged, Blind and Disabled
AAC	(1) Actual Acquisition Cost
	(2) Affirmative Action Clause
AAHP	American Association of Health Plans
AALL	American Association for Labor Legislation
AAP	Affirmative Action Program
AAPPO	American Association of Preferred Provider Organizations
AARP	American Association of Retired Persons
ABA	(1) American Bankers Association
	(2) American Bar Association
ABMT	Autologous Bone Marrow Transplant
ABO	Accumulated Benefit Obligation
ABP	(1) Account Balance Pension
	(2) Average Benefit Percentage
ACA	American Chiropractic Association
ACC	Ambulatory Care Center
ACLU	American Civil Liberties Union
ACP	(1) Actual Contribution Percentage
	(2) Average Contribution Percentage
ACR	(1) Actual Contribution Ratio
	(2) Adjusted Community Rating
ADA	(1) American Dental Association
	(2) American Diabetes Association
	(3) Americans with Disabilities Act of 1990
AD&D	Accidental Death and Dismemberment
ADEA	Age Discrimination in Employment Act of 1967
ADL	Activities of Daily Living
ADP	Actual Deferral Percentage

ADR	(1) Actual Deferral Ratio (2) Adverse Drug Reaction (3) Alternate Dispute Resolution (4) American Depository Receipt	APPWP	Association of Private Pension and Welfare Plans
ADS	Alternative Delivery System	AQL	Acceptable Quality Level
AFL-CIO	American Federation of Labor–Congress of Industrial Organizations	AR	Accounts Receivable
		ARC	(1) AIDS-Related Complex (2) American Red Cross
AFSCME	American Federation of State, County and Municipal Employees	ASA	Associate, Society of Actuaries
AGI	Adjusted Gross Income	ASC	(1) Administrative Services Contract (2) Ambulatory Surgery Center
AHA	American Hospital Association	ASCII	American Standard Code for Information Interchange
AHCPR	Agency for Health Care Policy and Research	ASO	Administrative Services Only
AI	(1) Aggregate Income (2) Artificial Intelligence	ASP	Application Service Provider
AICPA	American Institute of Certified Public Accountants	ASPA	(1) American Society for Personnel Administration (former name for SHRM) (2) American Society of Pension Actuaries
AIDS	Acquired Immune Deficiency Syndrome		
AIME	Average Indexed Monthly Earnings (Social Security)	ASTD	American Society for Training and Development
AIMR	Association for Investment Management and Research	AV	Audiovisual
aka	Also Known As	AWP	(1) Any Willing Provider (2) Average Wholesale Price
ALI-ABA	American Law Institute–American Bar Association	BC/BS	Blue Cross/Blue Shield
ALOS	Average Length of Stay	BFOQ	Bona Fide Occupational Qualification
AMA	(1) American Management Association (2) American Medical Association	BIC	Bank Investment Contract
		BLS	Bureau of Labor Statistics
AMEX	American Stock Exchange	BNA	Bureau of National Affairs
AML	Adjustable Mortgage Loan	bp	Basis Point
AMW	Average Monthly Wage (Social Security)	CA	(1) Chartered Accountant (2) Current Assets
ANA	American Nurses Association	CAD	Computer-Aided Design
ANSI	American National Standards Institute	CAI	Computer-Assisted Instruction
APA	(1) American Psychiatric Association (2) American Psychological Association	CalPERS	California Public Employees' Retirement System
APB	Accounting Principles Board	CAM	(1) Computer-Assisted Manufacturing (2) Complementary and Alternative Medicine
APHA	American Public Health Association		
		CAP	Closing Agreement Program

156

CAPM	Capital Asset Pricing Model	CFP	Certified Financial Planner
CAPP	Cash Account Pension Plan	CFR	Code of Federal Regulations
CAPPP™	Certificate of Achievement in Public Plan Policy™	CHAMPUS	Civilian Health and Medical Program of the Uniformed Services
CAPSA	Canadian Association of Pension Supervisory Authorities	ChFA	Chartered Financial Analyst
		ChFC	Chartered Financial Consultant
CAT	Computerized Axial Tomography Scanner (health diagnostic device)	CHPA	Community Health Purchasing Alliance
CB	Cumulative Bulletin (IRS)	CIMA	Certified Investment Management Analysis
CBA	Collective Bargaining Agreement		
CBO	Congressional Budget Office	CIO	(1) Chief Investment Officer (2) Congress of Industrial Organizations
CBP	Certified Benefits Professional		
CBOE	Chicago Board Options Exchange	CLU	Chartered Life Underwriter
CCA/ACR	Canadian Compensation Association/ Association Canadiénné de Remuneration	CLUW	Coalition of Labor Union Women (AFL-CIO)
		CM	Case Management
CCP	Certified Compensation Professional	CMO	Collateralized Mortgage Obligation
CCRA	Canada Customs and Revenue Agency	CMS	Centers for Medicare and Medicaid Services
CCRC	Continuing Care Retirement Community		
		CMV	Current Market Value
CCU	Coronary Care Unit	CNM	Certified Nurse Midwife
CCUS	Chamber of Commerce of the United States	COB	Coordination of Benefits
CD	(1) Certificate of Deposit (2) Compact Disk	COBRA	Consolidated Omnibus Budget Reconciliation Act of 1985
		CODA	Cash or Deferred Arrangement
CDC	(1) Centers for Disease Control (2) Community Development Corporation	COE	Center of Excellence
		C of C	Chamber of Commerce
CDIC	Canada Deposit Insurance Corporation	COLA	(1) Cost-of-Living Adjustment (2) Cost-of-Living Allowance
CD-ROM	Compact Disc Read-Only Memory		
		COLI	Corporate-Owned Life Insurance
CEAP	Certified Employee Assistance Provider	CON	Certificate of Need
CEB	Council on Employee Benefits	CONUS	Continental United States
CEBS®	Certified Employee Benefit Specialist®	COO	Chief Operating Officer
CEO	Chief Executive Officer	COPE	Committee on Political Education (AFL-CIO)
CERES	Coalition for Environmentally Responsible Economies		
		CPA	Certified Public Accountant
CFA	Chartered Financial Analyst	CPC	Certified Pension Consultant
CFO	Chief Financial Officer	CPCU	Chartered Property and Casualty Underwriter

CPI	Consumer Price Index	DOT	(1) Department of Transportation (2) *Dictionary of Occupational Titles*
CPP	Canada Pension Plan	DPSP	Deferred Profit Sharing Plan (Canada)
CPP/QPP	Canada Pension Plan/Quebec Pension Plan	DRG	Diagnosis-Related Group (also Diagnostic Related Group)
CPR	(1) Cardiopulmonary Resuscitation (2) Customary, Prevailing and Reasonable	DRIP	Dividend Reinvestment Plan
		DROP	Deferred Retirement Option Plan
CPT	Current Procedural Terminology	DTC	Depository Trust Company
CPU	Central Processing Unit	DUM	Drug Utilization Management
CQI	Continuous Quality Improvement	DUR	Drug Utilization Review
CRPC	Chartered Retirement Planning Counselor	DVD	(1) Digital Versatile Disk (2) Digital Video Disk
CRPS	Chartered Retirement Plans Specialist	DXL	Diagnostic X-Ray and Lab
CRT	Cathode Ray Tube		
CSRS	Civil Service Retirement System	EA	Enrolled Actuary
CTD	Cumulative Trauma Disorder (see also RSI)	EAFE	Europe, AustralAsia, Far East Stock Market Index
		EAP	Employee Assistance Program
DAW	Dispense As Written	EBC	Equity-Based Compensation
d/b/a	Doing Business As	EBI™	EMPLOYEE BENEFITS INFOSOURCE™
DBP	Defined Benefit Plan	EBIT	Earnings Before Interest and Taxes
DC	Doctor of Chiropractic	EBRI	Employee Benefit Research Institute
DCA	Dependent Care Account	EBSA	Employee Benefits Security Administration (formerly PWBA)
DCAP	Dependent Care Assistance Plan		
DCI	Duplicate Coverage Inquiry	EC	European Community (formerly EEC)
DCP	Defined Contribution Plan	ECF	Extended Care Facility
DEFRA	Deficit Reduction Act of 1984	EDGAR	Electronic Data Gathering, Analysis, and Retrieval System
DHHS	Department of Health and Human Services	EDI	Electronic Data Interchange
DI	(1) Disability Income (2) Disability Insurance	EDP	Electronic Data Processing
DJIA	Dow Jones Industrial Average	EEC	European Economic Community (former name for EC)
DME	Durable Medical Equipment	EEG	Electroencephalogram
DNR	(1) Department of Natural Resources (2) Do Not Renew (3) Do Not Resuscitate	EEO	Equal Employment Opportunity
		EEOC	Equal Employment Opportunity Commission
DO	Doctor of Osteopathy	EGTRRA	Economic Growth and Tax Relief Reconciliation Act of 2001
DOB	Date of Birth		
DOL	Department of Labor		

EI	Employment Insurance (Canada)	FAX	Facsimile
EIN	Employer Identification Number	FDA	Food and Drug Administration
EITC	Earned Income Tax Credit	FDIC	Federal Deposit Insurance Corporation
EKG	Electrocardiogram	FERS	Federal Employees Retirement System
ELOS	Estimated Length of Stay		
EMS	Emergency Medical Service	FFS	Fee for Service
EMU	European Monetary Union	FHA	Federal Housing Administration
ENT	Ear, Nose and Throat	FHLB	Federal Home Loan Bank
E&O	Errors and Omissions (Insurance)	FHLBB	Federal Home Loan Bank Board
EOB	Explanation of Benefits	FHLMC	Federal Home Loan Mortgage Corporation (Freddie Mac)
EOE	Equal Opportunity Employer	FI	Fiscal Intermediary
EP	Earned Premium	FICA	Federal Insurance Contributions Act (Social Security and Medicare)
EPA	(1) Environmental Protection Agency (2) Equal Pay Act		
EPCRS	Employee Plans Compliance Resolution System	FLMI	Fellow, Life Management Institute
		FLSA	Fair Labor Standards Act
EPEO	Employee Plans and Exempt Organizations (Division of IRS)	FMLA	Family and Medical Leave Act of 1993
		FMV	Fair Market Value
EPO	Exclusive Provider Organization	FNMA	Federal National Mortgage Association (Fannie Mae)
EPS	Earnings Per Share		
EPSDT	Early and Periodic Screening, Diagnosis and Treatment	FOMC	Federal Open Market Committee
		FR	Federal Register
ERA	(1) Equal Rights Amendment (2) Expense Reimbursement Allowance	FS	Financial Statement
		FSA	(1) Federal Security Agency (2) Fellow, Society of Actuaries (3) Flexible Spending Account (4) Flexible Spending Arrangement (5) Funding Standard Account
ERISA	Employee Retirement Income Security Act of 1974		
ERTA	Economic Recovery Tax Act of 1981	FSLIC	Federal Savings and Loan Insurance Corporation
ESOP	Employee Stock Ownership Plan		
ESRD	End Stage Renal Disease	FSPA	Fellow, Society of Pension Actuaries
ETI	Economically Targeted Investing	FTC	Federal Trade Commission
EU	European Union	FTE	Full-Time Equivalent
EVA	Economic Value Added	FUTA	Federal Unemployment Tax Act
EWL	Employer Withdrawal Liability	FY	Fiscal Year
FAQ	Frequently Asked Questions	GAAP	Generally Accepted Accounting Principles
FAS	Financial Accounting Standard		
FASB	Financial Accounting Standards Board	GAAS	Generally Accepted Auditing Standards

GAINS	Guaranteed Annual Income System (Canada)	HI	Hospital Insurance
GAO	General Accounting Office	HIAA	Health Insurance Association of America
GASB	Governmental Accounting Standards Board	HIPAA	Health Insurance Portability and Accountability Act
GATT	General Agreement on Tariffs and Trade	HIPC	(1) Health Insurance Purchasing Coalition
GAW	Guaranteed Annual Wage		(2) Health Insurance Purchasing Cooperative
GDP	Gross Domestic Product	HIV	Human Immunodeficiency Virus
GIC	(1) Guaranteed Investment Certificate (Canada)	HMO	Health Maintenance Organization
	(2) Guaranteed Investment Contract	HPA	Hospital-Physician Alliance
GIS	Guaranteed Income Supplement (Canada)	HPO	(1) Health Care Purchasing Organization
GLS	Group Legal Services		(2) Hospital-Physician Organization
GNMA	Government National Mortgage Association (Ginnie Mae)	HPPC	Health Plan Purchasing Cooperative
		HR	Human Resources
GNP	Gross National Product	HRA	(1) Health Reimbursement Account
GPM	Graduated Payment Mortgage		(2) Health Risk Assessment
GPO	(1) Government Printing Office	HRD	Human Resources Development
	(2) Guaranteed Purchase Option	HRIS	Human Resource Information System
GST	Goods and Services Tax (Canada)	HSA	Health Savings Account
GULP	Group Universal Life Plan	HSOP	Health Stock Ownership Plan
GUST	GATT, USERRA, SBJPA and TRA '97	HTML	Hypertext Markup Language
		http	Hypertext Transfer Protocol
HA	Health Alliance	HUD	(Department of) Housing and Urban Development
HCA	Health Care Account		
HCE	Highly Compensated Employee		
HCFA	Health Care Financing Administration	IB	Interpretive Bulletin
HCPCS	HCFA Common Procedural Coding System	IBA	International Bar Association
		IBNR	Incurred but Not Reported (Claims)
HEDIS	Health Plan Employer Data and Information Set	ICC	Interstate Commerce Commission
HEW	(Department of) Health, Education, and Welfare (now split into HHS and DOE)	ICD-9-CM	*International Classification of Diseases—9th Revision— Clinical Modification*
		ICF	Intermediate Care Facility
HHA	Home Health Agency	ICM	Individual Case Management
HHC	Home Health Care	ICU	Intensive Care Unit
HHS	(Department of) Health and Human Services	IDN	Integrated Delivery Network
		IDS	Integrated Delivery System

IFIC	Investment Funds Institute of Canada	JIT	Just-In-Time (System)
ILP	Independent Living Program	JOBS	Job Opportunities and Basic Skills Training
ILWU-PMA	International Longshoremen's and Warehousemen's Union-Pacific Maritime Association	J&S	Joint and Survivor (Annuity)
		JV	Joint Venture
IME	Independent Medical Examination		
IMF	International Monetary Fund	KBS	Knowledge-Based System
IO	Investment-Only (Contract)	KLN	Key Local National
IOMA	Institute of Management Administration	KSOP	401(k) Employee Stock Option Plan
IP	(1) Inpatient (2) Integrated Provider	LAN	Local Area Network
IPA	(1) Independent Practice Association (2) Individual Practice Association	LBO	Leveraged Buyout
		LCN	Local Country National
IPG	(Group) Immediate Participation Guarantee (Pension Plan)	LESOP	Leveraged Employee Stock Ownership Plan
IPO	Initial Public Offering	LIF	Life Income Fund
IRA	Individual Retirement Account	LIHEAP	Low-Income Home Energy Assistance Program
IRB	Internal Revenue Bulletin		
IRC	Internal Revenue Code	LLC	Limited Liability Corporation
IRR	Internal Rate of Return	LMRA	Labor-Management Relations Act of 1947 (Taft-Hartley Act)
IRRA	IRS Restructuring and Reform Act of 1998	LMRDA	Labor-Management Reporting and Disclosure Act of 1959
IRS	Internal Revenue Service	LOS	Length of Stay
ISCEBS	International Society of Certified Employee Benefit Specialists	LTC	Long-Term Care
ISO	(1) Incentive Stock Option (2) Insurance Services Office (3) International Standards Organization	LTD	Long-Term Disability
		M&A	Mergers and Acquisitions
ISOP	Investment Stock Option Plan	MAAC	Maximum Allowable Actual Charge
ITC	Investment Tax Credit	MAC	Maximum Allowable Cost (List)
IUC	Incurred but Unreported Claims	MAGI	Modified Adjusted Gross Income
IVR	Interactive Voice Response (System)	MC	Managed Care
		MCCA	Medicare Catastrophic Coverage Act of 1988
JATC	Joint Apprenticeship and Training Committee	MCM	Medical Case Management
JCAHO	Joint Commission on Accreditation of Healthcare Organizations	MCO	Managed Care Organization
		MDC	Major Diagnostic Category
JCWA	Job Creation and Workers Assistance Act of 2002	Medigap	Medical Supplement Insurance

Medsupp	Medicare Supplement Insurance	NHCAA	National Health Care Anti-Fraud Association
MET	Multiple Employer Trust	NHCE	Nonhighly Compensated Employee
MEWA	Multiple Employer Welfare Arrangement	NIH	National Institutes of Health
MFB	Maximum Family Benefit (Social Security)	NIMH	National Institute of Mental Health
		NIOSH	National Institute for Occupational Safety and Health
MGIC	Mortgage Guaranty Insurance Corporation	NLRA	National Labor Relations Act
MH/CD	Mental Health/Chemical Dependency	NLRB	National Labor Relations Board
MHPA	Mental Health Parity Act of 1995	NMB	National Mediation Board
MIS	Management Information System	NOW Account	Negotiable Order of Withdrawal Account
MIT	Modern Investment Theory	NP	Nurse Practitioner
MLR	(1) Medical Loss Ratio (2) Multiple Location Risk	NQA	National Quality Award
MMA	Medicare Prescription Drug, Improvement, and Modernization Act	NRA	Normal Retirement Age
		NRD	Normal Retirement Date
MNC	(1) Multinational Company (2) Multinational Corporation	NSF	Not Sufficient Funds
MPPAA	Multiemployer Pension Plan Amendments Act of 1980	NW	Net Worth
		NYSE	New York Stock Exchange
MPT	Modern Portfolio Theory		
MRI	Magnetic Resonance Imaging	OAA	Old Age Assistance
MSA	Medical Savings Account	OAS	Old Age Security (Canada)
MSCI	Morgan Stanley Capital International	OASDHI	Old-Age, Survivors, Disability, and Health Insurance
MSDS	Material Safety Data Sheets	OASDI	Old-Age, Survivors, and Disability Insurance
MSO	Management Services Organization		
MSP	Medicare Secondary Payer	OASI	Old-Age and Survivors Insurance
MSPA	Member, Society of Pension Actuaries	OBRA	Omnibus Budget Reconciliation Act
		OCC	Options Clearing Corporation
NA	Not Applicable	OCONUS	Outside the Continental United States
NAFTA	North American Free Trade Agreement	OD	(1) Occupational Disease (2) Organizational Development
NAIC	National Association of Insurance Commissioners	OECD	Organization for Economic Cooperation and Development
NASDAQ	National Association of Securities Dealers Automatic Quotation System	OEM	Original Equipment Manufacturer
NAV	Net Asset Value	OEO	Office of Economic Opportunity
NCQA	National Committee for Quality Assurance	OJT	On-the-Job Training
		OMB	Office of Management and Budget

OOA	Out of Area	PEBES	Personal Earnings and Benefit Estimate Statement
OOP	Out-of-Pocket Maximum	PEO	Professional Employer Organization
OP	Outpatient	PEPPRA	Public Employee Pension Plan Reporting and Accountability Act
OR	(1) Operating Room (2) Operations Research		
OSFI	Office of the Superintendent of Financial Institutions (Canada)	PERS	Public Employee Retirement System
		PFK	Pay for Knowledge and Skills Plan
OSHA	(1) Occupational Safety and Health Act (2) Occupational Safety and Health Administration	PHO	Physician-Hospital Organization
		PHR	Professional in Human Resources
		PHS	Public Health Service
OT	Occupational Therapy	PI	Personal Injury
OTC	Over the Counter	PIA	Primary Insurance Amount (Social Security)
OWBPA	Older Workers Benefit Protection Act		
		PIN	Personal Identification Number
PA	(1) Pension Adjustment (Canada) (2) Performance Appraisal (3) Physician's Assistant	PIPEDA	Personal Information Protection and Electronic Documents Act (Canada)
		PL	(1) Public Law (2) Public Liability
P/A	Power of Attorney	PLI	Professional Liability Insurance
PARCA	Patient Access to Responsible Health Care Act	PLR	Private Letter Ruling
PAT	Preadmission Testing	PMPM	Per Member Per Month
PAYSOP	Payroll-Based Stock Ownership (Option) Plan	POS	Point of Service
		PPA	(1) Patient Protection Act (2) Pension Protection Act of 1987
P/B	Price-To-Book (Ratio)		
PBGC	Pension Benefit Guaranty Corporation	PPD	Permanent Partial Disability
		PPO	Preferred Provider Organization
PBM	Pharmacy Benefits Management/Manager	PPS	Prospective Payment System
		PR	Pro Rata
PBO	Projected Benefit Obligation	PRD	Pro Rata Distribution
PC	(1) Participation Certificate (Mortgage) (2) Personal Computer (3) Professional Corporation	PRO	Peer Review Organization
		PSC	Personal Service Corporation
		PSO	Provider Sponsored Organization
PCN	(1) Primary Care Network (2) Primary Care Nurse	PSP	Performance Share Plan
		PSRO	Professional Standards Review Organization
PCP	Primary Care Physician		
PDA	(1) Pregnancy Discrimination Act of 1978 (2) Personal Digital Assistant	PT	(1) Physical Therapy (2) Prohibited Transaction
		PTCE	Prohibited Transaction Class Exemption
P/E	Price/Earnings (Ratio)		

PTD	Permanent and Total Disability	RICO	Racketeer Influenced Corrupt Organizations Act of 1971
PTE	Prohibited Transaction Exemption	RIPA	Retirement Income Policy Act of 1985
PTO	Paid Time Off	ROE	Return on Equity
PWA	Person With AIDS	ROI	Return on Investment
PWBA	Pension and Welfare Benefits Administration (former name for EBSA)	ROM	Range of Motion
		RPA	(1) Registered Pension Account (Canada) (2) Retirement Protection Act of 1994
QA	Quality Assurance	RPP	Registered Pension Plan
QC	(1) Quality Control (2) Quarter of Coverage (Social Security)	RRIF	Registered Retirement Income Fund (Canada)
QDEC	Qualified Deductible Employee Contribution	RRM	Renegotiable Rate Mortgage
		RRSP	Registered Retirement Savings Plan (Canada)
QDRO	Qualified Domestic Relations Order	RSI	Repetitive Strain Injury (see also CTD)
QJSA	Qualified Joint and Survivor Annuity		
QMAC	Qualified Matching Contributions	RTC	Residential Treatment Center
QMB	Qualified Medicare Beneficiary	RTK	Right to Know
QMCSO	Qualified Medical Child Support Order	RVS	Relative Value Scale (benefit determination system)
QNEC	Qualified Nonelective Contribution	R/W	Returned to Work
QPAM	Qualified Professional Asset Manager		
QPP	Quebec Pension Plan (Canada)	SAR	(1) Stock Appreciation Right (2) Summary Annual Report
QPSA	Qualified Preretirement Survivor Annuity	SARSEP	Salary Reduction Simplified Employee Pension Plan
QSLOB	Qualified Separate Line of Business	SAVER	Savings Are Vital to Everyone's Retirement Act of 1997
QTD	Qualified Total Distribution	SBA	Small Business Administration
RAM	Random Access Memory	SBJPA	Small Business Job Protection Act of 1996
RBRVS	Resource-Based Relative Value Scale	SDBA	Self-Directed Brokerage Account
R&C	Reasonable and Customary	SEC	Securities and Exchange Commission
REA	Retirement Equity Act of 1984	SEP	Simplified Employee Pension (Plan)
REIT	Real Estate Investment Trust	SEPPAA	Single Employer Pension Plan Amendments Act of 1986
RESP	Registered Education Savings Plan (Canada)		
RFI	Request for Information	SERP	Supplemental Executive Retirement Plan
RFP	(1) Registered Financial Planner (2) Request for Proposal	SERPS	State Earnings Related Pension Scheme

SFAS	Statements of Financial Accounting Standards	TDD/TTY	Telecommunications Device for the Deaf/Teletypewriter
SHRM	Society of Human Resource Management (formerly ASPA)	TDI	Temporary Disability Insurance (System)
SIIA	Self-Insurance Institute of America	TEFRA	Tax Equity and Fiscal Responsibility Act
SIMPLE	Savings Incentive Match Plan (for employees of small employers)	TI	Terminal Illness
SIPC	Securities Investor Protection Corporation	TIN	Taxpayer Identification Number
		TMJ	Temporomandibular Joint Dysfunction
SLMA	Student Loan Marketing Association (Sallie Mae)	TPA	Third-Party Administrator
SLOB	Separate Line of Business	TQM	Total Quality Management
SMI	(1) Supplementary Medical Insurance (2) Serious Mental Illness	TRA	(1) Tax Reform Acts 1984, 1986 (2) Taxpayer Relief Act of 1997
SMM	Summary of Material Modifications (summary of changes in an SPD)	TRASOP	Tax Reduction Act of 1975 (Employee) Stock Ownership Plan
SNF	Skilled Nursing Facility	TSA	Tax-Sheltered Annuity
SOP	Standard Operating Procedure	TWB	Taxable Wage Base
S&P	Standard & Poor's		
SPD	Summary Plan Description	UAW	United Auto Workers
SPDA	Single Premium Deferred Annuity	UBTI	Unrelated Business Taxable Income
SPHR	Senior Professional in Human Resources	UC	Unemployment Compensation
		U&C	Usual and Customary
SSA	(1) Social Security Act (2) Social Security Administration	UCC	Uniform Commercial Code
		UCCC	Uniform Consumer Credit Code
SSDI	Social Security Disability Insurance	UCD	Unemployment Compensation Disability
SSI	(1) Supplemental Security Income (Social Security) (2) Supplemental Security Insurance	UCI	Unemployment Compensation Insurance
SSOP	Second Surgical Opinion Program	UCR	Usual, Customary and Reasonable
SSRA	Social Security Retirement Age	UGMA	Uniform Gifts to Minors Act
STD	Short-Term Disability	UI	Unemployment Insurance
STIF	Short-Term Investment Fund	UM	Utilization Management
SUB	Supplemental Unemployment Benefit	UR	Utilization Review
		URAC	Utilization Review Accreditation Commission
TAMRA	Technical and Miscellaneous Revenue Act of 1988	URL	Uniform Resource Locator
TCN	Third Country National	URO	Utilization Review Organization
TDA	Tax-Deferred Annuity	U.S.C.	United States Code
TDB	Temporary Disability Benefits		

USERRA	Uniformed Services Employment and Reemployment Rights Act of 1994		W-2	Wage and Tax Statement
			WC	Workers' Compensation
USWA	United Steelworkers of America		WHEA	Women's Health Equity Act
UTMA	Uniform Transfers to Minors Act		WHO	World Health Organization
UTU	United Transportation Union		WPM	Words Per Minute
UVB	Unfunded Vested Benefits		WSJ	*Wall Street Journal*
UVL	Unfunded Vested Liability		WTO	World Trade Organization
			WWW	World Wide Web
VA	Veterans Administration			
VAT	Value-Added Tax		YMPE	Year's Maximum Pensionable Earnings (Canada)
VCR	(1) Variable Coupon Renewable (Notes) (2) Voluntary Compliance Resolution Program		YRT	Yearly Renewable Term
			YTD	Year to Date
VDT	Video or Visual Display Terminal			
VEBA	Voluntary Employees' Beneficiary Association		ZBB	Zero-Base Budget
			ZEBRA	Zero Balance Reimbursement Account
VNA	Visiting Nurse Association			
VRM	Variable Rate Mortgage		ZPG	Zero Population Growth